Social Science Research

'Drawing on her vast experience of ethnographic research, Barbara Czarniawska offers a brilliant guide to the beginning researcher.'
David Silverman, Professor Emeritus in Sociology, Goldsmiths' College, and Visiting Professor in Business, University of Technology, Sydney

'Written with much wry humor, the book – which is filled with practical advice, from how to treat sources, to why correct referencing is important – will be as enjoyable for an experienced researcher as it is for a neophyte. Read this book. Recommend it to your students, your colleagues, and your professors. Hats off to Barbara Czarniawska.'
Dvora Yanow, Professor of Organizational Studies, Keele University, and Guest Professor of Communication, Philosophy, & Technology, Wageningen University

'A lively, reflexive account of a variety of methodological approaches, some tried and true, some quirky and innovative. A thoughtful and creative methodological mapping, that is of equal value to the novice and the veteran researcher – both in and out of academic communities. A must read for those interested in cross-disciplinary work in social science.'
John Van Maanen, Professor of Management and Organization, MIT

'A goldmine of deep yet practical insights into the craft of doing high-quality field research. The book covers all relevant aspects of the research process, from study design over observation and interviewing to good academic writing. Barbara Czarniawska is a particularly trustworthy guide, because she so clearly practices what she preaches. This is a must-read for new and seasoned field researchers alike.'
Bent Flyvbjerg, Professor, Oxford University; author of *Making Social Science Matter*

Barbara
Czarniawska

Social
Science
Research

From Field to Desk

Los Angeles | London | New Delhi
Singapore | Washington DC

Los Angeles | London | New Delhi
Singapore | Washington DC

SAGE Publications Ltd
1 Oliver's Yard
55 City Road
London EC1Y 1SP

SAGE Publications Inc.
2455 Teller Road
Thousand Oaks, California 91320

SAGE Publications India Pvt Ltd
B 1/I 1 Mohan Cooperative Industrial Area
Mathura Road
New Delhi 110 044

SAGE Publications Asia-Pacific Pte Ltd
3 Church Street
#10-04 Samsung Hub
Singapore 049483

Editor: Jai Seaman
Editorial assistant: Lily Mehrbod
Production editor: Katherine Haw
Copyeditor: Jane Fricker
Marketing manager: Sally Ransom
Cover design: Francis Kenney
Typeset by: C&M Digitals (P) Ltd, Chennai, India
Printed and bound by: CPI Group (UK) Ltd,
   Croydon, CR0 4YY

© Barbara Czarniawska 2014

First published 2014

Library of Congress Control Number: 2013951860

British Library Cataloguing in Publication data

A catalogue record for this book is available from
the British Library

ISBN 978-1-4462-9393-5
ISBN 978-1-4462-9394-2 (pbk)

Contents

About the Author

Barbara Czarniawska (formerly known as Barbara Czarniawska-Joerges) is an organization theorist, best known for her contributions to constructivism theory in management studies as well as narrative analysis in studies of organizing. At present, she holds a Research Chair in Management Studies at Gothenburg Research Institute, School of Business, Economics and Law at the University of Gothenburg, Sweden.

Prologue: A Method Guide for the Perplexed

It has taken me some time to decide to start writing *Social Science Research: From Field to Desk*. In preparation, I collected various books and articles on methods used in social sciences, and was horrified by their number. Do social scientists really need yet another book? Finally, though, I decided that the current state of affairs is the very reason for writing this one: To guide young scholars through the jungle of methodology literature. What I hope to offer is a simple and pragmatic picture – from beginning to end – of a research process that includes fieldwork. This book is not designed to be of much help to people whose data have already been collected and processed – researchers using official statistics, for example. Neither do I review quantitative analysis techniques, although I mention these when relevant.

Yet for two reasons with one common historical cause, I prefer to speak of interpretative rather than qualitative studies.[1] The notion of 'qualitative studies' was coined in the 1960s as a means of defense against the wave of statistical procedures that were on their way to being declared the only truly scientific method. Many stories are told about the scholars who led the two groups: From the UK, Marie Jahoda defended qualitative methods; from the USA, her ex-husband, Paul Lazarsfeld, championed quantitative methods. But, as often happens, what seemed like a good solution in a certain time and place became a problem later. The consequences of the division are currently seen in both camps. Quantitative researchers have stopped interpreting their results and justifying their methods; they simply use methods common in their field and assume that numerical results speak for themselves. Unfortunately, the numbers do not speak for themselves, and never did. By way of contrast, one can look at the original positivists, who knew why they studied what they studied and why they studied it in the way they did – although at present we may not always be willing to accept their justifications.

Qualitative researchers, on the other hand, seem to consider it beneath their dignity even to count the pages in their work for fear of being seen as traitors to their field. But, as noted long ago by Gabriel Tarde, Director of the Statistics Bureau in Paris (1894–1900) and a most creative thinker and interpreter, there are always fascinating things to be counted, especially things that nobody counted before. I have two hopes, therefore: To convince researchers who rely on numbers to reflect on their provenance and interpret their meaning, and to convince researchers who are allergic to numbers to overcome this allergy. As Clive Seale (1999: 121) put it, count the countable – especially if you can do it yourself, rather than relying on calculations made in some unknown way for unknown purposes.

As I am an organization scholar, the examples I use often relate to studies of work. I would like to emphasize, however, that I study not organizations, but organizing – the activity of introducing order. This activity permeates all of life, from the family to the state.

The kind of research that I promote through this book relies on the assumption that the methods and the techniques must be adapted to the research problem – and to the personality of the researchers. There are several methodological approaches and a great variety of techniques from which to choose. So, this is my advice to a perplexed young scholar: Obtain the gist of what is possible, and then select the best fit for you and your problem.

One issue that will be resurfacing in all chapters is the ethical dimension of research. Most national research councils have now issued some type of ethical code, sharing the common spirit but differing somewhat among disciplines and countries. Yet there will never be a common code to cover every situation in the field or at the desk. Doing research means making moral choices, continuously, and often under time pressure. If there could be but one common maxim, perhaps it can be borrowed from medicine: *Primum non nocere!* (First, do not harm). While in medicine it means mostly physical harm, in the social sciences it means mostly psychical harm, usually unintended.

Finally, the *Further reading* list at the end of each chapter is exactly what it says: It lists works on the same theme or books containing chapters on the same theme, but not necessarily by authors sharing my opinions and preferences. Familiarizing oneself with diverse opinions can be useful.

Note

1. Schwartz-Shea and Yanow (2002) advocate a similar stance in relation to political science.

Acknowledgment

My most heartfelt thanks go to my English language editor, Professor Nina Lee Colwill, who did her utmost to make this text sing. If it does not, it is my voice that fails.

Further Acknowledgments

The author and publisher thank the following publishers for granting permission to reproduce their material:

Liber AB for excerpts from Barbara Czarniawska (2007) *Shadowing and other techniques for doing fieldwork in modern societies.*

Italian Paths of Culture for excerpts from Marianella Sclavi (2007) *An Italian lady goes to the Bronx.*

M.E. Sharpe for excerpts from Barbara Czarniawska (2013) 'The Uncertainties of Consulting', *International Studies of Management and Organization* 43(3): 11–21.

SAGE Publications Inc for excerpts from:
John Van Maanen (1991) 'Playing back the tape: Early days in the field' in William B. Shaffir and Robert A. Stebbins (eds.) *Experiencing fieldwork: An inside view of qualitative research*, 31–42.

Bent Flyvbjerg (2006) 'Five misunderstandings about case-study research', *Qualitative Inquiry* 12(2): 219–245.

Barbara Czarniawska (1997) *A narrative approach to organization studies.*

1

What, Why, and How?

In this chapter I attempt to recreate the researcher's situation at the beginning of a study, when major decisions are being made. Toward that end, the chapter is structured around the basic questions to be asked and answered.

WHAT DO YOU WANT TO STUDY?

What do you want to study? A new phenomenon that raised your curiosity? A phenomenon that raised someone else's curiosity? A phenomenon that has never been studied before? And if it has never been studied before, why not? A variety of answers to the latter is possible:

- It was under some sort of ideological, political, or religious taboo.

- It was taken for granted. Ethnomethodologists specialize in studying taken-for-granted phenomena; marketing scholars call such studies 'queries' (Carson et al., 2001).

- It has been studied, but not here and not now. Marketing scholars call that 'an inquiry', suggesting some doubts about the validity or generalizability of previous results (Carlson et al., 2001).

All these answers suggest preparatory interrogations, and such interrogations have the potential of yielding results even before the actual research project begins. But I want to focus first on a situation in which a new phenomenon raised your curiosity or your interest in what Green and Thorogood (2004: 29) called 'puzzles about the social world'.

Does this new phenomenon have a name? If so, who named it? If you did, you have already taken the first step in your analysis, even if you change your mind and re-name the phenomenon later. (Observe that this kind of iterative movement, from theorizing to description and from description – through analysis – to theory is not only common, but also a highly desirable process among social scientists.)

At any rate, there are at least three possibilities for naming. One is that the phenomenon has received a name from people who are involved in it. Let's say they called what they do 'risk management'. A second possibility is that you gave it a name – a perfectly reasonable first step in the analysis if you are prepared to change it when you learn more about the phenomenon during your study. A third, and in my opinion, the most risky possibility, is that you baptize the phenomenon with the name of an abstract concept already known in the literature. You may decide that you will be studying 'the institutionalization of risk management'. But what does an 'institutionalization' look like in the field? I would know how to study 'the history of the concept "risk management"' (Eriksson-Zetterquist, 2009) or even 'the spreading of the practice of "risk management"'. But 'institutionalization'?

You may want to tell me that 'institutionalization' can be 'operationalized'. Well, yes, but after you have translated this abstract term into concrete practices and studied it, it may turn out that there are other, better, abstract concepts to theorize about what you have discovered. Why not wait for a while before you start applying abstract terms?

As a famous sociologist, C. Wright Mills, wrote long ago (1959) in *The Sociological Imagination*, the issue at stake 'is to grasp what is going on in the world' (p. 7). Of course, this was a highly ambitious plan; so his followers, Erving Goffman and Herbert Blumer, simply asked, 'What's going on here?' thereby delimiting the scope of the research to a specific time and place – or times and places.

To return to my fictitious research problem: There are people who say that they practice 'risk management'. Isn't that curious? How can one manage risk? Let's go and see what is happening there! But before that, another question needs to be answered.

WHY DO YOU WANT TO STUDY THAT?

> … despite the conversions sure to occur with field experience, it is important for the would-be (and wanna-be) field worker to recognize as legitimate the personal matters that lead one into a project. (Van Maanen, 1991: 33)

As Silverman (1993/2011) and Carson et al. (2001) rightly pointed out, the 'why' question is key, although answers may vary significantly. To reflect on this matter early in the study can be useful later on, and it may help to avoid various complications in the future.

I begin with two obvious and apparently unproblematic answers: 'because it made me curious' and 'because it is a significant societal issue or problem'.

As for curiosity, it is the most laudable trait in a researcher, but it must be freed of hubris. Unlikely as it may sound, somebody else could have had the same idea and have already studied the same phenomenon in another context. This is why a literature review – the topic developed in the next chapter – is absolutely essential, no matter what theoretical and methodological approach is chosen.

'A significant societal issue' or, more often, 'a problem', has its own complications. As David Silverman (1993/2011) noted, the definition of a certain phenomenon as a problem often comes from the media or from a potential sponsor. The media may be turning a sporadic event into a societal problem because it makes a good story. Or the managers of a company may be willing to pay for a research project because of a hidden change agenda.

A researcher equipped with what Silverman called *sensitivity* attends to such signals, realizing that media and management 'problems' may be indicators of complex phenomena. But the sensitive researcher does not take them for granted. Problems that someone else has defined can detract from other problems and phenomena – an issue that requires some courage for a researcher to address. Journalists do not appreciate a reformulation of their statements, and sponsors do not like being told that they created the alleged 'problems' themselves. So courage is the second requirement of a social scientist's profession – right after curiosity.

'Why do you want to study this specific issue?' Some answers to that question may be less problematic than they appear. One possible answer is, 'Because it is (a variation on) a fashionable topic'.

Some people may sometimes consider the idea of researchers following fashions to be a preposterous notion. Some people sometimes, but not everyone always. Werner Sombart, whose *Luxury and Capitalism* (1913) has become one of the classics of fashion theory, took for granted that scientists followed what he called 'the science fashion of the time'. Forty years later, Pitirim Sorokin, a leading Harvard sociologist of Russian origin, published a book called *Fads and Foibles in Modern Sociology* (1956), which contained a vitriolic critique of 'fads and slavish imitation'. It is easy to agree with Sorokin that what is imitated – because it is fashionable – can be absurd or wrong. Revealing this fact could possibly change the direction of imitation, but never remove the phenomenon of fashion. Instead of moralizing about fashion, researchers should be trying to understand it – and their own place in relation to it. If you decide to follow research fashion, your chances of receiving grants and publishing the results are higher than if you decide to ignore the fashion. Ignoring it may make you a future fashion leader, but your present research life may prove somewhat trying.

Yet another answer to the question 'Why do you want to study that?' may appear equally problematic: 'Because my adviser or boss suggested it to me'. Acceptance of that suggestion may be read as an indication of conformism, just like the following of fashion could be. But again, it is not necessarily so. Your adviser or boss may be making the suggestion because there is research money for that topic, and how the two of you interpret it is merely a matter of your joint 'sociological imagination'. Alternatively, your adviser or boss may truly know better, unlikely as that may sound.

When I came to Sweden, I wanted to continue my research in the area of detail trade, which I had been studying in Poland and the USA (Czarniawska, 1985). My potential boss told me I could join his group if I were prepared to study public management. I thought that it was possibly the most boring topic in the world. My prejudice was based on the fact that at the time – in the 1980s – many studies of public administration consisted of a description of laws and regulations. Forced by the situation, though, I agreed, and never looked back. Public sector organizations turned out to be crammed with fascinating phenomena!

Once this question has been answered – once you know why you want to study that topic – the next question arises: 'How do you study what you want to know?' And in the chapters that follow, I focus primarily on one answer to that question: by doing fieldwork.

HOW TO STUDY WHAT YOU WANT TO STUDY

Why do fieldwork?

There is plenty of information around – information from, of, and about such phenomena as organizations, organizing, workplaces, management, production, consumption, and finance. It is no longer necessary to go to the library or buy a newspaper in order to collect that information. I receive the annual reports of several companies to which I am but vaguely connected: Scandinavian Airlines, an insurance company, and a housing cooperative. The mail and e-mail delivery of myriad advertisements combined with TV commercials could provide me with enough material to analyze the society in which I live throughout eternity. Global economies are at my fingertips on the Internet. Why go *to* the field, then? And where is that field?

In this text, the word 'field' is being used in the sense of a *field of practice*, where even theorizing is one type of practice. Because there is a 'turn to practice' in contemporary social theory (Schatzki et al., 2001), fieldwork in modern societies usually denotes the study of a field of practice, resulting in what Annemarie Mol (2002) has called a *praxiography* – a description of that practice. Its historical antecedents must be sought, on the one hand, in natural sciences and empiricism and, on the other hand, in studies of premodern societies.

Yet researchers whose goal is to describe practices can be seen as the opposite of traditional empiricists, with their motto, *Nullius in verba!* (On no man's word). In this type of fieldwork, the words of men and women in the field are as valid as the researchers' own words. If fieldwork must be seen as empirical, I would call this type of empiricism 'ethical'. Richard Rorty put it well in a passage that, to use Helen Sword's formulation, 'is dated in its gendered pronoun use but timeless in its sentiment' (2012: 10):

> [It is] a mistake to think of somebody's own account of his behavior or culture as epistemically privileged. He might have a good account of what he is doing or he might not, but it is *not* a mistake to think of it as morally privileged. We have a duty to listen to his account, not because he has privileged access to his own motives but because he is a human being like ourselves. (Rorty, 1982: 202)

The field is where other people live and work, which means that *my* life and work can also become elements of a field of practice to be studied. Fieldwork is an expression of curiosity about the Other – about people who construct their worlds differently than we researchers construct ours. I could study my own field – the practice of research – but in order to do so, I would have to become, at least temporarily, an observer of that practice. As Niklas Luhmann (1998) pointed out, the world as seen by actors is necessarily unlike the world seen by observers. Observers are able to see options – and to distinguish among them. But actors can see options only in the moment of reflection, of observing, of *not* acting. (The awareness of an alternative would be paralyzing – the condition from which Buridan's ass allegedly starved to death while trying to decide between a pail of water and a pile of hay.)[1] One must step back in order to observe – even to observe oneself at a different time – and, paradoxically, for researchers this backward step means stepping forward – into the field. The advantages are many.

Although all fields of practice currently produce many accounts of their activities, it is *in* the field that the actual *production* of accounts can be studied. Before a glossy brochure reaches my mailbox, there has been a long discussion about which accounting data to include and what tone the CEO's letter should strike – not to mention the three-month argument between the two schools of cover design. Sociologists of science and technology went to laboratories to see how facts were manufactured (Latour and Woolgar, 1979/1986; Knorr Cetina, 1981); medical anthropologists have gone to the field to see how health care is produced – together with both sick and healthy bodies (Mol, 2002).

There is another reason for 'stepping into' the field: Because both the actions and the accounts of action abound there. Of the many accounts produced in the field, its representatives send me one – the one they have decided is good for me as their client. As a student of their modes and mores, however, I may want to use a different selection principle. I may prefer to select the very accounts that they wish to hide from me, or those that they consider to be 'for internal use only'.

What is more, people in the field of practice both produce and consume a multitude of accounts and all types of narratives produced elsewhere. Their selection procedures are of obvious interest to an organization scholar, and it is equally obvious that it is easier to figure them out by observation than by speculation. What do they see? What do they read and hear? And why do they see, read, and hear these specific things?

As my colleagues and I have learned in preparing a collection of cases on organizing around threat and risk (Czarniawska, 2009), the Web is a practically infinite source of material. Because each day brings new contributions, going to the field can also be a way of *limiting* research material to manageable proportions – by allowing the practitioners to select material that they find relevant for their practice.

So researchers go into the field for at least three reasons: Because other people live and work there and can be observed, because that is where the accounts of their life and work is produced, and because that is where some of these accounts are 'consumed'.

An important source of inspiration for fieldwork is to be found in anthropological studies. Although there are a great many ethnographies of and from modern countries (Kunda, 1992/2006; Nigel Barley, 1995), they are adapted versions of techniques developed in studies of premodern societies.

Fieldwork in premodern societies

With the growth of what can be called 'contemporary ethnographies', there is much debate over the correct way to conduct studies of modern practices in an anthropological mode. Some researchers, like organization sociologist S. Paul Bate (1997), consider most such studies to be 'quick and dirty jobs' done on an 'in and out' basis, and they urge a return to traditional work ethnography:

> On closer examination 'thick description' invariably turns out to be 'quick description', yet another business case study or company history, a pale reflection of the experientially rich social science envisaged by early writers like [US anthropologist Michael] Agar. 'Prolonged contact with the field' means a series of flying visits rather than a long-term stay (jet plane ethnography). Organizational anthropologists rarely take a toothbrush with them these days. A journey into the organizational bush is often little more than a safe and closely chaperoned form of anthropological tourism. (Bate, 1997: 1150)

As Prasad and Prasad (2002) observed, Bate's critique is infused with a strong nostalgia for such 'heroic' ethnographies as those of Bronisław Malinowski. Although I agree with them, I am also sympathetic with Bate's critique of 'flying visits', on the grounds of their frequent cursoriness. Quite a few researchers reach profound conclusions about humanity on the basis of the answers given to abstract interview questions, which are assumed to be windows into the depths of reality.

This problem has no easy solution. Too much material and too little material may be equally problematic, as David Silverman (1993/2011) suggested, and as my research group's excursion into the Web has proven. As to the cardinal rule of ethnography – the necessity for a prolonged period of participant observation – it encounters four problems in research on such matters as contemporary organizing: problems of participation, of time, of space, and of invisibility (Czarniawska, 2007). I discuss them here one by one.

In the case of organization research, participant observation means that an employee becomes a researcher or a researcher becomes an employee – the method adopted by Melville Dalton (1959), a manager; by Michael Burawoy (1979), a machine-tool operator; by John Van Maanen (1982) and Jennifer Hunt (1984), police trainees; and by Robin Leidner (1993), a McDonald's employee and Combined Insurance trainee.

These examples indicate that such studies – no doubt superior to all other types of field studies – are possible to conduct only with exceptional luck in obtaining access or because the workplace of research interest does not require specific qualifications. I could probably try to play the role of a personnel manager, but it would require such effort that it would effectively prevent me from observing. It would take me years to obtain the state of 'detached involvement' that Severyn Bruyn (1966) considered ideal for a participant observer dropped into an alien culture.[2] Participation in a dance differs from participation in a top management emergency meeting. Prasad and Prasad (2002) claimed that top levels of the hierarchy are hidden from an ethnographic gaze for power-related reasons, but they overlooked the fact that these levels may simply be difficult to access in a participative mode. For researchers who are also practitioners in the field they study, however, or when the topic of the study is everyday life, self-observation (Brinkmann, 2012) can be extremely useful.

It is necessary to emphasize at this juncture that I have been using the term 'participant observation' literally, excluding the situations in which the researcher is present as an observer rather than a participant, as was the case with Gideon Kunda (1992/2006), who visited a hi-tech company; and Mitchel Abolafia (1996), who visited Wall Street. Such nonparticipant but direct observation is an obvious possibility for social scientists, and it is enhanced if the observation time is prolonged. Still, this is not to say the longer, the better.

The issue of time is especially problematic in organization studies. Consider, for example, the advice that science anthropologist Sharon Traweek has given to her colleagues in her article on fieldwork strategies in science studies:

> Our first field work should last a minimum of one year, preferably two; subsequent field trips can last as little as three months as long as they occur at least every three or four years. The questions and theories change, but we study the same people if they survive as a community, and maybe later on we also study some of their neighbors. (Traweek, 1992: 438)

My study of management in the City of Warsaw (Czarniawska, 2000) took me about 14 months. During that time, a new city council was elected, which meant that I lost half my interlocutors. Moreover, 'their neighbors', as Traweek called them, also changed as a result of an administrative reform. The point is that I was not studying a community of city managers but an *action net of city management*: interconnected acts of organizing (Czarniawska, 2002).

Traweek studied Japanese physicists for something like 20 years before she began to feel that she was getting the gist of their lives and activities. Suppose I had studied

Warsaw management for 20 more years. It would no doubt be a fascinating study, but I am not sure that there will be much about Warsaw's management in 2015 that was crucial in understanding the management of that city in 1995. I do not believe that there was some 'essence' that I could have revealed, given more time. Specific persons may retire or be exchanged as a result of the latest political coup, but the actions that constitute management remain. On the other hand, the form and content of actions may change drastically, even if the same people remain as a result of, say, a new information technology or a new fashion in big city management.

'Japanese physicists' may be creating an impression of stability quite incidentally, by remaining in the same space. But do they, actually? Researchers travel a lot nowadays. Time and space are inextricably intertwined in practice, although they become separated in theory. This separation facilitates specific theoretical biases. German anthropologist Johannes Fabian (1983) said that traditional anthropology counted the time of the Other in a different way than it counted 'our time'. In such a view, the Other's time goes more slowly than ours does, and it is not coeval (the Other is perceived as living in another era). Now, time in contemporary, complex organizations is condensed, and it is counted in many places concurrently. It is not merely coeval, but multiple. And it runs fast. The journalists in the news agencies I studied (Czarniawska, 2012) could not understand why I needed so much time to write my report or who was going to be interested in it a year later.

Hanns-Georg Brose (2004) suggested that contemporary western societies are characterized by three connected phenomena: acceleration, shortened time horizons, and increasing simultaneity of events. *Acceleration* refers to the hastening of social processes – the shorter life cycle of products, the faster pace of innovation – accompanied by such acts of resistance as the slow food movement. According to Brose, acceleration and resistance to acceleration must be studied together. A second phenomenon, related to the first and commented upon frequently by Zygmunt Bauman (e.g. 1995), is the *shortened time horizon* of expectations and orientations, resulting in a shorter duration of social structures and personal commitments. Both acceleration and shortened time horizon are causes and effects of a third phenomenon: an *increasing simultaneity of events* in what Schütz and Luckmann (1983) called 'the world at reach'. In this context, Brose formulated a question that is appropriate as a rationale for this text, especially if 'we' in his utterance is understood as 'we social scientists':

> More and more rapidly varying events seem to appear on our different screens, overlapping and blurring the rhythms of our everyday life (e.g. work and leisure) and life-courses, breaking the gendered coupling of work and education. As the functioning of the ordering principles (first things first) and synchronizing mechanisms (calendars and clocks) cannot be taken for granted any more, are we deemed – like with television – to zap around? (Brose, 2004: 7)

As our world at reach has widened, it has become increasingly difficult to record and interpret it. Zapping is one solution, a bird's-eye view another; but they hardly solve the quandary of contemporary fieldwork: How does one study the same object in different places at the same time?

Another difficulty is revealed here, resulting from an attempt to follow the anthropological tradition: dealing with space. An observer is usually situated in one room, one corridor, or one branch, although some excursions may occur, especially when the technique of shadowing is used (Chapter 5). Modern organizing, on the other hand, occurs in a net of fragmented, multiple contexts, through multitudes of kaleidoscopic movements. It happens in many places at once, and organizers move around quickly and frequently. As Lars Strannegård aptly noted in the title of his fascinating study of an IT company (complemented by the artwork of Maria Friberg), the people he studied were constantly 'already elsewhere' (Strannegård and Friberg, 2001).

Additionally, not all interactions require a physical presence. Knorr Cetina and Bruegger (2002) spoke about *embodied presence* and *response presence* (the latter not necessarily visible to an observer), as when people 'talk' to somebody via e-mail. As Barley and Kunda (2001: 85) noted, traditional observation is usually inadequate to capture any type of computer work, so they recommended a more sophisticated use of technical aids in observation (more on this in Chapter 9). Traditional techniques need to be updated if they are to be of use in the study of contemporary fields of practice. But before I move to that issue, it is necessary to attend to another activity typical of the early stages of social science research. It is imperative to check if somebody has not already made the same or a similar study. In other words, it is necessary to read the literature.

What do I want to know and why?

Answer the following questions about your own work:

1. What do I want to know?
2. Why do I want to know this?
3. How will I learn about it?

EXERCISE 1

FURTHER READING

Brinkmann, Svend (2012) *Qualitative Inquiry in everyday life: Working with everyday life materials.* London: Sage.

Carson, David, Gilmore, Audrey, Perry, Chad and Gronhaug, Kjell (2001) *Qualitative marketing research.* London: Sage.

Green, Judith and Thorogood, Nicki (2004) *Qualitative methods for health research.* London: Sage.

Silverman, David (1993/2011) *Interpreting qualitative data: Methods for analysing talk, text and interaction.* London: Sage.

Notes

1. In other versions of this apocryphal story (Buridan never wrote it himself), the donkey has to choose between two piles of hay, or between a pile of hay and a pile of oats. At any rate, in Luhmann's opinion (1995: 360), an actual donkey would survive, being an actor and not an observer …
2. He is emphatic, however, that detached involvement does not equal lack of bias; bias is both inevitable and revealing (Bruyn, 2002).

2
Reviewing Literature

The suggestions in this chapter have been drawn from the general theory of reading, and can be used when reading either scientific literature or written field material. Reporting and referencing of the literature can follow different templates; the emphasis here is on the key traits of any literature review.

DOING THE SEARCH

Having decided upon a research question to be answered or a research problem to be solved, the obvious next step is to check if somebody else has already done that study and answered that question. And in spite of the friendly presence of the Web, it is amazing how often people do not realize that an identical or highly similar study has already been done – often in a neighboring department or university, sometimes even in the same department. My guess is that all scholars, young and old, believe that it is impossible for anyone else to have had 'their' idea. Alas, as Robert Merton (1965/1985) has reminded his readers, all ideas are some place all the time; they merely change shape somewhat and become more or less visible. So, a thorough check is a must.

By a *thorough* check I mean *reading the texts*, as opposed to reading the abstracts – or reading only someone else's rendering of a study. It is, in fact, relatively easy to see from a text whether its author has read the referenced work or only skimmed the abstract. As you know, or soon will learn, writing abstracts is a skill in itself, and some authors are better at it than others. Additionally, the formal structuring of abstracts required by many journal publishers renders them a parody. I have submitted an article to a methodology journal in which the options in the category 'Paper type' (one is tempted to write 'Vellum') did not contain a method paper. Hopefully, a thorough check will end with the discovery that nobody has answered exactly the same question that you have asked. The search can yield at least two possible results. *First*, it is possible that although the specific question has not been answered, an existing theory satisfactorily explains a range of similar phenomena. In that case, there are at least two possible reactions: Drop the topic and look for another, unexplored problem, or decide to test the general theory on the specific case of the phenomenon. Your literature review would then consist of a thorough presentation of the theory in question, ending with an argument demonstrating that the theory needs to be tested and/or extended. *Second*, and more likely, the search will find neither an identical study nor an adequate theory of the phenomenon in question. Rather, the search will probably yield similar studies and theories concerning similar phenomena, which will constitute material for your literature review.

But what if there are a great many texts containing relevant material, as is likely to happen in these times of information overload? One answer to this question has already been given: Read the texts! Only then will you know what is truly relevant and what only seems so.

The next question to be asked is: 'In which way will I use this text in the argument to follow?' One such way is called *exegetic*: rendering the other author's text an object of criticism or material for a careful interpretation. The main thing then is to re-present the author as faithfully as possible (see next section), then take a stance: apologetic, critical, or a step beyond. Another way of referencing literature is *inspirational*, which is close to Michel de Certeau's (1984/1988) vision of reading as a poaching of ideas. I like the concept of emplotment, for instance, and I give Hayden White (1973) his due, but I use emplotment for my own purposes, in whatever way I see fit.

For some reason, the general assumption about literature reviews seems to be that the more references the better. This tactic leads to at least two curious practices. One is the referencing of clichés, like 'life is a theater'. But this expression has often been used, especially since Erving Goffman (1959); so, unless the researcher wants to use a Goffmanian frame, there should be no point in referencing this statement. Another peculiar practice is the quoting of sources that the author considers bad sources, on the assumption that all relevant literature must be mentioned. Because this strategy creates too many sources to allow for a thorough critique, scientific writers tend to save themselves by merely quoting the relevant authors in a long shopping list. The loser is the reader who must wade through piles of scientific products, only to discard them.

CLOSE READING

I find especially helpful the triad formulated by English literature theoretician Paul Hernadi (1987), who divided the act of interpretation of texts into three stages:

explication, explanation, and exploration. The attraction of his classification consists, among other things, of abolishing the traditional divides between 'interpretation' and 'explanation'. In a similar vein, the famous theoretician of literature Northrop Frye (1957/1990) spoke of 'standing under', 'standing over', and 'standing in for' a text. I combine both Hernadi's and Frye's triads in this section.

Explication is close to a reproduction; the interpreter chooses to *stand under* the text, aiming to understand it. Put simply, it answers the humble question: 'What does this text say?' The next stage, *explanation*, employs analytical moves; the reader *stands over* the text. The question to be answered is: 'Why does this text say what it says?' This question can be answered in many ways, depending on the reader's preference and the type of text. It can set the text in a wider context (*con-* other *texts*): of the same author (this stance is characteristic of this author), of others (this is typical of that school of thought, that time, or that place). Explanation can also start from an assumption held by historian and narratologist Hayden White (1987), who claimed that form also carries a message – that there is content in the form, and therefore the question 'why?' should be translated into questions 'how?' and 'how come?' These questions can be asked traditionally – that is politely – or with the intention of interrupting the text or even deconstructing it (see Chapter 11).

Scholars then proceed to the third stage of *exploration*, in which the readers *stand in for* the author, thus constructing a new text, although with an original one as a starting point. This stage may require the construction of a new text from scratch or a reconstruction of the existing one. In other words, it can be a critique or an espousal of the ideas or theories from the literature under scrutiny.

To illustrate the three stages, I am quoting my recent article (Czarniawska, 2013a) dedicated to a query concerning management consultants: Do they decrease or increase uncertainty in their clients? I searched for the answer to this question in the writings of four authors: Karl E. Weick, Niklas Luhmann, Gabriel Tarde, and James G. March (a social psychologist, two sociologists, and a political scientist). Here is my presentation of Niklas Luhmann's opinion, divided into Hernadi's three stages.

Explication

Luhmann doubted if the templates delivered by consultants arrive to clients in the same form as they were transmitted, whether they claim to deliver a theory or to instigate a practice. He questioned the possibility of a successful communication between consultants and their clients, as, in his view, their acts of communication form two distinct and closed systems (Luhmann 1989/2005; …). Such systems can only reproduce themselves, according to their blueprint, or 'DNA' – thus the term 'autopoiesis'. Although all energy systems are open systems (there is no *perpetuum mobile*), communication systems are autopoietic (Luhmann 1995).

… clients and consultants are unable to understand one another; they live in two worlds, and will never meet. So, yes, consultants merely plough through, unaware of the contradictions between their theories and their practices. This is because they see themselves as observers of other actors, and fail to see that they are actors, and not observers of their own practice (Luhmann 1995). Like every other actor, they have a blind spot where their own practice is concerned, but their practices are observed by their clients who, Luhmann suggested, actually select them on the basis of their blind spots (Luhmann 1989/2005).

Furthermore, the unsuccessful communication does not mean that management consulting is useless. According to Luhmann, the attempts at communication produced by management consultants serve as an irritant to the client system. Consultants do not 'know better'; they are able to observe the actors, and see them in another light than that in which the actors try to observe themselves. It is this difference in the observation points that can become 'irritating, stimulating, and eventually productive' (Luhmann 1989/2005: 364). Left to themselves, clients would be enacting their own visions of the world, perhaps until some crisis stopped them. Irritated by consultants, the clients may themselves arrive at a new and brilliant solution to their problems, which will still conform to the main traits of the system. ... (Czarniawska, 2013a: 13–14)

This is not the entire text of Luhmann's 1989 article of course; in my article, I have summarized only what is relevant to my argument, and I contextualized it referring to Luhmann's other work from 1995, which is the best known statement of his system theory. Observe that the three stages are rarely separated in writing practice; Hernadi's division is an heuristic device rather than an algorithm.

Explanation (by contextualization)

Clegg et al. (2004) have taken a somewhat similar approach, but one based on the ideas of Michel Serres rather than those of Luhmann. These authors used the term *parasites* to describe the relationship between consultants and their clients. ...

The conceptualization of consultants as parasites resonates with Luhmann's notion of consultants as external irritants who produce changes not by directly relating to clients, but by stimulating the client's social system from outside. ... Thus although their role can be seen as positive, in such a perspective consultants increase or even provoke uncertainty rather than helping to reduce it. They are helpful in the sense of disturbing routines and established truths, but can also increase ambiguity by offering interpretations alternative to the received ones. The system cannot incorporate the alternative, but it is shaken from its complacency by the awareness that an alternative interpretation exists. ...

The effective communication, however, is commonly taken for granted as a main connection between consultants and their clients. How else would consultants convince their clients to change their actions, which the consultants

promise to do and for which they are paid? Luhmann, who was interested
in the ideas of Gabriel Tarde before the present interest in Tarde began ... ,
pointed out that Tarde's theory of imitation explained how order could be possible without cognition (Luhmann, 1998). By the same token, consultants and
clients can act similarly without having succeeded to communicate.
(Czarniawska, 2013a: 14–15)

The explanation here proceeds by setting Luhmann's text beside other texts, this
time with texts that carry a similar message. One of those messages (Clegg et al.,
2004) was written later than Luhmann's and extends the context even further, by
referring to another philosopher. The other, the reference to Tarde's work, extends
the context back in time. These references are not disparate; as it happens, Michel
Serres (evoked by Clegg et al.) belongs to the same philosophical tradition as
Gabriel Tarde. The reference net is closed (for the time being), and embraces the
text in focus.

   I could have chosen to contrast Luhmann's ideas with opposing views, explaining
his position as a voice in a debate; or I could have focused on the way Luhmann
writes, explaining it through German sociological tradition or Luhmann's style. But
in this context, either of these choices would only deflect the reader's attention from
my main focus: the connection between management consultants and uncertainty.
Thus, after having reviewed texts by other authors, I move to my own exploration
of the theme.

Exploration

   In my reading, all the authors quoted by me here agree on all important points,
   although their theory of consulting seems to go against the commonly approved
   one. Consultants do not offer practical solutions, but serve as guides through the
   forest of managerial fashions; they are useful *because* they are unable to communicate in the same terms that their client systems employ; their advice needs be
   aesthetically attractive rather than correct. Consultants may come up with good
   stories themselves or merely provoke their clients to concoct some new ones, if
   by sheer irritation.

   From this perspective, it becomes obvious that consultants can both reduce and
   increase uncertainty. Furthermore, both reduction and increase can have positive
   or negative consequences for their clients. (Czarniawska, 2013a: 19)

I find Hernadi's triad helpful as a reminder of steps that need to be taken when
referring to the texts of other authors. The way of writing it up, as illustrated above,
is of course but one way of many (for example, the order could have been reversed).
Nevertheless, there are some general points about writing a literature review that
should be considered.

STRUCTURING THE REVIEW

> As civilized human beings, we are the inheritors neither of an inquiry about
> ourselves and the world, nor of an accumulating body of information, but of a
> conversation begun in the primeval forest and extended and made more articu-
> late in the course of centuries … (Oakeshott, 1959/1991: 490)

A literature chapter can be structured in at least two ways: chronologically or thematically. The thematic way sounds more ambitious, but if there is any truth in
Michael Oakeshott's claim that science is but a conversation, a chronological reporting helps to render that conversation visible. After all, scholars write their texts in
response to texts written earlier, and a chronological ordering also helps to locate
a given text in its time and place (provided that the first edition is always quoted).

For example, many commentators on Glaser and Strauss's (1967) grounded theory
forget that it was written in the California of the late 1960s, within the topical concerns and discussions of that time and place. This awareness, lacking in many other
renditions of grounded theory, makes Kathy Charmaz's (2006/2014) *Constructing
Grounded Theory* an excellent contemporary introduction to this approach.

Whether the literature review is structured chronologically or thematically, the
final part of the literature chapter must contain the following components, all drawn
from the literature already presented. The first component is a theoretical frame of
reference, and/or partial or complete theories of the phenomenon under study.
Even if there is no theory of the phenomenon – if a theory must be constructed
from the grounds of field material (see Chapter 3) – this very decision is the choice
of a theoretical frame of reference. The theory of truth as correspondence to reality and
the theory of truth as coherence (Rorty, 1980) are two contrasting theoretical reference frames, and a thoughtful choice must be made between them. The choice of a
theoretical frame of reference is followed, albeit not automatically, by the choice
of a methodology. Researchers espousing constructivism may choose an idealist version of Kenneth Gergen (1999/2009) or a materialist version of Actor-Network
Theory (Latour, 2005). The chosen approach will limit the choice of methods and
techniques to a certain extent, but there are so many possibilities that this is not
a concern. Rather, the concern should be for coherence: The chosen theoretical
frame, methodology, and techniques must match.

And so I come to the final component of the literature review, which should consist of indicating studies that will serve as a comparison to the study being planned.
They can be chosen for various reasons: because they are studies of the same or
similar phenomenon or because they used the same theoretical or methodological
frames on different phenomena or simply on different sites.

A grounded theory approach, which I present in the next chapter, allows theoretical associations to arise while the study is being conducted, but not in advance.
Whether to present them early, in the literature review – in the hindsight of known
results – or to wait until the field material justifies the reference is merely a stylistic

preference. Great scholars who were also great writers used both styles throughout the history of science – and not only the social sciences. Some readers hate to be surprised by new threads and references in the process of reading; others hate to be told in advance what is awaiting them in the text to follow. Do not believe people who tell you that the only scientific way is to summarize in advance.

David Silverman (1999/2009: Ch. 18) provided one unorthodox but pertinent piece of advice on timing the writing of a literature review. Many method books and many advisers tell students that a literature review must be done first. This advice is correct insofar as 'done' is not the synonym of 'written'. It is necessary to do a *literature search* – thorough reading and note taking – before starting a study, for the reasons I mentioned at the beginning of this chapter: To check if the study has already been done. But the writing should be done, Silverman suggested, 'after your other chapters' (p. 298). After all, you do not know which literature will be relevant until you have analyzed your field material. Only then can you decide about the location of references to various relevant texts. Basically, the entire document is best written backwards, because only after you have theorized your findings, will you know how much of the field material should be incorporated. Only then will you know the aspects of the methods that are worth explicating at length; and only then will you know exactly what literature is directly relevant. The introduction is best written last, of course. There is only one exception to that backward rule: The bibliography or references must truly be written last.

REFERENCING

In his gloomy but fascinating book, *The Decline of Discourse* (1990), Ben Agger compared academic writing to real estate business: In both practices everything is a matter of clever acquisitions and swift speculations. In this business, citations serve the main function of supporting the self-replication of the academic system, and copyrights concern not so much ideas as property rights – rights to a given place, or space, in the system. 'After all, academics write for themselves, and for others like them. They write not to be read but to command space, the basis of value in the academic world' (Agger, 1990: 136).

In order to be read, one must quote others; in order to continue to write, one must be quoted by others – so turn the mills of what Thomas Kuhn (1962/2012) has called 'normal science'. As Kaplan (1965: 181) has observed, citation practices solve the dilemma of knowledge as common property and individual property, based on priority. Scientists may not keep their products, but they are rewarded for production by points earned for early delivery.

Because I am propagating Oakeshott's idea of science as conversation in this chapter, it is crucial to note that references should be telling the story of this conversation. After all, the date of the original publication indicates when the conversation first occurred, although the date of publication actually quoted is helpful to the contemporary reader. The time of the original conversation is key, not because of some historical pedantry, but because it indicates its intended participants.

Roland Warren, Stephen Rose, and Ann Bergunder's *The Structure of Urban Reform* (1974) provides an example of a report that epitomizes organization studies done from an institutionalist perspective. But it was published at a time when the old institutionalism seemed to be buried for good in sociology, and the new institutionalism (usually dated since Meyer and Rowan's article published in 1977) had not yet emerged. The author most quoted in their book is Eric Trist ('sociotechnical systems'), who seems on the surface to be the least likely conversation partner for institutionalists. But in those days, the sociotechnical systems were a major topic of conversation, and it would be impolite, not to mention unpolitical, not to mention them. These and other stories can be read (or speculated about) from the reference list.

One sure way of killing the record of an important conversation is through ahistorical referencing, accomplished by alphabetical ordering and by quoting only the latest edition. My favorite such citation is 'Weber, 1964', from which it is easy to deduce that everything Max Weber knew about organizations he learned from March and Simon (1958/1993) – although he died in 1920. In fact, 'Weber, 1964' carries yet another story: Postwar German sociologists received Weber mostly in the guise of retranslations of his work by Parsons, Bendix, and other structural functionalists, and no (good) translation is literal. Comparisons with the original raise quite a few questions as to the exactness of those translations (see e.g. Kaelber, 2002).

Of course, if you cite Weber as '1947', which is when Talcott Parsons translated Weber's book into English, it is correct if you have never seen the original, and for all you know, Parsons might have invented the whole thing. But *Wirtschaft und Gesellschaft* was published posthumously in 1922, and that is historical fact. It may seem but a courtesy to remember who said what first, but in 1958 March and Simon were actually answering some questions that Weber posed in German in 1922 and Parsons posed in English in 1947.

Sometimes the reader has a feeling that referencing replaces the argument: 'Highlighting contradictions (Smith, 1987), we arrive at a stock-of-knowledge (Schutz, 1973) in order to be able to explore *la différance* proper (Derrida, 1967/1976)'. This quote is almost authentic (I changed it somewhat to avoid recognition). The sentence does not *say* anything, it only *does* something, as Silverman and Torode (1980) would put it. In this case, it shows the authors' familiarity with the jargon à la mode.

'Highlighting contradictions' is something that anybody can do – not only 'Smith, 1987'. Smith is a common surname in English, is it Dorothy? Then, certain authors have copyrights on certain vocabularies and neologisms: 'stock of knowledge' belongs to Alfred Schütz (1953/1973) and *la différance* to Jacques Derrida (1967/1976). But do readers know enough about these concepts to continue reading, or would they have to interrupt their reading to check Schütz and Derrida in order to understand the rest?

Another problem, felt most acutely by some readers, is counterargument referencing. In referencing a critical argument, it is often uncertain whether the author quoted is guilty of what is criticized or merely criticized it first. (Was Smith's argument contradictory or did she highlight somebody else's contradictions?) Similarly, in the case of 'stock of knowledge (Schutz, 1973)', the reader unfamiliar with Schütz's writings does not know if Schütz was someone with a stock of knowledge or the person who invented the expression. (Notice, also, that thanks to advancements in computer keyboard technology, Alfred Schütz can posthumously enjoy his name in its correct version: Schütz rather than 'Schutz'.)

If references are to tell a history of conversation, it makes sense to turn to historians and literary critics for models. In those disciplines, texts are seen as events, not merely as indices of legal rights and records of priority. Citing Merton's *On the Shoulders of Giants* as '1965/1985' is not analogous to establishing when cold fusion was first achieved. It tells the reader that a book that was written before 1965 became relevant (again?) in 1985. From that bit of information, one can speculate that the 1960s and the 1980s had more in common than the 1970s. It may be a wrong conclusion, but it is worth investigating. And so it goes, especially for exegetic approaches. First names make authors human and give women authors their overdue due. I am aware that some women authors in the USA are concerned that their feminine names will open their texts up to discriminatory reading. Correct as that suspicion may be, the practice of hiding gender only perpetuates the status quo. Many more women created organization studies than is commonly believed, but their first names have been hidden in their initials.

Exact references not only provide proof of a proper bibliographical work. They confirm the text's belongingness to a genre and a convention. It is social science, and social science is written predominantly in a realist convention. Although not experimentally established facts, references fulfill the same function: They promise that a text can be 'checked against reality'. Referencing may be but a routine resulting from the modern institution of copyrights, but discovering that the year of publication is wrong in some items can put at risk the credibility of the entire enterprise. When French novelist Jean d'Ormesson fakes all references in his pseudo-scientific historical novel, I am delighted. When the author of a purportedly scientific article fakes the sources in order to pull my leg, I am still delighted (see, for example, 'A surrealistic mega-analysis of redisorganization theories' by Oxman et al., 2006). When writers demanding serious attention do not get their references right, I am disenchanted.

As a writer of social science studies, I fight against memory lapses, vanishing traces, and tricky computers in order to keep my references straight. As a reader of social science studies, I hope to find in references a meta-story of the topic, a trace of conversations between texts, which occurred at a concrete time and in a concrete place. Past conversations, like personal memories, can be rewoven into present conversations and thus acquire meaning beyond the faithful remembrance of things past.

Explication, explanation, exploration

Take a short text of one of your favorite social science writers and go through Hernadi's three reading stages.

FURTHER READING

Hart, Chris (1998) *Doing a literature review: Releasing the social science research imagination.* London: Sage.

Oliver, Paul (2012) *Succeeding with your literature review: A handbook for students.* Maidenhead: Open University Press.

3

Designing the Study

When the decisions have been made about the phenomenon to be studied, and the predecessors have been found, or found missing, the time has come to answer in detail the question: How is the study to be conducted? This chapter presents a review of several options, based on examples of well-known works.

CASES, WINDOWS, SITES

> Case studies have been around as long as recorded history and today they account for a large proportion of books and articles in psychology, anthropology, sociology, history, political science, education, economics, management, biology, and medical science. (Flyvbjerg, 2011: 302)

When I refer to a case study in this text, I mean *a study of the occurrence of a phenomenon* – a chain of events, usually limited in time, usually studied retrospectively. The term is used in a great many, sometimes contradictory ways, however. Bent Flyvbjerg, a veteran of case studies, the best known of which is probably *Rationality and Power* (1998), has written an article entitled 'Five misunderstandings about case-study research' (2006), to which I could add at least three.

One misunderstanding consists of applying the term 'case study' to all *fieldwork*. This misunderstanding could have begun with the extremely popular yet misleading work of Robert Yin (1984), but it continues to be repeated almost 30 years later. His understanding of case studies as all fieldwork led him to claim that they are only studies of contemporary phenomena (Yin, 1984: 23). Yet the most famous case studies are historical (e.g. Ginzburg, 1966/1983, in anthropology; Chandler, 1977, in business history; Schama, 1987, in history).

The second misnomer is to use the term 'case study' for all types of *qualitative research*. The reasoning goes this way: If you do not perform statistics, you are surely doing a case study. This misunderstanding is as problematic as the previous one, because it conceals the fact that there can be, and are, well-executed and noteworthy quantitative case studies, such as Davis and MacNeilage's (1990) study from linguistics and the Schacter et al. (1982) study from psychology. Observe that the name of the phenomenon under study forms the title of both articles: 'Acquisition of correct vowel production' and 'Functional retrograde amnesia'.

But the most common error is definitely that of mistaking the site for the phenomenon under study. 'Volvo is my case', doctoral students tell me with pride. 'A case of what?' ask I, in what I hope is not an unfriendly way. They look at me, disconcerted.

I have long wondered about the reason for these misunderstandings. I hasten to explain that I am motivated not by semantic purism (How could I, not being a native English speaker?) Rather I am motivated by a commonsense approach to methodology. If case studies are all studies that use fieldwork, where does one categorize case studies based on secondhand data, as almost all historical case studies are? If case studies can only be qualitative studies, how does one classify quantitative case studies? (For why would the researcher not count if there is something relevant in the case to be counted?) And, finally, if cases are sites, what should be done if one site presents an opportunity to study several different phenomena – like most of the sites chosen by ethnologists and anthropologists? Or when a phenomenon occurs at several sites at once, as in management fashions?

Looking for the reasons behind this semantic mess, I turned to the history of case studies. Cases came to social science from medicine, particularly from psychiatry; and from law (the case method was imported into business education by early Harvard Business School professors who were lawyers; Muniesa, 2012). In both contexts, it was a *case of a phenomenon*: an illness in medicine and a crime in law. However – for reasons of brevity, I suppose – the name of the phenomenon in question, being obvious, has been omitted. Thus Conan Doyle's 'the case of the hansom cab killer' and Freud's[1] 'the case of Dora'.

Another reason for the semantic problem could be that the meaning of the term 'case' I am pleading for comes from grammar and from the declension of nouns; thus languages that do not decline their nouns do not evoke this meaning of the word 'case'. Yet even contemporary Italians such as Paolo Quattrone (2006) use 'case study' in the meaning of 'fieldwork'.

Flyvbjerg's critique (2006) was targeted primarily on these varied understandings of the term 'case study'. But one common criticism is independent of that issue: The alleged impossibility of generalizing from one case study. Recently, Carlo Ginzburg (2011) raised this issue in the thank-you speech he delivered when receiving the Prize Balzan 2010. Quoting Marcel Mauss, Ginzburg confirmed that an intense and extensive study of one case can be a basis for generalization (more about that in

Chapter 13). But, he added, this is especially so when the case is anomalous, because anomaly contains in itself the definition of 'normality'. This observation is especially pertinent when a field study is being designed, the point in time when beginning researchers are often concerned about the typicality of their case.

Nevertheless, there are possibilities other than case studies for doing fieldwork. Traditional anthropologists used to spend a long time with one tribe and describe not one, but all the phenomena they could observe. I called this type of study a *window study* – when a researcher opens an arbitrary window in time, and describes all that can be seen through it (Czarniawska, 1997). Studies of this kind are now commonly called 'ethnographies', as the methodological inspiration came from anthropology and ethnology, but that term is yet another misnomer. Field studies within social sciences rarely, if ever, describe a people's way of living (*ethno*), and they can be written (*graphy*) in numerous ways. More about that in Chapter 12. For the moment, I stick to my 'window studies', or to studies with a design that begins with the choice of a site.

A window study, or the choice of a site rather than a case, is usually dictated by an imprecise research question, but activated by information that something inter-esting is happening at a specific site, be that illegal Roma camps (Sigona, 2005) or a computer company that designs its own culture (Kunda, 1992/2006). A window study can turn into a case study if the researcher decides to follow a train of events; it can even turn into a series of mini-cases (Michael Burawoy's, 1998, 'extended case method' can be seen as an example). The result can be a full-fledged ethnography or a description of the way some people work (*ergonographies*, Czarniawska, 1997), or, most likely, what Annemarie Mol (2002) so aptly called *praxiography* – the descrip-tion of a practice, rather than the description of a tribe (a group, a profession).

An illustrative contrast between the two types of studies can be found by compar-ing two of Bruno Latour's works. One, *Aramis, or the Love of Technology* (1996), is a case study – the case of the introduction of a new technology that ended in failure. The other, *The Making of Law* (2010), is an ethnography of a French organization, the Council of State. Both studies are written in an original way. The former is a *Bildungsroman* – the story of someone's formative years – in this case the story of a young scholar learning his craft by studying the story of the unlucky train, Aramis. *The Making of Law* applies a narratological analysis. But the ways of choosing sources of information, sites, type of material differ, and are characteristic of those two types of research design.

But both studies required that choices be made. What phenomenon or practice should be the focus? Where to look for it? The grounded theory approach can be of great help here.

GROUNDED THEORY APPROACH

The 1960s are usually seen as the time when the popularity of the positivist approach in social sciences reached its peak. It demanded that young researchers test ('verify' or 'falsify', depending on the version of logical empiricism) the theories of their elders (usually speculatively deduced). Sociologists Barney G. Glaser and Anselm Strauss (1967) disagreed, however. They suggested that theories built inductively from empirical grounds are more useful – and more interesting – than those deduced from other theories or speculations. This claim, provocative at the time, is now, almost half a century later, practically taken for granted. The labels changed somewhat, however. In the meantime, the social sciences rediscovered the notion of *abduction*, coined by US pragmatist philosopher and semiotician Charles Sanders Peirce (1839–1914).

Abduction is a form of a logical inference that goes from a minute description of some event to an hypothesis (Peirce actually used the term 'guessing'; Sebeok and Sebeok, 1981). This explanation is then tried out ('tested') on the next observation. It has therefore been noted (see e.g. Jo Reichertz, 2010) that grounded theory follows not the precepts of induction, but rather the precepts of abduction – also called 'the logic of discovery'. Instead of amassing 'data', from which a theory can be 'induced', it does, in the words of Barney G. Glaser, 'a set of *double-back steps*' (1978: 16; italics in the original). It moves from the field to the desk and back, step-by-step, refining the 'emerging theory'.

Glaser and Strauss argued that it is more important to build new theories than to verify existing ones, because social reality changes constantly, and every social scientist should aim for a 'reality-fit'. Furthermore, it is this emerging theory rather than mechanical routines that should direct sampling, data collection, and data analysis. To aid this process, they introduced the concepts of *theoretical sampling* and *theoretical saturation*. The following eight steps outline the process of building a grounded theory, schematically presented in a more contemporary vocabulary (Glaser and Strauss's terms are in parentheses following each step).

1. Choose a site (a field of practice, an organization, a community, a group of people, a city, a family) where you are sure to find the phenomenon of interest to you (Theoretical Relevance).

2. Collect material of all accessible kinds, and continue to collect it as long as it brings you new information. As soon as you encounter two or three repetitions, check again, then stop collecting (Theoretical Saturation 1).

3. Decide which aspect of your up-until-now analysis (which you started with the first two pieces of data and continued all along) is the most important. Then look for another site/case that will be as similar as possible to the first (Difference Minimization).

4. Continue as in (2).

5. Is the same aspect still important? If not, repeat (3) from another perspective. If yes, look for a site/case that is as different as possible from the first two (Difference Maximization).

6. Continue as in (2).

7. Alternate between (3) and (5).

8. Stop:

    a) when your time and/or money runs out, or

    b) when you have a relatively consistent theory of the phenomenon (Theoretical Saturation 2).

Here is an example from my recent research. A group of ethnologists and management scholars have been studying the phenomenon of overflow and its management (Czarniawska and Löfgren, 2012). I knew from my earlier studies that news agencies overflow with information, and was curious to learn how they manage it. I procured access to the news agency closest to me: Sweden's *TT Nyhetsbyrån* (TT News Agency) (see Chapter 8 for a discussion of the vagaries of access). Having conducted a series of interviews and having read all possible documents, I concluded that the overflow of incoming data is no problem for them. To the contrary, because of changes in technology, news producers contribute to a general information overflow with the data they produce themselves. This means that there is no physical limit to the newswire, as there was before digitalization. The phenomenon I decided to study, therefore, was the cybernization and cyborgization of news production.

The TT News Agency could have been an exception, however, with its new offices, new computers, and the general computerization of Sweden. For that reason, I secured access to a second site – the Italian ANSA. It was slightly bigger, international rather than national, not English-speaking, and with offices in old buildings. The results were highly similar, so I then moved to a site where the differences were maximized: the global Reuters – huge, English-speaking, and the oldest surviving news agency. The final result was my theory of the cybernization and cyborgization of news production (Czarniawska, 2012).

I could imagine a slightly different route, still following grounded theory precepts. I could have begun with Reuters, then moved to the Associated Press (global, old, and using English), and then moved to, say, the Polish *Polska Agencja Prasowa* – PAP (national, relatively young, local language).

Thus the grounded theory approach advocates something that can be called a *continuous design*. The study is not designed at the outset, but is constantly redesigned. Indeed, the motto of grounded theory is 'constant comparative analysis': The collection of field materials, coding, analyzing, and theorizing are simultaneous, and continue throughout the entire study.

There have been various critiques of grounded theory, some of them based upon misinterpretation. One such comment, often coming from anthropologists, was that grounded theory is nothing but the commonsense of fieldwork. I would say that this is exactly the reason it has become so popular: because it summarizes the commonsense of fieldworking. Burawoy (1991: 274–275) put it more delicately, pointing out that Glaser and Strauss merely summarized recommendations formulated earlier by Robert Park, Ernest W. Burgess, Florian Znaniecki and Everett Hughes – the Chicago School of Sociology (with a pinch of Columbia University brought in by Barney Glaser, a student of Paul Lazarsfeld; Charmaz, 2006/2014).

The only problem with the commonsense of fieldwork is that it is not much appreciated by research foundations. An application must sound as if the researcher knew in advance exactly which steps needed to be taken and their results. As this is clearly an impossible task for any researcher, including positivist empiricists, it becomes obvious that an application is a genre in itself, a test of rhetorical skills probably best classified under science fiction.[2]

Another criticism concerned the starting point for grounded theory, supposedly a *tabula rasa* state of mind. Of course, this is sheer nonsense, because a person who knows nothing about anything would be unable to find the site where the study is to be done. There is a great difference, however, between finding the door bearing the name of the city mayor, and having an *a priori* theory of how city mayors manage their cities. If such a theory exists, there is no need for a further study. As I intended to show with my example of what turned out to be the nonexistent information overload at news agencies, one can even discover that the phenomenon originally in question is either absent on the site or not interesting enough, and therefore unworthy of further investigation. Other things may pop up. In this sense, grounded theory is close to another ancient method, which Thomas Huxley called 'a method of Zadig'[3] and others called 'serendipity' (Merton and Barber, 2004) – a method that consists not in accidental discoveries, as some will have it, but in inferential reasoning based on a detailed observation.

The following formulation by two experienced grounded theory researchers explains it well:

> The grounded theorist initially approaches an inquiry with a fairly open mind as to the kind of general theoretical account likely to emerge from the particular investigation. Preconceptions cannot, of course, be wholly abandoned, and we do not suggest that they should be. We do, however, encourage the investigator to commence by concentrating on a detailed inscription of the features of the data collected before attempting to produce more general theoretical statements. (Martin and Turner, 1986: 142–143)

What I have written to this point clearly indicates that, like ethnomethodologists (see e.g. Silverman, 2010), I attribute special value to what they called 'naturally occurring data'. I do have a problem with their vocabulary, however – or rather with two words: 'naturally' and 'data'. The concept of 'nature' has been thoroughly problematized since the development of ethnomethodology (Latour, 2004). It would be better to speak of *spontaneously occurring actions and events* – actions and events not elicited by the researcher. Another problem is that of 'data', the Latin word for 'givens'. If anything, they are 'takens', because even if some field material is given to researchers, it is the researcher who makes the final decision about what to consider and what not to consider. It is a pity that Ronald Laing's (1967) idea of replacing the term 'data' with 'capta' did not capture greater attention. I prefer in this book to use the term 'field material' – collected or manufactured – because I believe, for once not in agreement with David Silverman, that such material can be elicited and coproduced by the researchers, for specific reasons and specific purposes.

Study design also consists of choosing – or designing – field techniques and field equipment. But these issues deserve separate chapters, however.

Designing the study

Write a fictive research application using the template best known in your country and discipline.

EXERCISE 3

FURTHER READING

Charmaz, Kathy (2006/2014) *Constructing grounded theory*, 2nd edn. London: Sage.
Seale, Clive (2012) Generating grounded theory. In: Seale, Clive (ed.) *Researching society and culture*. London: Sage, 239–248.

Notes

1. Although Freud really needs to be absolved of this error. The 'case of Dora' (Ida) was described by Freud as *Brüchstücke einer Hysterie-Analyse* (1905), which was translated into English as 'Fragment of an analysis of a case of hysteria'. It was the later interpreters who shortened it to 'Dora's case' (see e.g. Bernheimer and Kahane, 1990 or Lakoff and Coyne, 1993).
2. David Silverman (1999/2009) and Michèle Lamont (2009) offered useful suggestions on how to write applications in the UK and USA, but the preferred rhetoric differs from one country to another and even from one foundation to another.
3. http://aleph0.clarku.edu/huxley/CE4/Zadig.html, accessed 7 December 2012.

4

Interviewing

Interviews are the most often used field technique in social science research. Yet they are not as simple as frequently assumed. Interviews can be seen as a site for the production of narratives, as a special type of observation, and as an opportunity to sample the dominant discourse. This chapter presents the advantages, complications, and multiple uses of interviewing.

WHAT IS AN INTERVIEW?

Elliot G. Mishler, an authority on narrative interviewing, suggested a very simple answer to this question: 'An interview is a joint product of what interviewees and interviewers talk about together and how they talk with each other' (Mishler, 1986/1991: viii). Absolutely correct, but perhaps not enough to help the beginning researchers to establish the status of the material they are collecting via interviews.

The ingenious spelling of the title of Steinar Kvale's 1996 book, *InterViews*, brought to the attention of researchers like myself at least two unpleasant insights about this much-used technique. The first concerned what, in its usual form, an interview is not: It is not a mutual exchange of views. A more correct name would perhaps be an 'inquisition' or an 'interrogation', quite in tune with the deplorable tradition of calling the interviewees 'informants'. The second insight concerned what, in its frequent version, an interview is: A collection of views and opinions on whatever topic is mentioned. This is not, of course, what most social scientists are after. They want to know facts or they want to know about attitudes or about many other things outside of the interview – the 'reality behind it', as it were.

But should a research interview be an exchange of views between two parties? Kvale claimed that as conversations are the main mode of knowledge production in our societies, conversation should indeed become the model for interviews. He believes that interviews should constitute dialogue: Two persons seeking knowledge and understanding in a common conversational endeavor.

As long as this postulate is crafted in abstract terms, there is no need to raise objections about the ideal, borrowed from philosophy. An interview is, indeed, a common enterprise in knowledge production. But the practice of research interviewing creates its own complications. Kvale pointed out that what he called a 'professional interview' takes a power asymmetry for granted: The 'professional' interrogates the 'object', or, in psychological parlance, the 'subject' responds to the best of his/her knowledge. No wonder that graduate students, at least in Sweden, used to call their interlocutors 'the interview victims'.

There is, however, a peculiar symmetry to this asymmetry. First of all, it is unrealistic to think about researchers as omniscient professionals. They may be professionals in research, but not in the profession of the interlocutor, whose profession is the topic of the conversation (this point is especially obvious in life stories, in which the narrators are the only experts in the matters of their own life). What the researchers have to offer in exchange is not their views, but their respectful and interested attention.

Interlocutors often want to know the opinion of the interviewer on the matter in question or they would like to know the stance of the discipline the researcher represents. But woe to the researcher who takes the request literally. In most cases, it is either a political trap (the interviewee wants to enlist the researcher's support in an ongoing conflict) or a simple rhetorical diving board. I must admit that I have fallen into this trap many a time and started to expand my views on the matter, only to notice the impatience with which my interlocutor waited for me to end my peroration and relinquish the floor.

The experience of more than 40 years of interviewing in five countries has taught me that professionals, especially those in managerial positions, are often quite lonely in their thoughts. Every exposition of their thinking with their own colleagues has political and practical consequences. At home, there is a limit to the amount of 'thinking aloud' that even the most loving family can take during the dinner hour. A research interview thus opens the possibility for an unusual but symmetrical exchange. The practitioners offer personal insight into the realities of their practice. The researchers offer something that our profession has in abundance, but others do not: An opportunity to test one's thoughts without practical consequences.

But none of this resolves the second doubt I raised at the outset: Are personal insights and subjective views all that an interview will yield a researcher? The symmetrical situation can be satisfactory to a therapist, but should it be acceptable to, let's say, a sociologist? Aren't social scientists hoping to get facts rather than opinions?

I understood just how vain that hope was when, in my early study of a reform in Swedish municipalities, the question 'When did you begin to plan this reform?' elicited responses that extended from the early 1930s to the late 1970s. It was valuable information, but not of the kind I expected. To begin with, an unaided memory always falters: People do not remember dates and numbers. There are documents where such facts can be found (always with a caveat that their production must be carefully examined). Furthermore, what people present in interviews are but their interpretations of the world. Still, these interpretations are extremely valuable to the researcher, who can assume that it is the same interpretations that informed their actions.

In order to exploit the technique in full, it is essential to understand that interviews do not stand for anything else; they merely represent an interaction that is recorded or inscribed. That is all they stand for, and it is more than enough. An interaction in which a practitioner is submitted to questioning from an external source is typical – and frequent – in the life and work of many people who, in a world of many and fast connections, must constantly explain themselves to strangers. These strangers can be journalists, social scientists, auditors, or recruitment officers. As noted by Atkinson and Silverman (1997; see also Gubrium and Holstein, 2002), we live in an 'interview society'. People are used to accounting for what they do. Although each of these accounts will be unique in the way every interaction is unique, it would be both presumptuous and unrealistic to assume that interviewees would invent a whole new story just for the sake of the researcher who happened to be interviewing them. The stories produced in interviews are often well rehearsed, and crafted in a legitimate logic.[1] Thus the interviews can be treated first, as an occasion for eliciting narratives (stories); second, as a special type of observation; and third, as an opportunity to collect samples of the prevalent logic of representation – in other words, of the dominant discourse.

A caveat is required here. In this chapter, I am avoiding the often-used term 'in-depth interview' because, trained as a psychologist in the 1960s, I apply this label only to interviews aimed at reaching deep into personal memories, and beginning with a question, 'What is the earliest memory you have?' Such interviews are beyond the moral mandate of social scientists, although Kathy Charmaz attempted to adapt them to a grounded-theory-type sociological inquiry by reformulating the question into 'When, if at all, did you first experience _____ [or notice _____]?' (2006/2014: 30), and she spoke of an 'in-depth exploration of a particular topic or experience' (2006/2014: 25). In much of the method literature, however, 'in-depth interview' denotes an interview longer than 20 minutes or so, which would be better called, following Charmaz (2006: 25), an 'intensive interview'. I am also omitting the label 'open-ended interviews' because I classify 'close-ended' questioning as surveys conducted orally.

THE INTERVIEW AS A SITE OF NARRATIVE RE-PRODUCTION

> Telling stories is far from unusual in everyday conversation, and it is apparently no more unusual for interviewees to respond to questions with narratives if they are given some room to speak. (Mishler, 1986/1991: 69)

Indeed, in many cases, answers given in an interview are spontaneously formed into narratives. This is usually the case with interviews aimed at life histories, or, in an organizational context, at career descriptions – cases in which a narrative is explicitly requested and delivered. This is also the case with interviews aimed at an historical description of a certain process. Such narratives have usually been collectively produced and rehearsed on many occasions, thereby producing great value for the researcher. The eliciting of narratives should be a key element of any interview.

When the topic of an interview is a chain of events that unfolds over time, there is nothing unusual in formulating a question that prompts a narrative. 'Could you tell me the story of the budget reform as you experienced it?' 'Can you recall when you first started to think about changing your career?' But in most cases, both sides must combat the shared conviction that the 'true knowledge' is not composed of narratives. The narrative may be seen only as an introduction to the 'interview proper', which would switch to an analytical mode aimed at producing the logico–scientific knowledge (Bruner, 1986, 1990). 'What were the reasons for the reform?' and 'What were the factors that prompted your change of mind?' are often considered to be truly scientific questions, prompting analytic answers.

This tendency is common among interviewers and interviewees alike (not to mention method books), and it apparently has long historical roots. Jack Goody, an anthropologist renowned for his comparative studies of literate and nonliterate societies (see e.g. Goody 1986), demonstrated that certain forms of knowledge and certain kinds of texts – tables and lists, and many models and taxonomies are complicated lists – became possible only when script arrived. Whereas a narrative can be easily remembered because of its chronological structure and the presence of the central personae, or Characters, tables and lists cannot. (Although even in oral cultures, mnemotechnical devices for the memorization of short lists existed.) Tables and lists, taxonomies and models, are thus props of modern knowledge, leaving stories to women, children, and 'savages' (Mitchell, 1987). A 'list of factors', delivered by an interviewee, lures the interviewer into a false impression of 'getting something concrete', an impression that lasts no longer than the interview itself. When it comes to interpretation, the 'knowledge' acquired disappears, and a desperate researcher is left with such ingenuous devices as counting the numbers of factors and comparing the frequencies with which various factors were mentioned.

In what follows, I quote two examples of my own battle against this tendency, both taken from my studies of big city management where, in the first stage of the project, I conducted a round of interviews with the politicians and officials managing the city, followed by shadowing (Czarniawska, 2007). The first example comes from Warsaw, the second from Stockholm, and it is probably incidental that the first interlocutor was a woman and the second a man.

> BC: Would you start by describing your work, please? What do you do? What are your responsibilities?
>
> I: No. Sorry, but in my case, I must begin with history.

The interlocutor's eagerness to start weaving a narrative could have been context-bound, as a conviction of the importance of history is pervasive in Poland. Whatever the reason, the fact is that the interview was saved at the outset, as my interlocutor took control of the interaction, much to my relief. I had no such luck in Stockholm, however:

> BC: What do you see as the main task in your work?
>
> I: My task is to fill the role of a group leader of the next-to-largest political party and to lead the opposition.
>
> BC: But what does it mean in terms of your job? What do you do?
>
> I: The political sciences state clearly that this role is that of a person who, in a democracy, was elected to be the foremost representative of some kind of a political movement or a group.
>
> BC: But what kind of tasks do you perform? You come here every morning, and then, what do you do?
>
> I: All that has to do with governance and management of the city.

We went on like that for a good while, until I struck a lucky solution: I asked my interlocutor (he was a political scientist by education) to describe his previous day in the office in detail. It resulted in the most minimalist kind of a narrative based solely on chronology ('In the morning I met my party colleagues …'). But the very poverty of this narrative prompted elaboration: 'You must know that, at present, we are trying to develop a new way of working together', and a story ensued. Almost every fragmented detail of the day served as an element in a story of its own.

I am quoting these excerpts not simply to document my clumsiness as an interviewer, lamentable as it may be. Latour (2005) noted a true irony: Whereas natural scientists encounter a continuous resistance in their objects, who do not want to do what researchers tell them to do, social scientists are faced with subjects who eagerly play the role of pliable objects when asked to do so in the name of Science.

Does it mean that there are no 'bad' interviews? Well, yes, it is possible to imagine a situation in which the interviewer talks incessantly, using a vocabulary alien to the interviewee. This is not merely a 'bad interview'; it is also 'bad manners'. As Cicourel (1964: 8) emphasized early on,

… [t]he subtleties which methodologists introduce to the novice interviewer can be read as properties to be found in everyday interaction between members of a society. Thus the principles of 'good and bad interviewing' can be read as basic features of social interaction which the social scientist presumably is seeking to study.

'Errors and mistakes happen in everyday interactions, too; in interviewing, they should be investigated rather than treated as problems', wrote Silverman (1993/2011: 97). In fact, the apparent misunderstanding between the second interlocutor and me reveals several noteworthy aspects about research interviews. In Scott and Lyman's (1968) terms, he tried to avoid giving me an account of his work.

An account is a linguistic device employed whenever an action is subjected to valuative inquiry. … An account is not called for when people engage in routine, common-sense behavior in a cultural environment that recognizes that behavior as such. (Scott and Lyman, 1968: 46–47)

Accounts are made to explain 'unanticipated or untoward behavior' (Scott and Lyman, 1968: 46). When the councilor does his work, he engages in routine, commonsense behavior in a cultural environment that recognizes his behavior as such. A research interview is a staged situation in which, by mutual consent, the recognition of a given behavior as 'routine and commonsense' is suspended. The researcher plays the role of a foreigner or a visitor from another planet, and the practitioners agree to explain their behavior as if it were not routine and commonsense. It is not surprising, then, that they may try to avoid giving an account of their work.

Avoiding accounts

Scott and Lyman mentioned three common strategies for avoiding accounts: mystification, referral, and identity switching. These strategies will all exclude or impoverish narratives in an interview.

Mystification occurs when 'an actor admits that he is not meeting the expectations of another, but follows this by pointing out that, although there are reasons for his unexpected actions, he cannot tell the inquirer what they are' (Scott and Lyman, 1968: 58). In some studies, mystification may have solid legal grounds, as when information is classified as confidential or when recounting somebody else's behavior can be read as slander. But it is the *referral* that is most commonly used: The interlocutor refers the researcher to a more competent source of information ('If you want to know what we do, look at the Web') or refuses to speculate about other people's perceptions ('I'm afraid you must ask her how she felt when this happened'). Another type of referral is the one that happened in the interview I mentioned previously, in which my interlocutor referred me to political sciences, where a legitimate account of his activities was to be found.

Identity switching, another frequently used strategy, refers to the suggestion that the researcher assumes another interlocutor's persona than the one he or she wishes to present: 'I am not a person who tells tales'. After all, to quote Scott and Lyman once more, 'every account is a manifestation of the underlying negotiation of identities' (1968: 59).

A notable addition to this list comes from science studies. The biochemists that Mulkay and Gilbert (1982) interviewed accounted for and told stories about errors and mistakes; they did not account for and thus did not produce narratives about what they considered *correct knowledge*. They were thereby confirming Scott and Lyman's observation that accounts consist mostly of excuses and justifications (1968: 47). In a narrative, excuses and justifications[2] usually serve as the points of the story, throwing additional light on my difficulties: Confronted with 'correct knowledge', I could hardly question it or feign ignorance. An impasse occurred, which could be resolved only by re-establishing the premises that made it legitimate for the interviewer to 'wonder'.

Prompting for narratives

How, then, to obtain narratives in a situation that offers many possibilities of avoiding an account? In his discussion of interview data, Silverman (1993/2011) recalled the importance that Harvey Sacks placed on the way 'membership categorization' is used in the construction of meaningful narratives (see also Sacks, 1992; Baker, 1997). Switching from the vocabulary of ethnomethodology to the vocabulary of narratology, one could say that membership categories are descriptions of Characters, one of the necessary elements of every narrative. 'I' is merely a personal pronoun, 'a woman of 50' is but a statistical category, but 'a mother of a family of five' is already the beginning of a narrative. This was, in fact, the ploy I used – unsuccessfully – in invoking the Character of an Opposition Leader. I met with a referral strategy in this case, but in many other cases this ploy has worked: Characters must know their lines and deliver them accordingly.

The other necessary element of a useful narrative is a Plot. Narratives based on sheer chronology are of little use in interpretation. The regular occurrence of Tuesdays after Mondays can hardly produce deeper insights into the nature of an activity, unless the construction of a calendar is being discussed. Although narratives always engage the *logic of succession* (albeit not always in a straightforward manner), they also involve the *logic of transformation* (Todorov, 1978/1990). The minimal plot consists of a passage from one state of equilibrium to another (more on this in Chapter 11). The second state of equilibrium may resemble the first only in that equilibrium also exists; it is not uncommon that its contents are the reverse of the first state of equilibrium. A company in trouble may reorganize and become profitable again; or it may go into bankruptcy, thereby restoring market equilibrium. Plots are usually much more complicated and contain chains of actions and events, oscillating states of affairs, apparent actions, and wrongly interpreted events; but a minimal plot is enough to make sense of a narrative. Thus the other common way of invoking narratives is to fish for a missing element in the minimal plot. Even a question like 'What made you change your mind?' is but a way of asking for the crucial element of the plot, the event of action around which the plot evolves. Similarly, when the manager in the first interview I quoted responded to my request that she describe her work by saying 'Sorry, but in my case, I must begin with history', it could be read as 'You are asking me to describe the last element in the plot; how can you expect to make sense of it without knowing about the elements that preceded it?'

Once the Characters and a Plot are in place, a narrative has been constructed. It must be added that Characters, unlike membership categories, do not have to be human. Many organizational narratives have as key characters a Computer, the Market, or an Equality Program. Furthermore, the accounting aspect of a narrative need not be explicit: The very way of structuring the elements of the plot – the form of the narrative – may serve as an explanation or a justification. Narratives mix humans with nonhumans, causes with reasons, explanations with interpretations. This makes them difficult, but also gratifying to interpret.

A crucial point of the quote from Mishler that began this section is contained in the last part of the sentence: 'if they are given some room to speak' (Mishler, 1986/1991: 69). Bombarding people with questions in a so-called structured or closed interview will, at best, limit the conversation to topics predetermined by the researcher. Then why not design a survey, and save the time of both the interviewer and the interviewee? At worst, it will focus the interviewee's attention entirely on the issues of proper impression management (Goffman, 1959). Still, impression management is an unavoidable part of every interaction, whether face-to-face or via survey questions. Respondents tend to answer questions in agreement with or opposition to what they consider to be the researchers' preferences – and in unknown proportions.

Consequently, not even narrative interviews (Mishler's 1986/1991 label) rule out impression management. To the contrary, they give free rein to such attempts. It is critical at this point to emphasize that, for Goffman, impression management did not equal intent to manipulate a person in an interaction into believing in a false version of an event; for him, impression management was a technique permitting the avoidance of 'performance disruptions' (1959: 208). In a narrative interview, interviewees are encouraged to control their own performances, rather than responding to the interviewer's cues. It is one of the aims of a research interview, therefore, to establish *what impression* the interviewees want to create and *which performance* they give, as it is likely that it is the same impression and performance they create in everyday practice. This is in contrast to a structured interview, in which the interviewer gives, whether intentionally or unintentionally, more or less explicit cues to the impression that should be created. The interviewee may accept or oppose these cues, but it will be the interviewer who manages the performance.

All this is not to diminish the role of interviews in social science research – perhaps only to recalibrate it. I started by painting a picture of disappointment in the old hope of seeing the interview as a source of facts or a philosophical exchange of views. But seeing the interview as a site of production and distribution of narratives, an opportunity to sample the dominant discourse via impression management, and as the observation of an actual interaction should more than compensate for this disappointment. I now turn to the observation.

INTERVIEWS AS OBSERVATION OPPORTUNITIES

Observing interviews

David Silverman (1993/2011) noted that an interview can be treated more or less as an observation of an interaction between the two people. He went further than the classic interactionists in problematizing the quasi-naturalist assumptions taken by symbolic interactionism, and in suggesting sensitive ways of minimizing the many traps connected with overconfidence in the interview as a 'natural' interaction. One such commonsensical but immensely valuable measure is to make the interviews accompany direct observation, a recommendation often made by ethnographers (see e.g. Hammersley and Atkinson, 1983/2007). Not only is there a shared experience to which both interlocutors can easily refer, but it makes it easier for the interviewer to visualize the scene in which the reported events are occurring, which greatly enhances understanding. Seeing a scene that someone has previously described always makes one realize how many cues we lose in our exaggerated reliance on verbal reports. This realization leads more and more researchers to use video equipment whenever possible, although videotaping exacts its price in making the observation more obtrusive (Jönsson, 2005). But there are no unobtrusive methods; indeed, there is no reason to expect that researchers can get a 'free ride' in the social world. Every interaction has its price, and it is part of the duty of every member of society to pay it as demanded.

An interview can therefore be treated as a recorded interaction and then submitted to a discourse or conversation analysis (see Chapter 10). In the rest of this chapter, I focus on the possibility of combining interviews with an observation proper – a procedure that, according to Annemarie Mol (2002), amounts to turning one's interlocutors into ethnographers.

The diary-interview or observant participation

As mentioned in the previous chapter, neither interviews nor direct observation are of much use in studying sensitive issues. Although drug use has been studied using participant observation (by Carlos Castaneda, 1968, for example, in his exploration of peyote-aided knowledge systems) or by ethnographic

interviews and direct observation (Rosen, 2002), it is not an easy phenomenon to document. Don H. Zimmerman and D. Lawrence Wieder (1977a, 1977b)
asked 60 members of a counter-culture community in Southern California to
keep diaries for seven days in a row. An analysis of the diaries was the basis for
subsequent biographical interviews; all this material was complemented by the
researchers' fieldnotes and those of their assistants. They called their technique a
'diary-interview method'.

Ignorant at the time of Zimmerman and Wieder's work, I designed a method
similar to theirs, which I later called *observant participation* (Czarniawska, 2007). In
the 1970s, I acted as a methodological consultant to a study of management of
consumer-goods-producing enterprises in Poland. The association of enterprises
(the equivalent of a corporation) included one central authority (the equivalent of
corporate headquarters) and 25 regional enterprises. We wanted to observe simultaneous reactions to the same central management initiatives in all regions, yet we
realized that it would be impossible to insert 25 researchers as observers into the
same association of enterprises. Even if it were possible logistically, it would take
some time for the researchers to become acculturated enough to begin their observations. This time lag would defy the aim of the research, the timing of which had
to run parallel with the time of the actors.[3]

The solution was to ask top managers in local organizations to document any
important decision-making event, under the guidance of a researcher who collaborated with them. The external observer (researcher) interviewed the internal
observer (manager), first in one-week and then in two-week periods.

I found this approach fruitful, and used it later on a somewhat smaller scale. When
told about my interest in declining organizations, a friend admitted that the large
multinational for which he worked was undergoing the same type of crisis, and
a variety of actions were being undertaken to prevent it. There was no question
of obtaining access; organizations in crisis do not welcome researchers unless they
come in the role of consultants. I suggested that he could write a diary, but he found
that too demanding. We settled upon something that could be seen as a variation
of what Spradley (1979) called an *ethnographic interview*: repetitive, open, extensive
interviews aimed at achieving an account of the events that occurred between the
interviews. I conducted 24 interviews with 'Bruno' as I called him (Czarniawska and
Rhodes, 2006) during a period of 14 months (a budgetary year plus two months – a
good period to study economic organizations).

In the late 1980s, I was still interested in the management of large and complex
organizations, but this time I switched to public administration in Sweden, with its
intriguing mixture of central steering and federative structures. I wanted to study
the relationships among the central government, local governments, and the Swedish
Association of Local Authorities; and the relationships among the National Social
Insurance Board, the Associations of Social Insurance Offices, and county-level social
insurance offices. I reckoned that I needed at least three municipalities and three
social insurance offices, but a simple calculation demonstrated that I needed to be

in ten places at the same time. This is where 'observant participation' turned out to be extremely useful indeed. I secured interlocutors in all these settings and returned to interview them every second week for 14 months. From what they told me, I selected 181 narratives that I later analyzed (Czarniawska, 1997). Although it was not planned this way, my contacts eventually began to resemble the 'diary-interview' method more and more, as my interlocutors told me that they had started to be much more careful with their personal diaries, in order to remember what to tell me on my next visit.

Although I value observation highly, especially shadowing, observant participation permitted me to learn about events that were occurring in several different but interconnected settings. But, did I learn what had *really* happened?

WHAT QUESTIONS DO THE INTERVIEWS ANSWER?

From what I have been saying, it may seem that I deny the possibility of learning 'what actually happened' with the help of an interview. Perhaps it would be helpful to return to the origins of this requirement. It was formulated by the famous German historian Leopold von Ranke (1795–1886), who said that history should reveal *wie es eigentlich gewesen ist* (what actually happened). By now the goal of reproducing history as it actually was has been abandoned by most historians (see White, 1973), but it still haunts the social sciences. Thus interviews have a bad reputation among serious fieldworkers, due to a misapprehension about the type of material they actually produce (on this point, see also Silverman, 1993/2011). The misapprehension consists of the fact that the interview material is seen as transparent, a window to something else: 'Now I have learned *how they make* strategic decisions here!' Wrong! 'Now you have learned *how they account for* their strategic decision making.' Whereas most talk is about something other than itself, it represents nothing but itself. But – and this is the most pertinent defense of the interview technique – this representation is important. Although an interview is what Van Maanen (1988) called 'representational data', 'doing representations' is a crucial part of social life – perhaps the most central (Goffman, 1959).

In my studies, I had no reason to suspect that my interlocutors were staging a completely new and unique representational mode for the benefit of one researcher. And even if that were the case, it would be easy to discover in the next interview with another interlocutor. It is impossible to imagine an entire organization staging a coherent performance for my benefit. As Becker put it,

> [T]he people the field worker observes are ordinarily constrained to act as they would have in his absence, by the very social constraints whose effects interest him; he therefore has little chance, compared to practitioners of other methods, to influence what they do, for more potent forces are operating. (1970: 43)

But what if I wanted to know how decisions were made in these organizations, and not how my interlocutors accounted for them? I could begin by interviewing several people who, to the best of my knowledge, participated in the decision making. Would that not be the way to learn only about the common thread in their way of accounting? Certainly, but this shared element in their accounts is critical; their accounts were inscriptions of the organizing that went into their production. As I noted in another context (Czarniawska, 2004), narrating helps in organizing, and organizing helps in narrating.

Next, I could start observing meetings in which the interlocutors claimed that strategic decisions were being made. And that is what I did, as I describe in the next chapter. But this does not mean that I know how the decisions were *really* made. I was merely able to add one more account – my own. The main advantage of my account is that it was what Marjorie DeVault (1990) called a *novel reading* – an account from a person who is not socialized into the same system of meaning, but is familiar enough with it to recognize its object. It may therefore vary from a standard account of the same event and provide new insights – a 'meaning added'.

It is also likely that the accounts I heard in the interviews were official versions, prepared for external use, possibly rehearsed in front of me, and *therefore* valuable. Saying this, I wish to challenge yet another myth behind 'how it really was'. The private versions of insiders, unless made official or officially subversive (in the sense of a shared counter-vision), have no impact on further developments. Organizations run on official representations and semi-official gossip. Idiosyncratic versions of reality are of no importance.

I am ending this section by recalling the two cases of observant participation or diary-interviews that I remember best. In one of the municipalities, I asked the Economic Director to become my interlocutor. He assented, but the Administrative Director, who was present at the introductory interview, demanded to be included. I agreed, but on the condition that I would speak to them separately. I conducted more than 20 interviews with the Administrative Director, and the contents were always the same. I always asked the same questions: 'What happened in the municipal government, and what have you been doing since I was there last?' He always answered in general terms that the municipal government was trying to improve the quality of its services. Then he compared municipal services to the services of a competent hairdresser, and would illustrate the importance of striving for the highest quality with the example of the then-world-champion high jumper, Patrick Sjöberg. He would first ask me if I knew who Patrick Sjöberg was (not being born a Swede, there was no guarantee that I did). During the first three or four interviews, I tried to fight back. I would explain my purpose and my method again and again. I would give him examples of events that could be of interest to me. In time, I gave up. Toward the end, I realized that I was no longer listening, merely giving the expected confirmations at right places ('Yes, I know who Patrick Sjöberg is'). In the meantime, the Economic Director provided me with material for one of the most interesting stories I was able to use. The point of this story is that no technique can guarantee the desired results.

I had quite a different experience in another setting within the same study. When I came for my last interview with a woman working in the central government office, she told me she had news for me: She was quitting her job. 'You know,' she said, 'when I had to tell you what I did during the last two weeks, I discovered that I didn't do that much.' (That had actually been my impression, too, but I chastised myself for signs of a patronizing attitude toward my interlocutors.) 'Mind you, it's not only your influence', she added. 'I participated in a course and discovered that there is another job I could do much better, so I applied. I also suggested to my boss that my job isn't needed.' Perhaps this is not much in terms of repaying people for their time and attention, but it is good to know that research may help some people some times.[4]

TRANSCRIPTION AND ITS PROBLEMS

It is more or less taken for granted nowadays that interviews are recorded and then transcribed. Of course, it happens – quite often – that interviewees refuse to be recorded or, at a certain point in the conversation, ask the interviewer to stop the recording. It also happens that interviewees add something after the recording has been stopped – because it was too sensitive to be recorded, or simply because they forgot to say it earlier. In all those cases, it is crucial to write down the unrecorded part as soon as possible. This material cannot be quoted *verbatim*, however, and cannot be used for discourse or conversation analysis, no matter how much the interviewer trusts memory.

Note taking is necessary even during the interview, partly to remind the researcher about the issues that need to be explained further, partly because the recording may fail. The Swedish author of detective stories Håkan Nesser provides an entertaining account of two policemen, one of them not too bright, going to an interview.[5] The less bright officer insists on making a double recording and brings an additional machine with him to do so. The result was that not only did the second recorder record nothing, but it emitted a noise that made the other recording unintelligible. Technical disasters do not have to be that dramatic, but they happen (more about technical tools in Chapter 7).

But even when recording is perfect, transcription is not without its problems. First, a decision must be made about the level of exactness required: all pauses in seconds, in order to make possible a sequential analysis of an interaction, or only the text, as most people do? Although conversation analysts may be using the instructions of Sacks et al. (1974) or an updated version of J.M. Atkinson and Heritage (1994), I would recommend the simple and clear 'Note on transcription conventions', the preface to Charlotte Linde's (1993: xi–xiv) *Life Stories: The Creation of Coherence*. For less ambitious transcribers, Mishler (1986/1991: 48) offered words of comfort:

There are many ways to prepare a transcript and each is only a partial representation of speech. Further, and most important, each representation is also a transformation. That is, each transcript includes some and excludes other features of speech and rearranges the flow of speech into lines of text within the limits of a page. Some features of speech, such as rapid changes in pitch, stress, volume, and rate, seem almost impossible to represent adequately while at the same time retaining the legibility of the text. Adding another complexity are the non-linguistic features of any speech situation, such as gestures, facial expressions, body movements, that are not captured on audiotape recordings and are difficult to describe and record from observations or videotapes. Lastly, it must be borne in mind that the initial record – audio- or videotape or running observation – is in itself only a partial representation of what 'actually' occurred.

An acceptance of the fact that all representations are necessarily partial, and that interviews, though not samples of 'natural' interactions, are of great utility, should help to understand both the value and the limitations of interviewing in social science research.

An interview

Record an interview from radio or television. (An alternative: Use a transcript of your own interview.) Does the interviewee give a proper account, or avoid it? What role is the interviewer playing? What expressions are most often used throughout the interview?

EXERCISE 4

FURTHER READING

Gubrium, Jaber F. and Holstein, James A. (eds.) (2002) *Handbook of interview research: Context and method.* Thousand Oaks, CA: Sage.

Gubrium, Jaber F., Holstein, James A., Marvasti, Amir B. and McKinney, Karyn (eds.) (2012) *The SAGE handbook of interview research: The complexity of the craft.* Thousand Oaks, CA: Sage.

Kvale, Steinar (1996) *InterViews: An introduction to qualitative research interviewing.* Thousand Oaks, CA: Sage.

Mishler, Elliot G. (1986/1991) *Research interviewing: Context and narrative.* Cambridge, MA: Harvard University Press.

Schaffer, Frederic Charles (2006) Ordinary language interviewing. In: Yanow, Dvora and Schwartz-Shea, Peregrine (eds.) *Interpretation and method: Empirical research methods and the interpretive turn.* New York: M.E. Sharpe, 150–160.

Silverman, David (1993/2011) *Interpreting qualitative data: Methods for analysing talk, text and interaction.* London: Sage.

Notes

1. As Charlotte Linde (1993: 59) pointed out, it is possible 'to structure an interview in a way that demands a type of speech that would not be produced in any other context'. It is usually done in experiments and results in a 'socially aberrant verbal output'.
2. More on justification in Boltanski and Thévenot (2006).
3. Nine years later, these enterprises ceased to exist.
4. More on the ethics of interviewing in Gubrium et al. (2012).
5. *De ensamma* (The Lonely), 2010.

5

Observation on the Move: Shadowing

The complexities of contemporary societies increase the difficulty of such traditional techniques of observation as participant observation and stationary direct observation. This chapter focuses on the technique of shadowing, as one way of avoiding those difficulties.

VARIETIES OF OBSERVATION

Most of the knowledge which people have about social relations is derived from uncontrolled observation, whether participant or nonparticipant. (Goode and Hatt, 1952: 120)

There are indeed variations in observation techniques, although they tend to blur in the field. The distinctions drawn here are merely to assist a methodological reflection by distilling traits that do not exist separately in research practice. The choice is always that of the researcher, and it is often an ethical as much as a methodological choice.

The anthropologist actually moves from one role to the other while in the field. He may, for example, go on a fishing trip as a participant, but during the preparations for an important religious ceremony he will interview formally the important participant, or record the ritual chants during the ceremony. This shift is made easier by the fact that the patterns of the society are not likely to be changed in important ways by the presence of an outsider, if the role of the latter is properly defined. (Goode and Hatt, 1952: 122)

More than a half century after Goode and Hatt wrote these words, social scientists are all ethnologists or anthropologists of contemporary societies – men and women alike. Yet we have inherited many of the field techniques of our predecessors.

Indirect observation (one-way mirror, hidden camera) is used in social work, psychology, and criminology, but is considered unethical whenever it is happening without legal justification and/or without the knowledge and approval of people observed.

Then there is *direct observation* (including open videotaping), which can be divided into *participant* and *nonparticipant observation*. As discussed in Chapter 1, there has been a great deal of debate over what is and what is not participant observation, and my definition is an answer to my pragmatic needs rather than an attempt to bring a final word to the matter. I believe that it makes sense to call it 'participant observation' when observers are doing the same things as the people (or some of the people) they are observing. Self-observation (Brinkmann, 2012) can be also counted as a kind of participant observation.[1]

Nonparticipant observation can be further divided into *shadowing* and *stationary observation*. Photography and video recording, used early on by anthropologists (Collier and Collier, 1986), can aid both of them, and are increasingly present in all social studies.

In what follows, I focus on those types of observation techniques I consider helpful in studying the ways of work and life of mobile people living in contemporary societies. I begin with *shadowing* – following selected people for a time in their everyday occupations. This approach allows the researcher to move with them.

A BRIEF HISTORY OF SHADOWING

I first encountered the technique of shadowing in the work of Italian sociologist Marianella Sclavi (1989), who, during a prolonged visit to the USA, followed a neighbor's daughter to school every day.

Sclavi saw Truman Capote as her role model. In his short story, 'A day's work' (1975), Capote told readers how, for the whole working day, he followed a cleaning woman who was everything he was not: woman, Hispanic, large, working class, heterosexual. In Capote's story, Sclavi saw an excellent example of an idea suggested by Russian philosopher and literary theorist Mikhail Bakhtin. Bakhtin (1981) argued that good novels – and he saw them as deeply sociological – require an author to assume an attitude of *outsidedness* that would provide different grounds for communication than does much-romanticized empathy. It aims at understanding not by identification (they are like us), but by the *recognition of differences* (we are different from them and they are different from us; by exploring these differences we will understand ourselves better).

As Bakhtin said in an interview, shortly before his death in 1975:

> In order to understand, it is immensely important for the person who under-stands to be *located outside* the object of his or her creative understanding – in time, in space, in culture. For one cannot ever really see one's own exterior and comprehend it as a whole, and no mirrors or photographs can help; our real exterior can be seen and understood only by other people, because they are located outside us in space, and because they are *others.* (Kelly, 1993: 61)

I found this stance attractive because it does not claim to represent the natives from an insider's perspective – a claim that has been rightly criticized for its colonial sedi-ments (see e.g. Prasad and Prasad, 2002). An observer can never know *better* than an actor; a stranger cannot say *more* about any culture than a native can, but observers and strangers can see *different* things than actors and natives can.[2] Bakhtin did not espouse the behaviorist idea of a complete separation between actors and observers, however; to the contrary, they may, and ought to, engage in a *dialogical relationship*.

The attitude of outsidedness replaces sentimental idealization with mutual respect between strangers – a symmetry. Rather than taming 'them' to become like 'us', we expect differences. These differences, in turn, are seen as a source of knowledge, not least about ourselves. This requirement of outsidedness is difficult to achieve, how-ever, not only in premodern societies, but also in such fields as organization studies, in which researchers often behave condescendingly toward practitioners by giving advice, establishing the 'best practice', or 'emancipating the oppressed'. Thus, shad-owing is a technique – and an attitude.

As often happens with innovations, shadowing seems to have been invented in several places in parallel. Or perhaps, as Robert Merton (1965/1985) noted, all ideas are around all the time, in some form or another. In 2000, another Italian sociolo-gist, Giampietro Gobo, asked well-known qualitative methodologist Jay Gubrium if he knew the origins of the shadowing technique (Gobo, 2005). Gubrium sent the query to all the contributors to the handbook he edited with James Holstein – including me. I did not answer, certain that my sources – Sclavi and Capote – would emerge without my intervention. They did not. Gobo did not know of Sclavi's studies, just as I had not known about Giuseppe Bonazzi's (1998) study until I read an article by Seonaidh McDonald (2005). Bonazzi had quoted as *his* models the studies of Mintzberg (1973) and Charles N. Walker, Robert H. Guest, and Arthur N. Turner's (1956) studies of foremen. He distanced himself from his predecessors, however, calling theirs 'quantitative studies, which made no concession to interac-tion between the researcher and the subjects observed' (Bonazzi, 1998: 223). On the other hand, he said, he constantly shuttled 'between hard data gathering and inter-action with the subjects' (p. 223).

This incomplete genealogy of shadowing is an illustration of the plurality of the social sciences, in which the Web is of great help in establishing connections, but makes us too certain of the completeness of our sources – a methodological point in its own right. Gobo's appeal located one main suspect, however: Oregon education scholar Harry F. Wolcott. In a letter to Jay Gubrium, Wolcott explained that during his study reported in *Man in the Principal's Office: An Ethnography* (1973/2003), he acquired a nickname 'the shadow', based on the old radio show[3] and as it well explained his role in the field, he used it himself in the book (Czarniawska, 2007: 24). Another discipline within the social sciences that uses shadowing – often without using the term – is consumer studies (see e.g. Miller, 1998). Shadowing is also used as an educational technique, particularly in teaching and nursing (Roan and Rooney, 2006; Lindberg and Czarniawska, 2006).[4]

In this chapter I present several shadowing studies to illustrate their advantages and some of the difficulties that may arise. I begin with a management study, followed by a school study, and finally a consumer study. The order in which they are presented is roughly chronological, to show that the perception of advantages and disadvantages changes over time, following the contemporary preoccupations of the social science community.

THE USES OF SHADOWING

'Structured observation' and the worries of its time

Henry Mintzberg, one of the most famous management researchers, began his introduction of what he called 'a structured observation' with a criticism of the diary studies of management, prevalent at that time (1970):

> Not one of these studies provides substantial insight into the actual content of managerial activities. ... The reader is told where managers spend their time, with whom they spend their time, how they interact (telephone, face-to-face, etc.) and so on. But the reader is never told *what* is transacted. (Mintzberg, 1970: 88; italics in the original)

The diary method assumed that the researcher already knew *what* managers were doing, and needed only to learn *how much* of *which*. 'But of which what?' asked Mintzberg. Surely nobody could use Fayol's categories (planning, organizing, coordinating, and controlling) to describe actual behavior? Some categories were necessary, Mintzberg reasoned; otherwise the researcher would be lost in the minutiae of everyday work. He suggested what he saw as a compromise solution:

> I use the label 'structured observation' to refer to a methodology which couples the flexibility of open-ended observation with the discipline of seeking certain types of structured data. The researcher observes the manager as he [Mintzberg

shadowed five men] performs his work. Each observed event (a verbal contact or a piece of incoming or outgoing mail) is categorized by the researcher in a number of ways (e.g., duration, participants, purpose) as in the diary method but with one vital difference. *The categories are developed as the observation takes place.* (Mintzberg, 1970: 90; italics in the original)

Readers in the second decade of the 21st century may wonder about this obsession with structure and categories, but at the time Mintzberg wrote, even direct observation was supposed to be strictly structured (social psychologist Robert Bales, 1950, had created a widely used form for recording observed interaction). Indeed, some pages after this quote, Mintzberg apologized to the reader who 'may feel that some of the categories are not sufficiently "neat" ' (p. 94). Again, in the 1970s, formal logic was considered an essential part of research training, and the categories were expected, at the very least, not to be overlapping, a requirement often neglected in contemporary classifications. Between listing the categories, Mintzberg gave examples of his field notes, showing that he had, in fact, shadowed 'Mr. M'. He sat in M's office and walked with M to the plant; they returned to the office, and then went to a meeting with consultants.

Mintzberg then produced examples of his coding procedures, which could have been included as illustrations to a textbook on grounded theory, although Glaser and Strauss (1967) are never quoted. The reason is, most likely, that grounded theory summarizes the commonsense of fieldwork, and at that time such commonsense did not require referencing.

Commenting on his method, Mintzberg referred to Rosemary Stewart's (1967) critique of observation techniques. She identified three problems: a lack of understanding about what was taking place, an exclusion from all confidential activities, and the size of the sample. Sampling was an issue for Mintzberg, whose ambition it was to turn his field material into quantifiable data. Because it is not an issue in the present context, however, I focus on the first two problems.

Mintzberg reformulated the critique concerning the possible lack of understanding into a problem of (proper) classification. As the article was written before 'the linguistic turn'[5] reached management studies, the idea of 'right' (valid) categories was still strong. At present, categories are evaluated in terms of their 'sensitizing'[6] power, whereas their validity (in the sense of being supported by the material, not in the sense of corresponding to reality) can be easily checked by NUD*IST-type software. The issue of understanding remains, but it has been resolved by the experience of science and technology scholars, who claim that a dedicated fieldworker can, after a time, understand even the work of quantum physicists (although they would *not* be able to perform it).

An analogy with traditional anthropology is often evoked: Anthropologists, too, needed time to understand the language and customs of the tribes they studied. The main difference was that they remained in the same village, whereas the village is now global. Acquiring an understanding has become a signal of satiation for a field researcher. The day when everything said at an observed meeting is fully understandable is the day to return to one's office – not only for reasons of efficient resource management, but because complete understanding means 'going native', at which point attention drops and outsidedness is at peril. When one understands everything, there is nothing left to explain.

The problem of exclusion from confidential activities was resolved by Mintzberg in conversations with shadowed managers, who reported to him what had taken place. Had they reported it all, and were their reports truthful? Yet if the confidential meetings were crucial, their outcome would soon become visible in future events. If not, it mattered little; nobody, not even the practitioners, could be everywhere, and many things were happening simultaneously. When shadowing a manager at a municipal company in Stockholm, I was excluded from appraisal interviews, which I thought was only fair. I do not allow shadowing of my advisory sessions, because I believe it is too trying for the doctoral student. Such encounters are deeply personal.

Mintzberg addressed other problematic aspects of his method, such as the possibility of a Hawthorne effect (in the sense of the possible impact of the researcher's presence and attention). He could see some of the effects of his presence, but he saw them as unimportant from the perspective of his research interests. The people being shadowed obviously explain to the researcher what they and others are doing, which increases the proportion of reflection in their daily work; but reflection can be triggered by other events and is usually considered beneficial. Other people contacting the shadowed person may watch their tongues, but they may also do the opposite, hoping that a witness can add weight to their utterances.

In general, however, one should remember Becker's (1970: 43) comment quoted in the previous chapter: People being shadowed need to transact their business and cannot suspend their activities for the sake of a performance that is specifically addressed to a researcher. Impression management requires effort and concentration, dedicated to keeping job performance undisrupted (Goffman, 1959) – and job performance is, after all, the topic of the study. What is more, people who meet the shadowed person and the researcher cannot risk a special performance without danger of exposure by the coworkers. In other words, it is unlikely that the shadowed people and the encountered others collude in staging and maintaining a special performance merely for the sake of the researcher. It has been my experience that after the initial curiosity has died off (usually a matter of a few minutes) people began to ignore me, as they usually have more important agendas to attend to.

Mintzberg's results were reported in *The Nature of Managerial Work* (1973), which has become a classic. The contents of the book are well advertised by its title, and I would claim that it was precisely the shadowing that made this 'nature' visible.[7] His study was repeated 30 years later by Stefan Tengblad, who shadowed Swedish managers (Tengblad, 2003, 2006).

The shadow in the principal's office

Harry F. Wolcott was an anthropologist who studied the Kwakiutl for his dissertation, then turned his attention to the field of education. Like Henry Mintzberg, he noticed that diary-type studies suffered from many shortcomings, and that they would not allow him to answer his central question: 'What do school principals actually do?' He did not seem to be aware of Mintzberg's study, not only because the two studies were done practically in parallel, but probably also because management was not yet perceived as a general profession in the 1970s, with precepts considered applicable everywhere. Wolcott decided to put his anthropological skills to work, but he realized from the beginning that his study, with its focus on one school principal, would differ markedly from studies of tribes or kinship (Wolcott, 1973/2003).

Wolcott specified a whole set of criteria before choosing a person to follow, but in the end he was eager to admit that 'good fortune' also played a part in his choice. He was looking for a person who was:

- a full-time, career principal (i.e. without teaching duties and not seeing his job as a step to another job);

- responsible for only one elementary school;

- experienced in his job;

- male (most principals were men, although most teachers were women); and

- likely to survive a two-year close contact with the researcher without personal hostilities.

This last criterion is especially significant. Although, to my knowledge, no other researcher who used shadowing has mentioned it, its lack can produce many unexpected results – as Chapter 8 will show. Wolcott admitted that he decided against following a certain principal because that man wore white socks with a dark business suit and talked patronizingly to pupils.

Wolcott first secured the cooperation of the principal, and then applied for formal acceptance higher up the hierarchy. 'By using this approach I felt I could avoid the possibility of having an overzealous superintendent summarily assign some fair-haired principal to be my cooperating subject or an underzealous one reject the project because he doubted that any of "the boys" would be interested' (1973/2003: 3). It needs to be added that cooperation from higher levels was necessary for shadowing, not least because Wolcott had the opportunity to meet the superintendent while achieving it.

> The superintendent looked quizzically at me as he stopped to chat with the members of the committee just before it convened. 'Say, you're not writing all this down, are you?' he asked. 'I write everything down,' I replied. I added that if

he was interested in the study I would welcome the chance to talk to him about it in detail. He was and I did. (1973/2003: 3)

The writing-down part of this exchange is familiar to me from my own shadowing experiences, but not a supervisor's interest in discussing the project – probably because my shadowing periods have been so much shorter: Two weeks in a row, after which I vanish, truly like a shadow. Neither is there any possibility of my becoming friends with the people I shadow – a realistic prospect in a two-year study – a situation that, as Wolcott pointed out, could be psychologically comforting, but may jeopardize contacts with coworkers, who may be unduly careful in their statements about the person shadowed.

Wolcott received the principal's permission to conduct virtually every activity that can be said to constitute shadowing: Recording in writing what was said and done, attending formal and informal meetings and conferences, interviewing him and other people who were encountered during the shadowing, and accessing various notes and documents. He also continued shadowing in the principal's private life.

Commenting on the effects of his stay in the field, Wolcott said:

It is tempting to report that after a brief 'period of adjustment' the researcher blended perfectly into the school setting and everyone at school continued about his business totally oblivious to him. Although my presence at the school was not intended to require major adaptations by those being observed, it seems unrealistic to insist that things were just the same with or without me there. (1973/2003: 11)

In making this comment, Wolcott echoed the sarcastic observation made by British anthropologist Nigel Barley: 'Much nonsense has been written, by people who should know better, about the anthropologist "being accepted" ' (Barley, 1983: 56). When the object of study is not an exotic tribe but a modern school or a corporation, however, an illusion of acceptance is more likely to arise ('You, coming from a business school, will surely agree ...', or 'You, who taught in school yourself ...', as Wolcott did). These tender illusions do not remove the basic sense of estrangement that becomes obvious under prolonged contact.

So, what difference did Wolcott's presence make? Wolcott did not believe that it made a great deal of difference to the principal's habitual ways of acting and speak-ing, but Wolcott's questioning (necessary in order to understand the principal's actions) was most likely achieving a change of frame: From the principal's taken-for-grantedness to an inspection, or even to a self-critique of his actions. His 'natural attitude' (Schütz, 1953/1973) probably gave way to a questioning attitude, or even to change. For instance, Wolcott administered a simple questionnaire concerning contacts among staff members. Its results made the principal realize that the staff did not have many occasions to meet socially. This and other comments seem to suggest that the impact of the shadowing was largely positive. As in Mintzberg's study, the researcher's presence was bound to facilitate reflection, but reflection is rarely detrimental, or so we are taught to believe.

Wolcott has also attracted attention to the drudgery of fieldwork: Long days, boredom, and doubts about whether or not the project made sense. The last aspect must have been the result of his long stay in the field. As he said, 'a lessening in note writing usually signaled the approaching finale to a productive observation period' (1973/2003: 16) and the advantages of a long period of shadowing the same person must be weighed against this disadvantage. As he noted, however, the principal he shadowed would fall asleep during some meetings, a liberty that his shadow could not afford to take.

Accompanying shoppers

Daniel Miller (1998) did not call his way of doing fieldwork shadowing, but I think that the following quote fully justifies my decision to include his work here:

> For a one-year period, 1994–1995, I attempted to conduct an ethnography of shopping on and around a street in North London. This was carried out in association with Alison Clarke [then Miller's doctoral student]. I say 'attempted' because, given the absence of community and the intensely private nature of London households, this could not be an ethnography in the conventional sense. Nevertheless through conversation, being present in the home and accompanying householders during their shopping, I tried to reach an understanding of the nature of shopping through greater or lesser exposure to seventy-six households. (1998: 9)

Miller, who, like Wolcott, is a trained anthropologist, sounds apologetic; but in fact he splendidly outlines the specificity of shadowing. His was not an ethnography for several reasons. His aim was not to describe 'the ways of life', but 'the nature of shopping', a phenomenon situated in time and place. And he did not study a tribe. He actually spoke of 'the absence of community', wishing to emphasize that some people are, or at least feel, outside of any community, isolated within a busy urban context. Shadowing, he claimed, is more suitable for describing the lives of such people than is standard ethnography (Miller, 2007).

The fact that Miller was interested in shopping meant that he undertook fascinating variations on straightforward shadowing. He followed a married couple, Sheila and Bob, while they shopped together, for example. In his reading, they both held conservative notions of gender differences, which provided grounds for a constant comic banter between the spouses as they shopped.

> A key element within this comic banter is her constant criticism of his lack of shopping skills. ... Taken in context, however, these criticisms are a mechanism she uses to affirm that as a man, although he may shop, he is not a natural shopper. He is thereby able to receive such 'criticisms' as praise for his natural manliness, something which he recognizes. (1998: 25)

A potential criticism of Miller's study is the type of critique from which Mintzberg defended himself: That the banter was produced for the benefit of the shadow. All the better, I say, and I would imagine that Marianella Sclavi would agree. A performance confirming the importance of the traditional gender division of labor can be seen as a message to the researcher, much stronger and more convincing than could any answer to an interview question. Again, impression management is a methodological problem only under the assumption that deeds and utterances of people under study should correspond one-on-one to some reality hidden behind appearances, to be revealed in the course of research. If this assumption is replaced by the Goffmanian premise that life is a theater, however, then that which is played is of central importance. Impression management, yes; but as I emphasized in the previous chapter, *what impression* are the performers trying to produce?

The complications of impression management became even more obvious when Miller shadowed a couple-to-be: a young divorced woman and her boyfriend.

> At this stage the crucial factor in shopping was my [Miller's] presence. This was an occasion to learn about each other's taste and forge a relationship in terms of shopping compatibility. But there was also a question as to how they appeared as a couple to an outsider. The sheer effort that I felt they were putting into showing me how happy they were together should not be seen as thereby false. It reflected their own question as to whether, when revealed in the reflected gaze of the anthropologist, they would find themselves to be in love. (1998: 29)

This was an intriguing situation, because this young couple, unlike Sheila and Bob, had not rehearsed their common performance many times. Theirs was a double trial – to perform together an act of acting together. One could venture a guess that the anthropologist's presence was beneficial to the couple, setting this double test for them. The anthropologist eventually managed to see more in their performance than they themselves knew. Although this was, by their own declaration, a couple that aimed at equality, the woman was trying to learn as much as possible about her boyfriend's habits and desires, while he was establishing his right to have the last word on everything. She could accept that, as long as he did not force her to acknowledge the fact. They did become engaged, however.

On the basis of his study, Miller constructed a theory of shopping, in which he claims that commodities are used primarily in shaping social relationships. The shoppers constantly buy things for others, or for themselves with others in mind. Buying goods for others expresses the hope 'to influence these others into becoming the kind of people who would be the appropriate recipients for that which is being bought' (1998: 8). Routine provisioning, on the other hand, can be seen as a devotional rite usually performed by women – a rite confirming a gender role.

One fascinating aspect of Miller's theorizing is his full awareness that the shoppers he shadowed did not share his theory. Most of them espoused a theory of shopping according to which shopping was an expression of deplorable hedonism and materialism; they also excluded provisioning from the definition of shopping. Miller noted the paradox implicit in the ethical requirement of fieldwork: respect for the 'informants'' opinions. It is assumed that, short of accusing them of suffering from false consciousness, respectful fieldworkers must faithfully render the views of the natives. But there is another way: Fieldworkers can try to advance their own views, neither surrendering them to the views received nor asserting their supremacy, but simply adding to the views from the field. This is, in fact, the core of the dialogical relationship recommended by Bakhtin (1981), for whom it was obvious that the views of the observer and the views of the actors may clash. A dialogue need not be a duet.

The reader may think that it was still relatively easy for Miller to maintain his outsidedness, considering that shopping turned out to be strongly gendered. In a later study, Alison Clarke and Daniel Miller (2002) followed women when they shopped for clothes, and Clarke characterized their study as one that included participant observation. Miller sees it differently. He believes that fieldworkers must often:

> ... transform themselves into something quite distinct from people's initial assumptions, often occupying many different persona in order to work with many different kinds of people. I assume it is my job to try and become the kind of person that the other individual prefers to spend time with, if I want them to spend a considerable time with me, so I will shift from being young, old, male, female, comic, serious, etc all the time. Similarly when working with a colleague, Alison or another, we try to exaggerate differences to give people an opportunity to respond to the kind of personality they prefer out of this choice based on our distinction. I don't see this as manipulative, I see it as part of our responsibility to make the experience comfortable for the people who are giving us this time and information. (Miller, 2007)

This stance corresponds to one suggested by Rosalie Wax:

> Perhaps good fieldwork is more like play-acting than most of us are willing to admit. Respondents rarely resent a fieldworker's 'acting like them' or 'learning their ways' as long as the fieldworker makes it clear that he knows he is only playing a part and that his newly acquired skills do not entitle him to any privileges which they are not willing to offer him. (1971/1985: 197)

Although Wax and Miller agree on the main point, the small differences between their utterances illustrate well the difference between studying a strange culture and studying one's own. Miller's domestic skills did not have to be acquired for the purpose of the study (he declared that he had a life-long hobby of cake decoration), but they do not *entitle* him to the privilege of sharing people's time and attention – he has to earn it. Prasad and Prasad have quoted the same passage from Wax, but they concluded that, for Wax, 'the most effective form of going native takes place when it is performed as a *masquerade*, played out within clearly delineated rules and limits' (2002: 194). To my reading, Wax and Miller are saying that in fieldwork as in everyday life, exotic cultures or not, strangers would do well to play likeable personae if they want people's time and attention. Sociologists from Goffman to Garfinkel have made it known that rules and limits are never clearly delineated, but known through transgressions and continuously renegotiated. This time it is Prasad and Prasad who are guilty of romanticizing; there is a visible trace of the myth of 'an authentic presence' behind their critique.

THE SHADOWY SIDE OF SHADOWING

Shadowing is easier than participant observation because shadowing does not require simultaneous action and observation and because participation in complex, professional activities would be impossible for most researchers. In terms of methodological gains, it permits one to preserve an attitude of outsidedness, whereas participant observation creates many opportunities for 'going native'. Yet shadowing does not prohibit the feeling or expressing of emotions, making them, as Sclavi (2007) rightly said, the main instrument of cognition. The point is never to behave like a fly on the wall (what a peculiar metaphor, considering what happens to the flies on the wall, once they have been noticed), but to behave like a responsible adult, showing respect and sympathy for others.

The main advantage of shadowing over stationary observation is, by definition, its mobility. The matter is, however, more complicated than is the sheer act of movement. After all, not even observers whom I call 'stationary' remain immobile in the same place during their study. Shadowing creates a peculiar duo: the person shadowed and the person doing the shadowing. This is where the dynamics of cognition become complex indeed, as I have tried to illustrate in this chapter. There is mutual observation, an establishing of similarities and differences; then there is a focus produced by the movements of the person shadowed, creating the double perception, as it were. The researcher guesses (and asks about) perceptions of the events being perceived as well: a camera with a mirror lens, to use a technical analogy.

I return to the issues of psychic discomfort and its role as a source of insight in Chapter 8. Here it is enough to say that perhaps shadowing meddles with the taken-for-granted, making threats to the personal and professional identity of the researcher unavoidable. But the psychological discomfort seems to be a necessary price of learning, as ethnomethodologists noticed long ago. The bonus lies in the extra self-knowledge that researchers can gain. The main compensation is a problematized picture of social reality that carries the possibility of liberation for those observed – if they happen to suffer from the reality they were led to construct – and the promise of a nontrivial story for the researcher.

Then there is the issue of blending in, or 'passing' (Hammersley and Atkinson, 1983/2007), not least in terms of clothing. Although the relationship between the person shadowed and the person shadowing can be resolved in several ways, blending in is necessary in order not to attract attention to the activity of shadowing. In organization studies, it appears that male researchers have fewer problems blending in than female researchers do, as the dress code for men is much more limited than it is for women (McDowell, 1997, called men's clothing 'unmarked', in contrast to women's 'marked' outfits). In Warsaw, I did not know how to blend in, other than not dressing in any way that could attract attention. In Stockholm there was a clear dress code for professional women in public administration: jeans, shirt, and a jacket (the shirt has now been replaced by a low-cut top, with an obligatory necklace). This camouflage worked well, apart from the fact that when my identity was revealed, I was told that I 'did not look like a professor'. Alas, I was not able to establish how a professor should look, apart from a serious suspicion that I should have been a man. I chose to interpret it as confirmation of the right choice of camouflage, as the norm seems to be that it is doctoral students who do fieldwork. Of course, these are minor worries compared to those of the fieldworkers who studied outlaw bikers, the police, or the homeless (Hammersley and Atkinson, 1983/2007).

Yet another practical difficulty is the need for note taking, while being constantly on the move. All solutions are welcome: Taking notes whenever seated; dictating reflections whenever alone; and finally, writing up as much as possible at the end of each day (the most difficult of all, as shadowing is extremely tiring). Perhaps Reporter-type digital tools (Chapter 7) will become more accessible and easy to use.

The last point I would like to raise here is the possible effects of shadowing for and on the person shadowed. Truman Capote's shadowing ended with the cleaning woman losing her job – but, I hasten to add, this was because Capote changed into a participant observer, and they both smoked hash at her workplace. At least one of my shadowings has boosted the morale of the person shadowed, who fell victim to a hasty restructuring. The principal shadowed by Harry Wolcott assured him that it contributed to his professional growth, and although Wolcott read it as due to the principal's tendency to create something positive from every situation, he accepted the statement with gratitude. More striking was a comment from the superintendent, who told Wolcott, 'We're thinking of having you fellows start paying for information. You never help us with our problems anyway – you just study what interests you' (1973/2003: 15). Wolcott said that that was a comment the anthropologists of the day were often prone to hear – upon returning to their homelands from exotic sites, I assume – but I have never met with that reaction. One reason is that within my discipline it is only recently that researchers stopped playing 'company doctors', and began studying that which interests us, rather than what the company wants us to study. Another reason is that I and the people I study have been deeply indoctrinated into the belief that research ultimately helps practice, no matter what twisted routes it may take to get there. Van Maanen (1991: 34) was probably right when he said that fieldworkers must recognize that they cannot offer much of obvious value to those who are studied.

But shadowing isn't restricted to following humans. The idea has recently been extended to include nonhumans – more exactly, objects and quasi-objects. Following objects rather than people is an innovation introduced in studies of science and technology, an innovation that is the topic of the next chapter.

Shadowing

Shadow a person you know who agrees to be shadowed; someone as different as possible from you in as many ways as possible. Shadow that person for some hours, reflect over everything that struck you as strange, and consider what it tells you about yourself.[8]

FURTHER READING

Brinkmann, Svend (2012) *Qualitative inquiry in everyday life.* London: Sage.
Collier, John Jr. and Collier, Malcolm (1967/1986) *Visual anthropology: Photography as a research method.* Albuquerque, NM: University of New Mexico Press.
Czarniawska, Barbara (2007) *Shadowing, and other techniques for doing fieldwork in modern societies.* Malmö/Copenhagen: Liber/CBS Press.
McDonald, Seonaidh and Simpson, Barbara (eds.) (2014) Special issue on shadowing research in organizations. *Qualitative Research in Organizations and Management.*
Wolcott, Harry F. (2008) *Ethnography: A way of seeing.* Lanham, MD: AltaMira Press.

Notes

1. I avoid the term 'autoethnography' because, as literally understood, it would assume a multiple personality disorder (*ethnos* means 'people'). Also, it is not clear if by 'autoethnography' the researchers signal the use of self-observation, a study of his or her own group, or both.
2. Bakhtin's stance, similar to Bruyn's (1966) 'detached involvement', finds corroboration in Niklas Luhmann's theory (Luhmann, 1998; Seidl and Becker, 2005).
3. The radio program *The Shadow* (there were many versions in other media) started on 31 July 1930. Each episode began with the narrator saying, 'Who knows what evil lurks in the hearts of men? The Shadow knows!' and ended with 'Crime does not pay ... The Shadow knows!' (en.wikipedia.org/wiki/The_Shadow, accessed 21 April 2013).
4. For a thorough and detailed review of the uses of shadowing, see McDonald (2005). She has used the technique in the study of team leaders in a hi-tech organization.
5. It is generally agreed that the expression, 'the linguistic turn', originated with *The Linguistic Turn: Essays in Philosophical Method*, a 1967 anthology edited by Richard Rorty. It was at least another decade before this perspective trickled sideways from philosophy to the social sciences.
6. The notion of 'sensitizing concepts' was launched in 1954 by Chicago sociologist Herbert Blumer, in his critique of contemporary social theory. Again, it took several decades to make the idea popular.
7. Joyce Fletcher (1999) used Mintzberg's study as a model for her shadowing of female design engineers.
8. This exercise was inspired by one that Edgar Schein (1999) recommended for his students.

6

Following Objects and Quasi-objects

Following objects is a technique close to shadowing, but the researcher is targeting things rather than persons. This chapter contains a brief history of the technique, three examples of its application, and ends with a discussion of its usefulness.

REDISCOVERING THINGS: ACTOR–NETWORK THEORY

The idea of following objects is usually associated with Actor-Network Theory (ANT) a narratology-inspired approach to science and technology studies, especially as practiced by Bruno Latour (2005). The assumptions behind ANT can be briefly summarized as follows: Although not all people structure their experiences as narratives, the narrative form is the dominant form of knowledge, even in modern societies. Narratologists (in this case, Lithuanian–French semiologist Algirdas J. Greimas) have studied the typical narrative structure, revealing several characteristics that can be useful in social science studies (Czarniawska and Hernes, 2005).

Greimasian narratology (see e.g. Greimas and Courtés, 1982) starts from the observation that a Character acquires its traits through its actions throughout a story. At the beginning, the only thing that can be distinguished is anything that acts or is acted upon; Greimas called it 'an actant'. An actant that succeeds in its action programs may become an actor or even a hero or a macro-actor. In various tales, such actants can be objects (scarecrows, magic wands), animals (as in all allegoric tales), or humans. The lessons for the social sciences, thought Latour, are several. First, if the Characters are known from the beginning, there is no story to tell; if powerful actors can do what they want, there is nothing more to say. From an ANT perspective, one should ask: 'By what route have certain actants become powerful actors and others have not; or how is power constructed?' The second lesson is that by jumping to conclusions about power as the cause of events, social scientists spend too little time studying objects and too much time studying humans, misled by the fact that humans can talk and can therefore be spokespersons, even for networks primarily comprising nonhumans. This asymmetry should be redressed, and the encouragement to follow objects is one consequence of that ambition.

Additionally, the shadowing of objects should, in most cases, help to avoid at least some of the ethical problems related to the shadowing of humans. The relief that this knowledge provides is balanced by a need for a constant renegotiating of access, however (see also Chapter 8).

In what follows, I present the Latour study that is most quoted in this context, and then two studies of his followers.

THE TRAVELS OF THE SOIL FROM THE AMAZON FOREST

There is an ever-returning question in methodology in general and in science studies in particular: What is the connection between things and words, between objects and their representations? One way of concretizing this question is to ask: How are scientific papers produced? Bruno Latour (1995/1999) followed the chain of transformations that changed the soil samples taken in the Amazon forest into a scientific paper, a voice in the debate over whether the forest advances or retreats, whether or not it was being eaten up by savanna.

In October 1991, Latour was allowed to accompany a research group comprising a botanist, a geographer, and a pedologist (pedology is a science of soil) on their excursion into the Amazon forest near Boa Vista, a small town in Brazil. They worked, and he photographed and described what they did. Their fieldwork concerned the Amazon forest; his fieldwork concerned their research.

In Latour's story, the botanist became allied with the forest, the pedologist with the savanna. Who would win this tug-of-war? The pedologist asked another pedologist to help. Now they were two. The group consisted of two women, two men; two Brazilians, two foreigners. The observer (a man, a philosopher, and an anthropologist) was the fifth member of the expedition.

They first had to decide where to take the samples. They chose the spot on a map of the territory, which they spread out on a restaurant table. This double presence fascinated Latour: By putting her finger on a place on the map and on the table, the botanist actually touched the heart of the forest, or so they seemed to believe.

They were right. They discovered the referent of her finger after a one-hour jeep ride. But they were able to find the place on the map because the botanist had prepared the forest during the many years she had worked there; there were tags on patches of the forest that corresponded to the marks on the map. Now the botanist could start collecting plant specimens, which she said she recognized as well as the members of her family. But in this case, the opposite of that of the family, the recognition begins with a reference to an existing taxonomy of plants. Nobody consults the family tree in order to recognize their close living relatives, but the botanist goes to the family tree in order to name the individual specimen.

Reference, Latour reminded the reader, comes from Latin *referre*, to bring back. Back to where? To the place where taxonomies live. Bring back what? Two features of reference can be recognized in the botanist's way of collecting specimens: the *economy* (one blade of grass to represent thousands of blades of grass) and the *evidence* (in case her colleagues start doubting her words). The botanist saw to it that the plants she had collected were well preserved and annotated them for further use. Next, she would take them to her office and add them to her collection, where they would be carefully conserved, minutely described, and arranged into a system permitting easy identification. No wonder flowers are used for preserving memories.

But there are difficulties in the botanists' work that are unknown to nonprofessional flower collectors. Sooner or later each botanist has a pile of specimens requiring classification. A cleaning person's mistake or even the botanist's mistake, and the sample returns to its original state, no longer having any meaning. The overload of information is ubiquitous, and classification is the main way of managing it in sciences (Bowker, 2006).

In the meantime, the pedologists dug soil samples. The excursion had been founded on a conciliatory hypothesis: Neither the forest nor the savanna were receding or advancing; the border that separates them reflects a difference in soil. But at the depth of 50 centimeters, the soil was exactly the same in two holes: one under the forest, the other under the savanna.

At this point, the observer was allowed to participate. Because he is tall, he was used by the pedologists as an alignment pole (equivalent to being used as a coffee maker while observing a management meeting). The pedologists used a device that allowed them to turn the entire terrain of interest into a set of triangles from which the soil samples would be taken. The samples were stored in plastic bags on which was recorded the number of the hole and the depth at which the samples were taken. The pedologists made some qualitative observations, all of which were quickly written down, but the soil was to be systematically analyzed in laboratories, located in various places around the world. In order to transport the samples, they were first put into a pedocomparator – a drawer with compartments – which could

then be stored in a cabinet-type suitcase. Locating samples in different compartments of the pedocomparator was another step in the process of classification; even
for a non-pedologist, the differences in soil became visible. From there, it was possible to prepare a diagram, which at first merely summarized what could be seen
in the pedocomparator (the soil changing along the sampling line), but which later
would be included in a published paper.

Why were all these transformations necessary? Latour had an answer: Because it
was not possible to include the forest in the debate! Things need to be changed into
words and pictures (signs), in order to enter a debate. But what was the principle
of this transformation? Were the words used similar to the things they represented?

> ... these acts of reference are all the more assured since they rely not so much
> on resemblance as on a regulated series of transformations, transmutations, and
> translations.[1] A thing can remain more durable and be transported farther and
> more quickly if it continues to undergo transformations at each stage of this
> long cascade.
>
> It seems that reference is not simply the act of pointing or a way of keeping,
> on the outside, some material guarantee for the truth of a statement; rather it
> is our way of keeping something *constant* through a series of transformations.
> Knowledge does not reflect a real external world that it resembles via mimesis,
> but rather a real internal world, the coherence and continuity of which it helps
> to ensure. (Latour, 1995/1999: 58)

Later, the diagram would be compared to other diagrams, photographs to other
photographs, and what the members of the excursion said to what their colleagues
had written. The process would re-enter the realm of rhetoric and discourse, and
from there it was an easy route to a scientific paper. The pedologist wrote the final
version of the report on his laptop computer, from which it began to circulate,
coming in contact with other texts. The report would change into the draft of a
paper, the draft into a published article. If all transformations were done correctly,
the process could be reversed: From the published paper to the Amazon soil, with
no changes. The account of Latour's experience became yet another paper, as well
as the book chapter which I am using here as a reference – both of which joined
the circuit.

FOLLOWING THE AIR AND THE WATER IN STOCKHOLM

There are many people and instruments involved in producing air and water quality
for the City of Stockholm, and Petra Adolfsson (2005a, 2005b) repeated Latour's
procedure in an urban environment, in order to study those processes. Although the
production process resembles that of the production of a scientific paper, the results
are more numerous and more surprising.

As in the case of the Amazon forest, the process begins with coordinates. A unit at Stockholm Municipality offices was in possession of a detailed map of the Stockholm area, on which their predecessors had marked appropriate places for measuring the characteristics of the air over Stockholm. There were three types of measuring stations: temporary projects; automatic measurements, in which the instruments located in the measuring stations were sending data to the central computer every hour; and so-called passive or sampling stations, where pollutants (specifically, sulfur dioxide and nitrogen dioxide) accreted on sampling tools. Samples were collected from these three stations once a month and sent to the laboratory for analysis.

It was on one of those collection excursions that Adolfsson followed 'Pernilla', an employee of the air pollution unit. Before they left the office, Pernilla collected a plastic bag containing sampler jars with red locks for nitrogen dioxide and blue locks for sulfur dioxide. Petra and Pernilla took a ladder with them and drove away, following a list of 14 stations that Pernilla was to visit. The samplers had a small roof to protect the samples from the weather, and were located on street lamps, trees, and roofs. Pernilla would climb the ladder and exchange the old sampler for a new one, then put the old sampler in a jar marked with the type of sample and the location. She added the date and time of the exchange of samplers on the jar's label. Back in the office, she placed all the jars in a row according to their numbers, to ensure that none was missing; stored them in a plastic bag; and sent them to the laboratory in Gothenburg. Upon receiving a report from the laboratory, she typed the results on an Excel sheet and turned them into a diagram. The diagram was made at the request of a road construction company, but it is the type of diagram used for the prognosis of air pollution, and was made public on the unit's homepage.

The construction of a diagram was performed by computer, but the coordinates were set by the European Union. There are legal texts and international standards determining what to measure, how to measure it, and how to present the results. The results, in graphic form, travel further. They are used daily in newspapers to inform citizens about the degree of pollution. They arrive semi-annually in the form of a report at meetings of the committee appointed by the City Council. They usually comprise the last point on the agenda, rarely producing much debate, for the air in Stockholm is relatively clean. They can be seen on the computers of the City Public Library, where visitors can interact with the measurement group. They were used in an urban planning debate that was stirring up both the politicians and the citizens of Stockholm at the time of the study. But they also earned other applications, as Adolfsson was to discover following the transformation of samples with her camera and her notebook. An energy company used the graphs as the advertisement for their method of energy production and as an adornment during a public exhibition.

Adolfsson followed Stockholm's water in a similar way: from boats distributed throughout Stockholm's archipelago, where the sampling was done, to the laboratory of the Water Company, to the computers and statistical programs, to daily reports, and on to scientific papers. She followed water sampled at public drinking places and she followed samples from the sewers.

Following air and water finally led Adolfsson to the least expected place: the Royal Environmental Monument inaugurated by His Majesty King Carl XVI Gustaf (Adolfsson, 2005b). The monument consists of two obelisks. On one, a shiny zigzag of colorful light shows the state of water in the city; on the other, the light shows the state of the air. The play of light is steered by the Water Company's computers, but the stone obelisks also contain metal plates with engravings demonstrating long-term changes (Stockholm is said to be in the unique position of having these data dating back many years). The study allowed Adolfsson to conclude that the transformations of water and air into information and from information into various types of aesthetic objects are part of the larger process of organizing and running the city. Thus nature has been co-opted and pressed into the service of a macro-actor – the City of Stockholm – to serve its inhabitants and to attract its tourists.

The next example is of the study of a software used in a hospital that was to serve the patients and the medical personnel alike.

SHADOWING SOFTWARE

Attila Bruni (2005) studied the introduction of an electronic patient record (EPR) system in an Italian hospital. The EPR had been introduced there after a year-long participatory design process, during which information engineers collaborated with physicians. Bruni's aim was to conduct a structured observation of certain organizational events, but he became interested in the EPR's presence in some times and places, but not in others.

This trait, in my opinion, is typical for quasi-objects; now you see them, now you don't. Ann-Christine Frandsen (2009) followed a quasi-object in the form of a bill, an economic report. This was an actual object, however – a piece of paper – and it was relatively easy to trace back to its origin. Attila Bruni's quasi-object may be more precisely called a virtual object, in the sense of two of three meanings of the word 'virtual' listed by Marie-Laure Ryan (2001): Virtual in the sense of containing the potential of many different actualizations, and virtual in the sense of being computer-mediated.

Bruni was fascinated with this vanishing object and decided to follow the software for a month. He immediately discovered the first actualization of the EPR. The computer that contained the EPR used by nurses was located in the patient reception area. At the time of the study, an electronic document of virtual existence had no legal validity. Thus each EPR document was printed in order to be signed by the physician and the chief consultant, and then inserted in the folder containing all the documents concerning a specific patient.

A typical EPR-mediated interaction developed between a patient and a nurse. Patients presented themselves at reception, told the nurse their names, so their appointments could be checked on a computer or a printout, and, depending on the situation, either delivered their latest test results to the nurse or received them from the nurse, who had retrieved them from the computer. Then the EPR provided the basis for a key decision concerning the color of the slip of paper that a patient received, together with a queuing number. The EPR showed if the results of the tests differed from the previous treatment. If not, the patient was given a green slip; if yes, a yellow one. The color indicated the type of treatment the patient was to receive.

Bruni's peculiar situation as an observer of a software is evident here. Sitting in the reception room, he witnessed many interactions between patient and nurse and among the relatives accompanying patients. But although the EPR software was, in a sense, always there, he could glimpse it only now and then. Once he realized its importance, however, he started visiting other premises where the EPR could show up: the laboratory, the hospitalization ward, the therapy preparation room, and the infusion zone.

The significance of this presence is well illustrated in a vignette showing the beginning of the day at a day hospital. The head nurse opened the door, switched on the lights, and turned on the computer, waking up the EPR. The nurse then engaged in what might be considered more proper nursing activities (preparing drips, beginning therapies for patients who did not require a check by the physician, for instance). An hour later, another nurse arrived and contacted the EPR. She checked all the clinical records that had been completed for patients expected to arrive that day; she printed the list of appointments and stacked the patients' clinical records in the order indicated by the computer. She also printed the EPR records for the new patients and initiated new folders for them.

A physician who wanted to scan the test results jammed the operating system. A computer technician was asked to help, and was able to start the system again, but he made it clear that if he started tinkering with the scanner, the nurse would not be able to use the EPR. The EPR won, and the scanner program had to wait.

There were also complaints about the EPR's behavior. One nurse told the other to be careful, because the computer had printed the wrong therapy. The nurse explained to Attila Bruni that,

> ... the program is a bit rigid in its structure. ... When the cycle requires a particular order, a particular drug, and then for some reason it has to be reduced ... you have to be very careful because he [the software] always sets the same therapy at 100%. So that he [the physician] often says 'Reduce the dose', but he [the software] doesn't reduce it, because you have to go into the first ... first memory'. (Bruni, 2005: 371)

The 'he' suggests that the physician and the EPR ended up on the same level, cooperating – or, as the case may be, not cooperating. The EPR actually had some stable character defects; it consistently made mistakes with one type of therapy. The computer technicians had been told that, but did nothing. As it happened, the physicians also made mistakes with the same type of therapy, partly because they relied on computers and did not realize that changes in the original inscriptions had to be made to ensure that this mistake would not happen. So it was the nurses (and the technicians, when they were in the mood) who had to correct the mistakes of the software – and of the physicians.

One could ask about the sense in which Attila Bruni was 'shadowing' the software. He was merely sitting in one room or another, as any direct observer would do, watching the nurses, the patients, the physicians, and the technicians. A direct observer could have been inclined to notice merely that nurses 'do something on the computer'. But Bruni was focusing on the EPR software, watching its appearances and disappearances, following its actions and its interactions.

WHY FOLLOW THE OBJECTS?

There are more gains to be expected from following objects than those mentioned previously, namely that it may be easier in the psychological if not the physical sense to follow objects rather than people, and that shadowing objects completes the picture of the activity or way of life under study. In order to explain further advantages of this approach, however, I need to return to the times when Bruno Latour and Michel Callon (1981) introduced Actor-Network Theory to the social sciences.

Latour and Callon claimed that social scientists are often in awe of the powerful macro-actors they study, and whether they criticize or admire them, they take their greatness for granted. This greatness is but an optical illusion, claimed Latour and Callon, a trick that requires myriad successful actions, multiple connections, and many stabilizers. The trick is to present a large network of heterogeneous parts (people, objects, animals, quasi-objects) as one actor that speaks in one voice. This is indeed the trick behind the state, as illustrated by the mythical figure of Leviathan. But the task of social scientists should be not so much to criticize or applaud actors that seem larger than life, but try to answer a question: Why do certain actors grow into macro-actors, while others remain medium or micro-actors, and yet others remain forever merely actants upon which others act?

One obvious way of trying to answer these questions is through historical case studies. This was how Karl Polanyi (1944) traced the formation of such macro-actors as industrial capitalist economies, and Bruno Latour (1986) showed how an unknown biologist called Louis Pasteur became an institution. What is necessary in such cases is a significant temporal distance and solid documentation.

Another way is to follow the formation of a macro-actor prospectively, while the act is in progress. There are two usual obstacles hindering that procedure, however. The main one is that it is difficult to know which actant will become a macro-actor, as Tom Peters and Robert H. Waterman discovered. Their 1982 bestseller, *In Search of Excellence*, proudly presented 200 excellent US companies, half of which no longer existed 15 years later. Stories of failure should be, at least in principle, as fascinating as stories of success, but they reintroduce the other difficulty: The first signs of failure are difficult to recognize, and when failure is undeniable, the researchers are no longer welcome. Perhaps the studies of both successes and failures in macro–actor construction are best studied retrospectively.

In most research, social scientists meet with fully developed macro- (or at least solid) actors that do two things. They hide their humble actant's origins (unless they have already become legendary, like Ingvar Kamprad, the founder of IKEA, in whose case the legend successfully stylizes the actual origins). They make connections between heterogeneous actants that form their network invisible. This is why Actor-Network Theory suggests a focus on the humblest of actants – those deeply ingrained in an existing network. Watching how that actant moves through the network allows for the discovery of many other actants, otherwise hidden in black boxes; to inspect various connections among them, and to examine their stability or fragility. The shadowing of people reveals more about their actions than about their networks, and is more likely to reveal the ways in which their actions are connected to other actions (Czarniawska, 1997). And following objects diminishes the risk of focusing merely on people and neglecting other actants present in every network.

Following the objects

Choose an object or a quasi-object (an idea, a document, a model) crucial for the practice of interest to you and follow its trajectory through space and time (as far and as long as you can).

EXERCISE 6

FURTHER READING

Czarniawska, Barbara (2007) *Shadowing, and other techniques for doing fieldwork in modern societies*. Malmö/Copenhagen: Liber/CBS Press.

Latour, Bruno (2005) *Reassembling the social: An introduction to Actor-Network Theory*. Oxford: Oxford University Press.

Note

1. Latour used the word here, not in its linguistic meaning, but in the original meaning retrieved by philosopher Michel Serres: *trans-latio*, putting things in another place, which changes them into different things.

7

Tools for Fieldwork

Since the earliest attempts at fieldwork, fieldworkers have gone to the field well equipped, but their equipment constantly changes. Nowadays, most of it is digital. What follows is a short review of tools specifically invented or adapted for purposes of fieldwork.

DIARY STUDIES IN THE DIGITAL ERA

It so happens that diary studies – as a means of self-observation or in a diary-interview technique – are highly popular among researchers active in the field of computer–human interaction. Many such studies aim not at contributing theoretical insights, but at developing new or improving existing computer technologies. This practical orientation does not make the studies uninteresting for theoretically oriented researchers; to the contrary, they may find much of value in that approach. Additionally, the technologies thus developed may prove to be of significant aid to fieldworkers, independent of their perspective and orientation. And self-observation usually takes the form of some type of diary.[1]

It may be said that most attempts at using computers in the aid of fieldwork aim at eliminating or reducing what are seen as problems of conventional techniques:

- obtrusiveness of observational techniques,
- additional workload of self-observational techniques such as diaries,
- recall problems in interviews and diary-interviews (see Chapter 4).

In what follows I have chosen five examples. One demonstrates how a diary could be made easier with the aid of computer technologies; the next two illustrate the use of an enhanced diary technique in researching uses of a specific technology; the fourth and the fifth aim at developing a technology for field studies.

The first example concerns tools designed to study work fragmentation. Czerwinski et al. (2004) addressed this issue by starting from the observation that it is not only managers whose work is fragmented; all professionals suffer (or enjoy) the same fate. (Indeed, I interrupted the writing of this chapter to answer my mail, sometimes forgetting my train of thought as the result, and I answered both the stationary and the mobile phones.) Thus Czerwinski and his colleagues asked experienced computer users – three women and eight men – representing a variety of occupations, such as stockbroker, professor of computer science, web designer, software developer, boat salesman, and network administrator – to complete diary entries for one week. They were given a Microsoft Excel spreadsheet, which contained worksheets for each weekday, and an additional one with instructions. The columns were called: Time of Task Start, Difficulty Switching to the Task, What Documents Were Included in the Task, What Was Forgotten if Anything, Comments, and the Number of Interruptions Experienced. It turned out that different diarists chose to register task switches in different levels of detail, and these differences appeared to be related to their occupations. The stockbroker, for example, unlike the others, considered each telephone call a separate task. Two researchers later coded all the diaries from the first day, in order to achieve agreement on a common coding scheme. The diarists were obviously proud of their ability to multitask, and claimed that it brought fun and variety to their work.

Nevertheless, I estimate the time needed for recording task switches and providing explanations for them at something like 1 to 90 minutes a day, quite a bit of time for information workers, especially those working against deadlines. Thus the main concern of Barry Brown et al. (2000) was to simplify the diary procedure further. Their starting point was the assumption that most people nowadays search and find information as part of their work, something Brown and his colleagues called 'information capture'. Their ambition was to design a new kind of capture device – a handheld document scanner. They recruited diarists, all PC and e-mail users; 13 were from Hewlett-Packard (the producer of the capture device) and nine from outside HP, representing a diverse mix of occupations. They were divided into 'multimedia capture' and 'paper capture' groups, given digital cameras, and told to photograph any information they wanted to capture over the next seven days. The multimedia group was told to photograph any information source, whereas the paper group members were to limit themselves to any type of paper document. The pictures (219 from the multimedia group and 162 from the paper group) were then used 'as memory joggers in semi-structured interviews' (Brown et al., 2000: 440), a procedure repeated three times over the week. The authors ended their paper on a methodological note:

By using digital cameras to support diary-keeping, one can collect naturalistic data without the large overhead of observational approaches. Since the photographs are taken at the site of action, and interviews about the photos are carried out within a couple of days, subjects showed few recall problems when prompted by photos even on the relatively low resolution screen used on current digital cameras. This method also reduced the demand on the subjects themselves as taking pictures was easier for them than writing notes. (Brown et al., 2000: 445)

Although it is easy to agree with these conclusions, it is also obvious that the photo-diary technique may be disturbing in social contexts. Similarly, one can imagine that the 'beeper technique' Jane Hannaway (1989) used in her study of 52 managers in the central office of a large school district in the USA must have been rather obtrusive. The managers wore random-signal-generator devices and answered a set of ten questions when the beeper sounded. And they did it every working day for six weeks. The questions concerned, among other things, the type of task they were involved in, the content focus of the task, the ideal task performer, the special focus of the task, the expected disposition of the task, and the initiator of the activity (1989: 45). Although Hannaway did not report any disadvantages of her technique, one cannot but wonder at the patience of the managers and the bewilderment of people who were talking to them when their beepers sent them off to their diaries.

Leysia Palen and Marilyn Salzman's studies (2002) were among several within the computer–human interaction community in which the technology for conducting the study was also the study object – in this case, mobile telephones. The researchers' starting point was the need to depict mobility. Their diarists, who were paid for their participation, reported events connected to the use of mobile telephones on a dedicated voicemail line. In their first study of 19 novice mobile phone users, Palen and Salzman did not instruct the diarists to contact voicemail via their mobile phones, because the uses of their newly acquired phones was one of the research questions. The instructions were relatively open: The diarists were supposed to report when they first used their telephones in a new environment, when they used them in an unexpected way, when they did not use them for an extended period, when they used a new feature, and when they experienced problems.

In their second study, 200 novice users were followed for a year after the acquisition of their first phones. Considering the size of the sample, the responses had to be more structured, and the voicemail included prompts that gave instructions about the contents of the reports. Palen and Salzman (2002: 91) were satisfied with their method, because, in their reading, it 'yielded rich descriptions of activity and experiences that fleshed out findings emerging from other data sources'; the researchers also used a quantitative telephone survey, face-to-face interviews, and focus groups.

Palen and Salzman made another critical observation: In the usual discussion over the advantages and the disadvantages of open versus structured techniques the preferences of respondents are rarely discussed. As Galen Strawson (2004) noted when arguing convincingly against a romanticized view of narrativity, not all people structure their experience in a narrative form. Some people prefer closed questions or multiple-choice items to open questions; indeed, some people prefer surveys to interviews. Charmaz (2006/2014) has also noted, for instance, that anonymous elicited texts can provide opportunities for disclosures that are not likely to be revealed in an interview. All of this is also contingent upon the writing skills of the diarists. An alternative would be to allow diarists to choose a form that fits them best, or to combine techniques.

Carter and Mankoff (2005) ran a diary study during a jazz festival, in which two diarists were told to use digital cameras, two others to use digital audio recorders, two were asked to collect tangible objects in a bag, and one was expected to do audio recording and collect objects. A great many instructive insights emerged from these methodological experiments. The collection of tangible objects, for example, is certainly a highly unusual and therefore appealing approach, but Carter and Mankoff were disappointed in its results. One woman brought three flowers to illustrate various tonalities of jazz she heard, which the researchers were lost on how to interpret. They were most pleased with the photo-diaries, but found audio recordings easy to annotate and considered them the least obtrusive. Their conclusion was not unexpected: A hybrid photo/audio technology would be the most appropriate. Consequently, they designed Reporter, a tool for diary studies.[2] Reporter lets one take photographs, record voice memos, and annotate them.

While Carter and Mankoff continued to test their Reporter and other fieldwork technologies, like video recordings, Brandt et al. (2007) also tried to lessen the burden for the diarists under mobile conditions. They developed a technology for capturing and transmitting *snippets* of information: bits of text, audio or pictures that could be transmitted by voicemail, SMS, or MMS, and used to compose complete diary entries at leisure. The advantages, as they see it, are threefold: It diminishes data input; it relies on a device that most people now carry on them (the mobile phone); and it allows the diarists to choose the medium that suits them best.

Do these technologies solve the contemporary fieldwork problems I listed in Chapter 1? To people like me, who adopt the pragmatist stance[3] of fieldwork, only the overload of work caused by diaries is a difficulty to be alleviated. In this aspect, digital technologies are a great help.

As to the traditionally emphasized problem of the obtrusive presence of an observer, an observer in a society that observes itself was, to Niklas Luhmann (1998), a characteristic trait of modern societies. In Swedish municipalities, because of free access to all nonconfidential dealings of the public administration, there are sometimes more researchers than administrators in sight. In companies, the researchers compete with journalists and with visitors from abroad and from headquarters. In the interview society (Atkinson and Silverman, 1997), which, according to Giampietro Gobo (2008), has also become an observation society in which *Big Brother* is the favorite TV show, the idea of unobtrusive methods seems quaint. The problems created by obtrusiveness are moral rather than methodological. Digital technologies are a great help, given their speed and ease of use; observers and diarists can forget, feel confused, and tire. It is necessary to return to the traditional sensitivities of anthropology, however, and to ask oneself if photography and audio recording is ethical – if it offends or otherwise harms those who are observed in such a way.

The traditional anthropologists and ethnographers first used photographs, then films. Although both are now digitalized and were therefore mentioned in this section, they deserve separate attention.

THE EYE OF THE CAMERA

> The camera's aid to observation is not new; Leonardo da Vinci described its principles. (Collier and Collier, 1967/1986: 7)

The Colliers were of the opinion that modern people are poor observers and that field researchers receive literary rather than visual training – perhaps with the exception of psychologists. Urban dwellers, when forced to observe in detail, rely on some type of technology: microscopes, telescopes, and, increasingly, cameras.

As mentioned, anthropologists made early use of cameras. But the original enthusiasm for photographs as the most objective observation technique gave way to doubts based on the fact that photographs depend not merely on cameras, but also on photographers. Thus anthropologists later used photos as illustrations only (Collier and Collier, 1967/1986). At present, however, with smart phones equipped with cameras, photography and video recordings occupy more and more space in social science studies.

Photography can be used as a tool for mapping, literally or metaphorically – for gaining orientation in a site, then introducing the reader to it in a visual way. As I am not adept at 'painting with words', I used photographs to introduce readers to the three news agencies I studied (Czarniawska, 2012). Photography can also be used as a 'cultural inventory' (Collier and Collier, 1967/1986), not only by anthropologists, but also by marketing scholars. Cecilia Cassinger (2010), for example, asked Japanese IKEA customers to photograph their acquisitions in their homes. Thus photographs can be taken both by researchers and by the people under study; they can document observations or be used to elicit commentaries in an interview (more about it in Chapter 10).

Like photographs, films can be treated as field material, but also be part or all of a final report. Video recording presently exists primarily as stationary observation (Jönsson, 2005; Kokk and Jönsson, 2013), but that limitation could be removed through technological development (smaller and lighter cameras) and the growing skills of social scientists. Not many of us can use a movie camera effectively. Again, anthropologists are at the forefront of this technology, although they apparently need the frequent assistance of professional filmmakers (Collier and Collier, 1967/1986).

The use of digital cameras has much to do with another type of fieldwork: virtual ethnographies and other types of virtual studies, both of which I address in Chapter 9. The physical presence in the field, however, is related to many practical and ethical complications, which I discuss in the next chapter.

> ## Research tools
>
> Complete your research application (Exercise 3) by including the list (and prices!) of the tools you will need to conduct your study.

FURTHER READING

Fetterman, David M. (1988/2010) *Ethnography: Step by step*. London: Sage (see esp. Chapter 4: Gearing up: Ethnographic equipment).

Harper, Douglas (2012) *Visual sociology*. Abingdon: Routledge.

Notes

1. Barrett and Barrett (2001) and Brinkmann (2012) list some other, less well known forms of self-observation, used mostly in psychological research.
2. Reporter aids researchers performing diary studies that involve digital capture of media such as audio and photographs. It enables communication between study participants and researchers, and allows sharing and annotation of captured media.
3. In philosophy, this is best represented at present by Richard Rorty, see, for example, interviews with Rorty edited by Mendieta (2006). I explained this stance in relation to fieldwork in Czarniawska (1997).

8

Surviving in the Field: Practicalities and Personalities

It is the actual work in the field that presents the most problems, as there can be no prescription that fits every possible situation. This chapter, then, is only a review of some of the most common complications: The need to obtain and maintain access, the variety of relationships between the researcher and the people under study, and the impact of gender and social stratification on the course of research.

ACCESS

Access problems and their solutions are usually described in a section of a method book dedicated to study design. Fieldwork, especially shadowing, quickly reveals that access is a continuing problem, from beginning to end.[1] Different people, different days, different situations, and even different moods require continuous renegotiation of access. In the rest of this chapter, I discuss problems related to access to so-called closed settings, although even in studies of public settings, researchers can encounter access difficulties (see e.g. Hammersley and Atkinson, 1983/2007).

What is more, the difference between closed and public settings is not always clear in the field.

Marianella Sclavi, still on the prolonged visit to the USA described in Chapter 5, decided to undertake another shadowing project. She presented it in the following terms to her sociology colleagues in a college located on the border between the Bronx and Westchester in New York City, where she was teaching at the time.

> *The Program*: 'What I want to do is to visit a part of the Bronx where the people have gotten organized and are trying to save their neighborhoods, both morally and physically.'
>
> *The Method*: 'I need a few names and telephone numbers for people who're involved in this kind of work, and who might be willing to let me *shadow* them in the course of their daily lives.'
>
> *The Approach*: 'All I want to do up there is to look and listen. I want to take a good look at my difficulties in communicating with the people who live there, and at theirs in communicating with me. At the things that get on our nerves, at my own discomfort.'
>
> *The General Goal*: 'I want to find out what they do and how they live, what they believe in, what kind of hopes they have and what kind of difficulties they have to meet as people who have refused to resign themselves to catastrophe.'
>
> *The Specific Goal*: 'I hope to collect a lot of little clues that will fit together like the pieces of a puzzle. And at the end of it all, I might just come away with a better idea of the intellectual and moral climate of certain areas of the Bronx today.' (Sclavi, 2007: 231)

Her colleagues' reactions were almost entirely negative. In the first place, they found her methodological approach faulty. They believed that she ought to have started with a complete review of the literature dedicated to the Bronx. (Hopefully they had only urban studies in mind.) That would allow for the formulation of one or several hypotheses, to be tested in a properly designed study. Second, and this was the main objection, the Bronx was too dangerous to be studied by a middle-aged Italian woman. Third, and this objection represented the only real problem in Marianella Sclavi's eyes, nobody knew how to make contact with somebody from the 'real' Bronx. Sclavi wanted to shadow some of the college teachers who taught in the Bronx, but the teachers did not consider it doable. They went to the Bronx as if they were going on a dangerous but necessary excursion, from which one returns as quickly as possible.

Sclavi's project was saved by the two factors behind every successful field study: chance and persistence. At a Christmas dinner party organized by the company employing her husband, she was placed next to a lawyer who, while awaiting the main dish, told her that his son, also a lawyer, specialized in legal services to the poor and worked 'in the heart of the Bronx'. She asked for the son's telephone number and received it.

Two years passed before she was ready to begin her fieldwork. It turned out that the young lawyer had already moved to Florida, but he knew immediately what she needed. The Banana Kelly Community (BKC) was a committee formed at the end of the 1970s by a black worker's family and a social worker of Italian origin living on Kelly Street – after the dramatic events that had made the Bronx notorious.

Sclavi did have some qualms before her first trip to the Bronx, so she formulated an instruction for herself: 'A white, affluent, middle-class Italian woman is alone on a subway on her first trip to the South Bronx. Let's try to take a look at the way she's looking at things!' (2007: 12). She was following a well-known fieldwork rule: '[R]ecognize your feelings and relate them to the phenomenon' (Kleinman, 1991: 191). This self-observation immediately helped her to discover three of her own implicit assumptions: that men are more dangerous than women, that those who look unemployed and/or homeless are dangerous, and that young people are more dangerous than older ones. 'You deserve to be mugged by a calm, middle-aged woman who looks like a secretary', she told herself (Sclavi, 2007: 12).

Physical access can present complications even in apparently nonthreatening environments. Here is a story of 'My worst day in the field', written by and used with the permission of one of my doctoral students, who did not want to be identified (Czarniawska, 1998).

Strange stories of my adventurous life

It was my first day in Budapest, in the city summer heat. I had an appointment scheduled with the Director of Western Electronics in Hungary, an impressive and busy 'Herr Doktor', who had nevertheless given me a slot for an interview in our brief telephone conversation. Now, half an hour before our meeting, I was standing in my suit and tie, in an East European streetcar, exchanging stares with my fellow travelers. As I carefully traced the advance of the streetcar on my city map, I felt the tiredness of a sleepless night overcoming me. A new city, a new apartment, a new interview. I had arrived the day before, and a good friend had given me a guided tour of the city. Western Electronics was located on the outskirts, whereas I lived downtown. But the streetcars were a reliable means of transportation. My friend helped me locate the yellow streetcar track on the map. It was supposed to pass right by the street I wanted.

Now I was standing here, holding onto a handle as we slowly left downtown. Colorful sequences of images passed by: The brown Danube, roads swarming with small East European cars, beautifully decorated house fronts still bearing the marks of war damage, street signs with the names crossed out, plane trees along the street. It was like seeing scenes from a picturesque movie. But after a while, the road and sidewalks became filthy and rough. The streetcar passed by housing areas that looked like barracks, row after row of dilapidated yellow tenements. Children with grimy faces were running around; the women seemed to be on their way to some strenuous cleaning or industrial jobs. There were some men sitting around a table with wine bottles, playing cards.

I looked at my watch. It was twenty to nine, and the streetcar had barely idled its way over two-thirds of the distance. The car turned alongside a graveyard and came to a three-way crossroads. To my alarm, I noticed that the yellow track on the map split two ways, and I had missed it. I didn't know which way my street-car was turning. I held my breath and heaved a sigh of relief as it turned 'my way'. The car inched its way past another row of barracks and a couple of broad streets with heavy traffic. I asked one of the passengers about my stop. There it was, a bit further down the street. It was a big junction for streetcars, buses, and the subway along the wide street *ut Kerepsi*.

I was standing with my map in the middle of the morning rush, with people swarming in all directions. Which way to go now? I asked a pleasant-looking young woman (perhaps a service-minded secretary with language skills, recently employed at one of the Western companies?). She turned my map around a few times, pointed along the busy street, and disappeared into the crowd. It was almost ten to nine. I started to run. I crossed the street with a herd of other people and continued to jog down the road. There were four lanes on each side, no sidewalks, and the street was lined with ongoing roadwork, forcing me toward the rushing traffic. Inhaling the exhaust fumes felt like smoking ten Hungarian cigarettes at once. The next side street was in sight, but the name wasn't right. I had been running in the wrong direction.

I turned around, crossed the street again, and headed back to the junction, the camera dangled round my neck. I held my briefcase with my papers, passport and tape recorder out in front of me, so I could run better. My tie whirled and my jacket fluttered around me. The waving of pedestrians and honking of drivers signaled that I looked very funny, or possibly threatening. More roadwork and another crossroads with a policeman directing the traffic appeared before me. He pointed me in the direction of a side street.

Here it was calm, not a car in sight. Shabby military barracks on both sides. A littered sidewalk, where I was greeted by stray, mangy dogs and groups of equally stray, mangy Russian soldiers (at least that was what I assumed). Unshaven and wearing dirty, wrinkled uniforms, they appeared to lack morale or any belief in the future. They watched me, a foreigner with all the paraphernalia of prosperity, eyeing me from top to toe as if wondering if they could sell my camera on the black market. I dared not meet the eyes of either dogs or soldiers.

I progressed with hurried steps. Finally I spotted the right street. But what a street it was! Even shabbier than the one with the dogs and soldiers. It was five to nine. I ran and saw a sign that said 'Electra'. It has to be here! Western Electronics had probably taken over a Hungarian company by that name and moved into its premises. I rushed into the reception area, where three Hungarians were standing engaged in conversation. I announced my meeting with 'Herr Doktor' and Western Electronics. 'Can you show me to his office, please?' Communication breakdown. I tried again, this time in German. The language confusion became even worse. French? No, mission impossible. Maybe if I write it down? No response. Western Electronics was an unknown concept in this world. They had never heard of such a company here.

Out on the street again. I considered giving up, turning around to hail a cab downtown. Then, suddenly, the street changed. The misery faded, the shabbiness disappeared and normal buildings with normal people and normal cars came in sight. Now what? The street ended. An anonymous building complex, brown, functional style, no numbers, no signs. It can't possibly be here, can it? I ran through one of the gates. Oh yes, Western Electronics, third floor. I was ten minutes late. I ran up the stairs and was met in the corridor by a secretary. 'Herr Doktor' would receive me soon. I had time for a quick run to the bathroom to wash my hands and face. 'Herr Doktor' came out, speaking German and sounding somewhat irritated. 'Wasn't hard to find now, was it? The streetcar runs right by here.' I nodded and accepted a cup of coffee.

The problem of physical access, trivial as it may seem, is known to all field researchers and does not abate with age or experience. Getting to an unknown place on time is one of the recurring research nightmares, as it symbolizes much more than an organizing failure; it symbolizes the fear of entering an alien landscape. In the student's story, there is a palpable sense of danger, culminating in the meeting with dogs and Russian soldiers, who acquire a terrifying air, becoming monsters from a fairy tale. Like Sclavi, the author caught himself evoking standard prejudices (women are secretaries and Russian soldiers represent a potential threat).

It is true that difficulties in securing formal permission to do a study can be formidable and in some extreme cases produce the only story there is (see e.g. Silverman, 2000: Ch. 17). But seeking access continues throughout the entire study; there exists no such felicitous moment when the study can continue without any hindrance to access. This problem intensifies with the kind of fieldwork I am advocating here, characterized by multi-site observations and by the mobility of study objects and thus, necessarily, of the researcher. Access is never secured 'once and for all', but is always precarious, in need of constant maintenance. The multiple thresholds contribute to the feeling that there is no 'inside', where researchers can safely reside – merely a series of antechambers. Inside one is still outside another.

This is not to say that problems of this kind are new and unique to contemporary researchers. A collection of access stories in organization studies by Colin Brown et al. (1976) sought to reveal the tacit dimensions of research practices. UK scholar Nigel Nicholson told a story from the field about negotiating research in industrial relations, in which access had to be simultaneously obtained from management and from unions:

I suppose I feel that in situations like these people are less interested in precisely what you want to do than what sort of person you are: whether you will put people's backs up, that you are trustworthy, not a left-wing infiltrator, that you are impartial, that you are not an idiot. The details of your programme tend only to be a major concern when you are on some specific problem solving exercise. (Brown et al., 1976: 93)

The main gist of Nicholson's account is that both parties – management and unions – followed their routine interaction patterns throughout, rendering the researcher's access a bargaining issue. Nicholson almost left the field (especially when explicitly instructed to do so), before learning not to take routine cues too literally, and before understanding that the content of his study was not an issue – the *fact* of his study was.

I selected this quote from Nicholson's story because it struck me as based on an implicit assumption that cannot be adopted in all cases: That the researchers, the managers, and the stewards were all made of the same clay, that they were able to estimate each other's trustworthiness and political allegiances. In many cases, where the researcher is a woman in a male-dominated organization or a foreigner and thus an alien, this would not work. Nevertheless, it does not mean that field studies in a familiar culture are always easier than fieldwork in an alien culture. Ann Fischer (1970/1986) found that it was easier to be a fieldworker in Japan than in her home country of USA, and Charles McMillan found it easier doing research in Japan than in Britain:

I think there was a certain fascination in having a Canadian coming from Britain and someone from an American university to study their companies. They were curious to know what we wanted to study and they had an appreciation of the distance we had come. They felt, too, that they were legitimizing a kind of research that other countries undertook and Japan did not do and, therefore, they not only wanted it done but have it seen to be done. In terms of managerial issues, I don't think they were all that optimistic that we were going to give them really practical suggestions about how to improve anything. (Brown et al., 1976: 137–138)

Once detected, similar themes can be found in many access reports, old and new. They are not apprentice fears, because they do not abate with experience. They are not 'arrival problems', either; at least, I suffer such 'arrival problems' every day in the field, though their character changes daily. Perhaps when they are no longer felt, it is time to go home; the feeling of outsidedness is gone, and with it the main source of insight. The interviewers are 'interview victims' more often than the interviewees are. This has certainly been my experience, and I would like to point out that, in fact, there is nothing surprising about it – except perhaps that the theme of threatened identity does not figure prominently in access stories.

My impression is that access issues were more openly discussed in anthropology than in other research areas, especially during the 1970s, when Fischer and McMillan were seeking access to research sites. Women – never quite properly enculturated into male fields of endeavor – were especially prone to talk about the never-ending process of renegotiating their presence in the field (Wax, 1971/1985; Golde, 1970/1986). When men mentioned such matters, as Malinowski (1967/1989) did in his (in)famous diary, it was answered with censoring attempts by the research community.[2] The picture of a researcher's identity threatened by fieldwork violates the image of a mature adult and a competent professional.

As fully socialized adults, or 'competent members', as ethnomethodologists put it, researchers are supposed to possess a continuous personal identity. The emphasis placed on the stability of personal identity, however, conceals the fact that it is accompanied by 'discontinuous personal diversity' (Davies and Harré, 1991: 46). Continuous personal identity grows from the repetitiveness of interactions in which people engage. Discontinuous personal diversity is the result of a steady element of novelty in various interactions. Davies and Harré suggested, therefore, that instead of speaking of a 'self' possessing an essence (or expressing the essence of a person), it would be more useful to speak of *positioning*, which they defined as 'the discursive process whereby selves are located in conversations as observably and subjectively coherent participants in jointly produced story lines' (1991: 48). I would add that the process is not only discursive (the body and its accouterments play a key role), and that the self consists not only of an identity (Who am I like?), but also of an alterity (How do I differ from others?) (Czarniawska, 2013c). Nevertheless, the image of oneself is supposed to be well established in a mature person. But, as Davies and Harré have suggested, it is constantly challenged and re-established via positioning.

Positioning need not be intentional (every act can be interpreted as positioning), but it often is – particularly in interactions with unknown people and in new contexts. Entrance into a new field begins with extensive positioning, especially on the part of the researcher. It may be successful – or not.

POSITIONING IN THE FIELD

One of the often neglected but important symmetries in fieldwork is the fact that the researchers are not the only ones engaged in observation: they are themselves an object of observation. This symmetry needs to be emphasized, because, as John Van Maanen (1991: 31) put it, 'the success of any fieldwork endeavor depends inherently on the results of the unofficial study the observed undertake of the observer'.

Marianella Sclavi's study in the Bronx is an excellent example of this statement. Her first visit to BKC initiated a series of snowballing contacts, and she kept asking people she met for permission to shadow them for one day. The first was one of BKC's pioneers, Pearl White, a black mother of eight, a hairdresser and beautician, a Baptist. Here is the first encounter between Pearl and Maria (Marianella Sclavi):

During the first ten minutes of their conversation, Pearl and Maria had continued to study one another. They found each other disconcerting; they were also drawn to one another and aroused each other's curiosity. Both of them were tall and solid, with a touch of irony in their eyes, a mouth that could broaden into a wide, winning smile, lively faces and a carriage like the Queen of England. 'A bit stiff and withdrawn, too much composure. Who knows what she's like when she lets herself go?' they each thought of the other. They were both forty-eight years old. (Sclavi, 2007: 49)

Sclavi followed Pearl White many times; and on many occasions, including a visit to the church, she stayed at Pearl's house for a couple of days. While she interviewed Pearl about the history of BKC, the shadowing enabled her to experience life in the Bronx firsthand.

Sclavi emphasized the advantages of shadowing as a methodology in which the researcher does not try to avoid problems caused by the unexpected or by discomforts related to the strangeness of the Other. On the contrary, shadowing places those factors squarely at the center of the researcher's attention. Psychic discomfort and communication problems are turned into resources, permitting us to understand ourselves and Others' selves in interaction. Her approach guided me through my own difficulties in the field.

In the course of my study of big city management (Czarniawska, 2002), I shadowed, among others, a Finance Director (FD) — a woman of my own age with a diploma in economics from Warsaw School of Agriculture. My PhD is from Warsaw School of Economics, and the two universities are across the street from each other.

I interviewed her for the first time in February. Her first sentence was to tell me that she was busy, as the Mayor was waiting for her; in her second sentence, she admitted to never having seen my introductory letter; yet in her third, she agreed to be shadowed for two weeks in March. Here are some excerpts from my fieldnotes:

Warsaw, March 7.

9:35 — I am truly dragging my feet on my way to the Finance Director's office. I am clearly afraid — but of what? I am fairly sure of FD's sincere intentions. There may be some minor troubles and difficulties along the way in our ten working days together, but there always are. Nobody wishes me ill. Why be afraid? Because of my total dependence and the necessary passivity, that's why. I am not used to other people controlling my life so literally.

Despite my slow pace I arrive at the office too early. I go down a wrong corridor first, but then arrive at the right door. Will I recognize FD? A woman dressed to go out passes me in the door — is it her? No, but she comes next, carrying her fur coat on her arm, ready to meet the Deputy Mayor before the council session we are all to attend. FD directs me to her deputy, promises to send her car for us, and gives me a draft of the budget to study in the meantime. And a very good thing too, as otherwise I wouldn't have been able to understand much of the session.

...

12:00 – End of the session. I am waiting for FD at the door. FD clearly expects me to go home, but I protest. We return to the office in her car. I follow her into the back seat, but she stops me and tells me to sit in front next to the driver. I am sure my ears are red, but I try not to show my humiliation.

FD is planning to meet the Deputy Mayor. I summon all my courage and ask: 'May I go with you?' 'No, these matters are not intended for the ears of strangers.'

I go into her office, where I claim a place at the conference table, which is to be mine in the days to come. She comes in and goes out of the office without explanation. The secretary makes tea for her and she eats her lunch sandwich while looking at her papers.

14:00 – FD calls her first deputy: 'Take Madam [that's me] to the cafeteria, I am leaving now'.

...

15:30 – I am back in the office when FD returns. 'I'm still busy', she says before leaving the office again. She comes back after a while: 'Are you still waiting for me?' I smile bravely (or so I think) and promise to be there tomorrow at 8:00. FD protests. This is not how she imagined it. She can't work this way. She thought that I would only be appearing now and then. I feel that I am sinking, but I try to stay up, and once again to explain to her my way of working. The compromise reached is that I may come the next day at 14:00, after all her important meetings.

Warsaw, March 8.

14:00 – As I enter the secretary's office, she says: 'Madam Finance Director is busy'. 'I will wait then.' 'But she has other meetings afterwards.' I smile coolly (or so I think) and say: 'She told me to come at 14:00'. I take my coat off and hang it on a hanger, close to FD's. 'At least let her finish this telephone call', says the secretary.

I sit down and prepare to wait. Several people go into FD's office and come out again. I am beginning to feel serious apprehension, when FD finally appears herself: 'Are you waiting for me already?' I go into her office and begin to flatter her. 'Your budget was accepted in great style! No wonder the telephone never stops ringing. You're the name of the day!' FD smiles thinly but does not send me away [this comment turns out to represent the peak of my shadowing success in the days to come].

'Perhaps you can tell me about your plans for the next few days so I can try not to tire you too much?' The next day she is meeting the City Mayor, after which they will both go to meet representatives of a Big Bank – my presence is out of the question. I can come to the office at 14:00. The day after that she's going to Łódź to meet other city finance directors. Too far for me (in her opinion).

And the following day again she's visiting one of the districts, but won't be staying long. After that I can hang around, if I insist.

…

FD seems to be reconciled to my presence, and she promises to arrange an interview with the Deputy Mayor for me, which I had failed to do on my own. She calls his secretary and presents my business in great and incorrect detail, and sends me along there. It is next door. The secretary's office/waiting room is enormous. There are two people sitting there, the secretary and a man whom I assume to be a bodyguard. The secretary talks on the phone while the guard asks me to state my business. I do and he bids me to wait. The secretary stops talking, takes my business card and my letter of introduction and says that the Deputy Mayor is very busy. Right now he is talking to a journalist. I produce my best smile [I was told afterwards by an honest respondent that I smiled far too much for the local custom],[3] and explain that any time during my stay in Warsaw would do.

The Deputy's door opens and the journalist comes out. The secretary goes into the office and returns with the Deputy, who shakes my hand without kissing it (What a relief!) and says that he has heard of me but that he's awfully busy. I reply that I haven't counted on meeting him today, but perhaps sometime during the week … He and his secretary lean over his completely blank diary and bombard me with his appointments: bus factory all day Wednesday, London on Thursday … [I am not suggesting they were inventing all this. As far as I could establish, nobody used calendars for writing down their appointments. They looked at them to remember days and dates.] I say that I'll be back; he says that he may not be Deputy Mayor any longer; I say, even better, he would have more time for reflection; he says, not before retirement; I say that would be too long to wait; he says not at all; I say that, after all, we are the same age, and he studied at the University with my first husband … 'Put her in on Wednesday', he says to his secretary. 'Which Wednesday? There's a press conference this Wednesday'. We decide the date, the day, the hour. [The secretary canceled the appointment later.] … He leaves, the telephone rings. The secretary answers: 'He just left'. She turns to me, sighing: 'Poor man, everybody wants him … He should change his name to "Wanted" '. I would have some less flattering suggestions, but I do not share those with her. I take several deep breaths and return to the FD's office.

My coat is not on the hanger, but lying on a chair. Had I forgotten to hang it up after all? Had somebody taken it down thinking FD's fur coat was too crowded? The etiquette of fieldwork seems to be beyond my capacity.

FD is talking with her deputy about public tenders. I ask if they can explain some matters to me that I don't understand. FD agrees – either she is in a good mood or feeling guilty for systematically neglecting me.

I wish I could report that my relationship with FD improved, but it didn't. It didn't get worse either. One thing is clear: I could never have spent two years shadowing her, as Wolcott did with the school principal. But could I have guessed that from the outset? She did not wear white socks; perhaps the fur coat was the cue I missed. At any rate, she regularly left me for business meetings and for business gossip (of which there was a great deal, given that a major reform was in the offing). She took me to some other meetings, all of which were engrossing. I spent hours in the secretary's office, overhearing conversations that were both entertaining and informative, talking to FD's deputies and reading various documents. As I was not allowed to spend all the working day in the FD's office, I had a great deal of time to brood over my inadequacies as a field researcher.

It seemed to me that the Finance Director and I were too alike to achieve an easy distance, and yet too alien to become close. Indeed, we perceived each other as similar and as being in symmetrical positions, unlike the traditional anthropologists in relation to the native inhabitants of the colonies (Geertz, 1967). She likely compared herself to me, just as I compared myself to her. Similarly, I achieved access to the Deputy Mayor – or what appeared at the moment to be access – by pointing out the similarity of our ages and our common acquaintances. The issue of similarity also arose in my relationships with other people in the field, some of whom I shadowed later. But it was not easy. Similarity, it seems, can both hamper and facilitate fieldwork. As mentioned, Ann Fischer, comparing her fieldwork in five cultures, noticed (with some surprise) that a study of one's own culture could be as traumatic as that done in an alien land. 'In a foreign culture a participant-observer can play the pleasanter role of a "naive child," but not so in American culture' (Fischer, 1970/1986: 272–273).

As far as I can judge, Henry Mintzberg and Harry Wolcott were similar to the people they shadowed – in gender and age at least – which can be deduced from the fact that they do not mention the issue. Marianella Sclavi attempted to find similarities while assessing differences in her first study, and found Pearl White to be a mirror image in the second. A gay entrepreneur shadowed by Attila Bruni (Bruni and Gherardi, 2002) assumed that Attila, too, was homosexual. Establishing similarities may be a psychological remedy against the researcher's feelings of discomfort with outsideness and against uncommon closeness for the person shadowed. But then again, it may produce further discomforts – all instructive for the researcher. Why was I expecting smooth cooperation from FD? On the basis of the solidarity of sisterhood? Peer camaraderie? Economists' commonality? Common first language? All of the above, probably, and in that order. Did my strangeness (a professor from Sweden) win out? Self-observation and introspection, critical sources of knowledge, as Sclavi noted, may be activated more often during shadowing than during traditional types of observation. Movement attracts and focuses attention – the attention of the others and of those who move.

FIELDWORK IS INTERSECTED

As I compared my experience of shadowing FD with my shadowing of other people, the notion of intersectionality helped me to interpret my experience. Above all, it helped me to understand what may have been the norm, what may have been a deviation from the norm, and how far and long the deviation could be tolerated.

'Intersectionality' is a term introduced by US law scholar Kimberlé Crenshaw Williams (1994), to emphasize the fact that scholars focusing on gender, race, or class are often blind to the fact that these social categories intersect in human interactions. In my case, there were intersections among such categories as gender, nationality, profession, age, and hierarchical position.

I conducted my fieldwork in three places: Warsaw, Stockholm, and Rome, in that order. I could not do any shadowing in Rome; the implicit but strong norm seemed to be:

Researchers do not follow practitioners in their daily activities (shadowing is weird).

The existence of this norm was fully corroborated by Donatella Cozzi (2004), an Italian anthropologist who sent her students out to do shadowing. A great protest ensued, and it was justified with: Shadowing is not scientific! Contrasting cases come from the work of Attila Bruni (Bruni and Gherardi, 2001; 2002), who was allowed to shadow a gay entrepreneur and a newly hired employee in a consulting firm. Both Cozzi's students and I approached people in managerial positions in the public sector, however, whereas Bruni's objects were young, a homosexual, and a woman, the last hired, and in small private companies.

I suspect that even I could have pulled it off in Rome had I been an Italian researcher with a good *renomé*. But I was a foreigner of no importance to the local practitioners. I settled for intense interviewing, which gave me the opportunity to make short observations, confirming my present reasoning.

The same rule seemed to operate in Poland, with the additional nuance that seemed to specify that professors (people in high academic positions) do not do fieldwork (as Wolcott confirmed, fieldwork is assumed to be the domain of graduate students). Yet I was allowed to shadow three persons: one woman, two men; one accountant, two engineers. The shadowing of the woman – the Finance Director – was filled with the small troubles and embarrassments that I have described. The shadowing of one of the men went smoothly and without memorable events; the shadowing of the other man, although it had many a dangerous moment (like when I was invited to do ad hoc consulting; see Czarniawska, 2001), seemed to be pleasurable for both of us.

There is no doubt that what is usually called 'personal chemistry' plays a role in shadowing; nevertheless, this chemistry is not particularly strong in organizational shadowing (Wolcott's impression, too), and can be kept under the control of sheer politeness. Why, then, did I encounter more troubles in shadowing the woman than the men, especially considering our other similarities?

My tentative answer is that the norm from Rome was in place even in Warsaw, but that I was allowed to do the shadowing for two reasons. One was that I was a 'halfie', to borrow Lila Abu-Lughod's (1991:138) term for 'people whose national or cultural identity is mixed by virtue of migration, overseas education or parentage': a Polish Swede or a Swedish Pole. They could have stopped a 'real' foreigner by refer- ring to existing or invented laws or customs, but they knew I could check any such statements. And whereas the politicians and officials in the Municipality of Rome did not care how a Swedish researcher would present them, the people in Warsaw did. Poland was an economy in transition, with a positive image to maintain abroad, particularly in Sweden. So, both my cultural halves worked in my favor. My gender worked for and against me. As I see it, the implicit norm in Poland was:

People in high positions do not follow practitioners in their daily activities (shadowing is weird, and shadowing done by full professors especially so).

When shadowing men, my gender de-positioned me somewhat:[4] It is 'natural' that women in professional contexts wish to learn things from men in high positions. I similarly suspect that Bruni's gender 'promoted' him when he was shadowing the newly hired woman, because a male researcher is in a higher position than a young female consultant; thus it was 'natural' that she agreed to be shadowed.

In Sweden, I shadowed two people in high positions: a man and a woman, an econo- mist and a natural scientist. Shadowing was a relatively unusual technique, but fieldwork was not. As Sweden's transparency law guarantees access to public administrations, these organizations are filled with researchers: sociologists, political scientists, ethnologists, and management scholars. Compared to my colleagues video recording meetings at Volvo (Jönsson, 2005), shadowing seemed positively harmless. And yet it was easier to shadow the man than the woman. The reasons could be many: the similarity of my profession and the man's and our earlier contacts during another study, to name two possibilities. But I would venture a guess as to another unspoken norm that was being transgressed:

Women in high positions do not follow women in high positions in their daily activities.

I would claim that this norm is based purely on frequency rather than a clash in values. Joyce K. Fletcher (1999) shadowed six female design engineers from the same team, and they were all eager to collaborate, knowing that the others would be shadowed as well. Additionally, Fletcher was a member of an all-female research team ('Ladies from Ford Foundation', p. 42), which normalized her approach.[5] There are still few women in high positions in Sweden, so the situation would have been unusual. One way of resolving its abnormality would be to lower the status of one of the two people involved. A feminist sociologist friend of mine, who conducted several studies of unemployed women, was startled by her experiences during a new project involving top female politicians and administrators. 'I always thought I had very good contact with the women in the field', she said to me. 'I still think so. But I was sent packing several times, and I spent a lot of time in waiting rooms expecting them to eventually find time for an interview they'd agreed to in advance.' Her original impression was based on her earlier studies. Later, she realized that much of her excellent contact with unemployed women depended on the shared assumption that it was all 'for their own good'. Helen Schwartzman (1993) alluded to this notion when quoting anthropologist Laura Nader's (1974) distinction between 'studying up' and 'studying down' (pp. 27–46). And in further reference to Nader's notions, Joke Schrijvers (1991) spoke of 'studying sideways', claiming that it presents the best conditions for a dialogical relationship with the field. I could not agree more, but I cannot but point out that manipulating status differences – for example, framing fieldwork as studying up – often happens in the field. After having conducted two barely 20-minute interviews with a female top administrator in Rome, who was not only the same age but also a friend of a close friend, I asked when I could see her again. 'Hopefully never', was her answer. What for me was studying sideways, for her was studying up. I did cry a bit on the bus on the way home.

The reverse problem is related to studying down, or what may be perceived in that way. In organization studies, the necessary permission of top-level executives may lead to a suspicion that the researcher is a spy for them; in community studies the suspicion may be that the researcher is collecting information for future investors. Thus, as Van Maanen suggested, fieldworkers should, as soon as possible, 'dissociate themselves as best they can from the interest and control the third party may have over those who are studied' (1991: 34).

Are these methodological problems? No, this is field material. The dynamics of intersectionality and status manipulations, much as they may be considered inconvenient or even psychologically costly, offer a source of insight about social norms – one's own and the Other's.

Surviving in the field

Write a story entitled 'My worst day in the field'.

EXERCISE 8

FURTHER READING

Feldman, Martha S., Bell, Jeannine and Berger, Michele Tracy (2003) *Gaining access: A practical and theoretical guide for qualitative researchers.* Walnut Creek, CA: AltaMira Press.

Hammersley, Martyn and Atkinson, Paul (1983/2007) *Ethnography: Principles in practice.* London: Routledge.

Kostera, Monika (2007) *Organizational ethnography: Methods and inspirations.* Lund: Studentlitteratur.

Neyland, Daniel (2007) *Organizational ethnography.* London: Sage.

Notes

1. Burgess (1991: 52) called it 'a social process that occurs throughout a research project'.
2. Clifford Geertz (1967) defended him, however.
3. Ann Fischer (1970/1986: 278) called such reactions a 'counter-cultural shock'.
4. For more on gender and fieldwork, see Järviluoma et al. (2003).
5. One aspect of Fletcher's experience seems to be unique – or at least nobody else, to my knowledge, has mentioned it, and I certainly never experienced it in my field-work. As she put it, 'All the subjects seemed to be quite conscientious about being a good shadowee, sometimes even asking me if they should do what they normally do or do something more interesting or interactive' (1999: 42). That could be incidental, locally specific, or due to the fame of the Ford Foundation.

9

Excursions into Cyberspace

Social scientists are making increasing use of computers in their work. Meanwhile, more and more studies focus on computerized work and on free-time activities at the computer. Cyberspace, once merely a tool for researchers, has become a research field of its own. This chapter addresses new opportunities and new complications resulting from this development.

FIELDWORK VIA CYBERSPACE

Stephen R. Barley and Gideon Kunda (2001: 85) were among the first to notice that, as a growing proportion of contemporary work involves computer use, fieldworkers need to follow, both by using digital devices themselves, and finding ways to study such computer-enhanced work. Indeed, as most people have now become information workers, the ways of observing this work must be improved. Although life in cyberspace and virtual reality attract a great deal of attention (for a well-balanced review, see Marie Laure Ryan, 2001), the literature on fieldwork through, about, and in cyberspace only now begins to accumulate. Many techniques are simply being transferred from the physical field to the virtual field, but some new ones are beginning to emerge as well.

Computer work

When, during my study of news agencies (Czarniawska, 2012), I managed to secure permission to observe and shadow people in the Italian news agency ANSA, I was both elated and worried. From my previous visits to the Swedish TT News Agency, I knew that news producers work primarily at, and through, their computers. In the past, I had been frequently observing managers who used their computers sporadically. Barley and Kunda noticed in 2001 that ways of studying people working with computers were not well developed, apart from computer studies, which have a different purpose. Since then, some forays into this domain have been made (for a review, see Jemielniak and Kociatkiewicz, 2009).

Much to my relief, it was my hosts at ANSA who taught me how to study what they did. They simply gave me a place at a computer, such as they were using themselves, and although I could not intervene, I could see 'the desk' and 'the wire' and follow the news through the production process. When a discussion started in the newsroom concerning a specific piece of news, I could trace it in the database (I had two screens at my disposal) and know what they were talking about. Contrary to Knorr Cetina and Bruegger's (2002) claim that traders (whose job is similar to that of news producers) are involved in a network of post-social connections (between humans and computers), and in accordance with what Kociatkiewicz (2004) and Beunza and Stark (2005) documented, there is constant interaction between the physical and the virtual world in computer-based workplaces.

Not even shadowing seemed to be a problem. After all, shadowing consists of watching over people's shoulders as they work, and receiving explanations, and the journalists in the newsroom were certainly used to that process, as can be seen in

Figure 9.1 Shadowing at work

Figure 9.1. It is common for colleagues – invited or uninvited – to watch over each other's shoulders as they work. It is also common for the person doing the work to explain what is being done and to invite comments and questions. So the journalists saw nothing peculiar about my wanting to observe their work at the computer.

My later fieldwork at Reuters was similar to my work at ANSA – attending meetings, shadowing people at work, following the news on the screen, and completing interviews. The main difficulty was my inability to look at more than two windows at a time (I believe that some of the journalists had up to six windows open at the same time).

Somewhat surprisingly, studies of nomadic workers and nomadic computing rely primarily on traditional interviews, although Makoto Su and Mark (2008) also did shadowing. One reason for this reliance on interviews could be that, unlike most social scientists who find cyberspace exotic, informatics scholars look with greater interest at offline activities. A key difference lies in the amount of attention IT researchers dedicate to objects and technologies, comparable only to science and technology studies (STS).

Information gathering

Megens and Martin (2003) listed several methods of information gathering in cyberspace: web browsing, web data collecting, hacking (or merely lurking), and surveillance. Obviously, only the first two are legitimate and ethically permissible for social scientists. But if lurking mirrors the practices of ordinary members of a virtual community and if surveillance comes in the form of consented observation, those two methods can also be included (more on that in the section on virtual ethnographies in this chapter).

Eriksson and Kovalainen (2008) referred to information gathering in cyberspace as 'electronic research' and noticed its increasing relevance in reviewing research literature and collecting field material. In both cases, the main problem is how to navigate in cyberspace – how to find what is needed and how to assess its usefulness. They provided a useful guide for evaluating web pages that consisted of answering two questions: Who? and What?

Who?

- Whose web address is it (e.g. is it a university address, company address, online journal address; in which country)?

- Who is the author of the information presented on the site or web page (e.g. academic author, market researcher, consultant, teacher, political activist)?

- For whom was the information written or compiled (e.g. researchers, business people, students, consumers)?

What?

- What is the purpose of the site or web page (e.g. informing, entertaining, advertising)?

- What is the content of the site or web page (e.g. information, advertisements, public opinions)?

- What is the currency of the information (e.g. publication years of the references, last update of the site)?

- What is the accuracy and completeness of the information (e.g. how many references are given)? (Eriksson and Kovalainen, 2008: 100)

One additional difficulty lies in the fact that many web pages are created with the intention of misleading the reader about their nature: Political propaganda is presented as fact; academic authors take the opportunity to criticize their personal enemies. But experience helps, and it may be consoling to know that journalists must constantly and rapidly evaluate their sources in this way.

Eliciting field material

The Internet created the possibility of producing field material analogous to material elicited offline: online synchronous interviews, online asynchronous interviews, virtual focus groups, and web questionnaires (Meho, 2006). Online asynchronous interviews are, to my eye, the most promising form, usually conducted via several e-mail exchanges between the interviewer and the interviewee. As Meho noted, this form of interview is especially useful for interviewers and interviewees who are geographically separated or for approaching people who do not want to be interviewed face-to-face. But it is also useful for interviewers who do not feel at ease in face-to-face interactions.

Lokman I. Meho reviewed studies in which e-mail interviews were used prior to 2006, and developed a list of advantages and disadvantages related to this technique. E-mail interviews are undoubtedly cheaper to conduct and transcribe than either telephone or face-to-face interviews. In his opinion, they also democratize and internationalize research, although limiting research to people with access to the Internet. As access continues to grow, however, this difficulty diminishes.

One complication related to e-mail interviews is the issue of confidentiality, which remains ambiguous, as some people believe that online communication is anonymous, while others are suspicious and afraid of leaving non-erasable traces. In any case, research foundations in most countries and in all disciplines are developing appropriate ethical guidelines concerning online research.

Meho (2006) claimed that the specificity of the medium means that many non-verbal clues are lost. On the one hand, this consequence is negative, for it means impoverishment of the material; on the other hand, it is positive, for it means a removal of most unconscious reactions to race, gender, age, and voice – of both the interviewer and the interviewee. Similarly ambiguous is the fact that some interviewees may be not as effective writers as they are speakers, but this is only the reverse of the usual difficulty related to face-to-face and telephone interviews, for many people interviewed in the traditional way may, in fact, be more effective writers.

FIELDWORK ABOUT CYBERSPACE

The Internet is commonly described as a new forum for exchange and interaction between people and organizations. Businesses of all types moved part or all of their services from people, telephones, and fax machines to interactive websites. It is now relatively common to see human-like personal assistants performing services on the Internet. Eva Gustavsson (Gustavsson and Czarniawska, 2004; Gustavsson, 2005) observed that most of these human-like animated interface agents were female, and decided to study this phenomenon. In her opinion, there were at least two reasons for the increasing popularity of humanoid assistants, apart from the obvious fact that the technology was available. First, cost reduction and quality improvement are expected effects of the virtualization of services. Second, there is a 'persona effect' claimed by the researchers in the area of human–computer interaction. Beginning in the 1990s, a special line of research was established to improve human–computer interaction by computer mimicking of human behavior. This research has resulted in many new software products that promise to make the sales even less troublesome for service providers in the future. Software providers have argued that animated interface agents mimicking human behavior will improve human–computer inter-actions because 'they allow us to draw on communication and interaction styles with which humans are already familiar' (André and Rist, 2001: 53). Other researchers have been less optimistic. The controversy continues over the interpretation of this statement and how the 'persona effect' is actually created.

Gustavsson (2005) began to collect examples of virtual assistants (VAs) in the beginning of 2001. At this time, most VAs were demos, and the producers' websites described future applications of VAs, rather than actual products. In time, they multiplied and became more commonly used. There are also many types of virtual characters that perform services on the Internet. Gustavsson focused on *chatbots* with human-like conversation skills, of which there are many (Google returned 1,820,000 results on 21 December 2012, compared with 30,000 when Gustavsson did her study in 2004), but many of them noncommercial. Of course, the exact number of VAs on the Internet cannot be known. Gustavsson located approxi-mately 50 human-like VAs, chatted with 30 of them, and then interviewed them, using questions intended to reveal the extent to which the VAs were equipped with human characteristics:

- Q1: How old are you?
- Q2: Where do you live?
- Q3: What hobbies do you have?
- Q4: Have you ever been ill?
- Q5: Do you have a family?
- Q6: Do you have children?
- Q7: Do you have brothers and sisters? (Gustavsson, 2005: 407)

Interviews were conducted in VAs' 'native tongues', and Gustavsson conducted several follow-up interviews exploring their repertoires. She analyzed the physical image of the VAs and discovered that male VAs were more often presented as 'photoreals', and female VAs as animated pictures. Gustavsson has also contacted some of the producers, discovering, for example, that they denied or appeared to ignore the significance of gender in their choices, although they clearly favored female characters for virtual services. She concluded with two possible explanations for the results of her study. For one thing, the stereotyped image of women assumes that they are by nature more suited for service work and that VA producers, probably unintentionally, replicate this stereotype (Gustavsson and Czarniawska, 2004). Furthermore, the Internet became populated by virtual women in its early days – women that were designed and programmed by men – and there were, therefore, more such models in cyberspace that guided and inspired VA designers in their work.

Most studies of the Web are conducted within media studies, which treat 'internet media like any other popular media that appeals to people' (Gauntlett, 2004: 3). Scholars interested in financial reporting (see e.g. Abdelsalam and Street, 2007) study it on the Internet, but treat it like any other type of corporate reporting, focusing as it does on the amount of disclosed information. Gustavsson's study, original in the way it approached the connections between offline and online worlds, is close to the growing number of virtual ethnographies (Hine, 2000) or netnographies (Kozinets, 2009).

FIELDWORK IN CYBERSPACE

In the questions of presence and role, virtual ethnography need not entail drastically different dilemmas from more traditional face-to-face ethnographies. All ethnographers have to decide where to go and what to do when they get there. (Hine, 2008: 261)

Early days

In her brief history of virtual ethnographies, Christine Hine (2008) rightly identified that their origin could be connected to popular science fiction novels – especially

William Gibson's *Neuromancer* (1984) and Neal Stephenson's *Snow Crash* (1992). And '[a]lthough the technologies that they described were not yet in existence, these fictional visions helped to fuel both a generation of computer scientists aiming to realise them and a swathe of commentators aiming to explore their social implications' (Hine, 2008: 258). They were soon joined by researchers, who reflected on methodological complications – and opportunities – offered by the Web. Time has shown that what seemed to be the main difficulty – the uncertain relationship between online and offline life – became one of the main foci of interest.

Early ethnographies of everyday life on the Internet have typically used the Internet-as-culture metaphor in their descriptions of such website inventions as multi-user domains (MUDs), newsgroups, bulletin boards, and role-playing environments (Hine, 2000). Hine suggested, however, that this approach could be problematic if it were based on the assumption of some sort of corresponding 'real' culture or 'real' identities – some target group of individuals who are identifiable from either their offline or online identities. In her study of virtual identities, Sherry Turkle solved this difficulty by inviting MUDers in her neighborhood to a series of pizza parties, and by visiting places such as computer laboratories and programming classes where she was likely to meet the kind of users she was looking for (Turkle, 1996: 323). Turkle described her approach as 'conservative' and with a 'real life bias' (1996: 324) because she used material only from people she had met offline. One could say that in this way she 'realized' the virtual groups, but in doing so reduced the unique character of virtual interaction to an interaction that signals only the 'real world'. As noted by Christine Hine (2000: 28), the online reality is both produced and consumed in multiple locations and institutions and by many individuals. But how is it possible to comprehend the virtual world in relation to the real world unless the virtual is properly anchored in the real? One possibility is to break free from the duality and assume that the virtual world is simply part of the real world. Life online and life offline are connected, but only partly mirror or symbolize one another.

Hine also argued early on that the Internet-as-culture metaphor neglects critical aspects of its construction (2000: 39). The space and its offerings are there for the culture to feed upon, but the organization that guides its actions has already been established, and its coordinating devices are hidden 'behind' the screen.

True enough, 'virtual reality offers a pure form of "organization" in which every decision and action is completely, and literally, accountable' (Warren Smith, 1998: 229). Yet the coordination of the technology for Internet-based service encounters is beyond the reach of laypeople, even when we are given computer access. To overcome these dilemmas, Hine (2000) proposed a complementary perspective – treating the Internet as a cultural artifact. In doing so, she drew on the work of Grint and Woolgar (1997), who treat technology as texts, and suggested that the Internet could be seen as 'textual twice over: as a discursively performed culture and as a cultural artefact, the technology text' (Hine, 2000: 39). Thus, the Internet comes to be treated literally rather than metaphorically, as a part of culture. Overemphasis on the textuality of cyberspace, however, may hide its other aspects, rather than helping to reveal them.

The blooming of virtual ethnography

Virtual ethnographies are multiplying daily, partly because of a general fashion for ethnography in social science studies and partly because of the relative ease of working in the virtual field compared to a physical field. Hine (2008) predicted that 'virtual ethnography' will soon cease to be a special kind of approach, as the border between online and offline communities continues to blur. The proliferation of public events organized via the Web (from the fights of football hooligans to political demonstrations, see e.g. Shirky, 2008) illustrates it well.

Extended opportunities brought about new sets of dilemmas. One of these dilemmas concerns technical skills – especially for researchers interested in fast-paced gaming. Although Hine (2008) offered sensible suggestions on finding a golden mean between total technical competence and total lack of it, it must be noted that many, if not all, researchers interested in gaming are gamers themselves. Another is the problem of authenticity, although the Goffmanian vision of the world-as-theater applies even better to the virtual than the physical world. If anything, the overt possibility of cyberspace 'playing a role' makes the issue of authenticity irrelevant, and renders role-playing central to the analysis. Furthermore, the researcher has to negotiate access and create an acceptable persona online in the same way (although not with the same means) as offline.

Virtual ethnographies can be divided into two types: those dedicated to the exploration of social phenomena and those intended to produce some practical recommendations, concerning system design or marketing, for example. They could be called theoretical and applied (with a caveat that nothing prevents theory from being applied, and an application from being based on a theory). Here I quote examples of both.

Ulrike Schultze (2011, 2012, 2014) is interested in identity performances in virtual worlds, but also in their material (bodies and things) premises:

> … virtual worlds provide users with a virtual body, or avatar, that acts within a digitally material world consisting of others, objects, and landscapes. As such, virtual worlds are simulations of the actual world, that is, places with their own materiality, constraints and possibilities that nevertheless mimic actual reality. At the same time, they are utterly contrived and artificial … , thus making room to question taken-for-granted, supposedly naturally occurring binaries such as subjects/objects, male/female, human/nonhuman, work/play, and reality/fantasy. (Schultze, 2011: 2)

Schultze conducted face-to-face interviews with 35 participants of the virtual world Second Life, and asked them to conduct weekly photo-diaries for three weeks. They were asked to take snapshots (Second Life has a snapshot feature) of incidents that were important to them in some way, and to paste them into the photo-diary template provided. The template required annotations concerning 'when, what, why, who, how' questions. A weekly telephone interview gathered additional explanations and focused on the relationships of the interviewees with their avatars. Among many fascinating results, Schultze noticed that the participants in Second Life tended to confuse their online and offline identities, their selves with their avatars, which led her to suggest the notion of 'cyborgian identity performances' (Schultze, 2012).

Robert Kozinets' 'netnography' (2009) is meant specifically for marketing scholars, which may partly explain its more positivistic ambitions. It uses the information publicly accessible on the online fora of consumers to deduce preferences for a specific consumer group. In Kozinets' opinion, netnography is less time consuming and less elaborate than traditional market-oriented ethnographies, and – if the researcher wants it to be so – completely unobtrusive.

Kozinets (2009: 84) identified five types of online communities of interest to marketing netnographers: electronic bulletin boards, web pages, listservs (e-mailing address lists around a specific topic), MUDs, and chatrooms. The collection of material can be passive (copying the information and communications provided by the community) or active, using e-mail interviews. Kozinets warned of the danger of data overflow, unknown to traditional ethnographers, but well known to all contemporary scholars, in both the social and natural sciences (see e.g. Sands et al., 2012; Löfgren, 2013). In general, Kozinets suggested a grounded theory approach to study design: Material collection should cease as soon as no new insights on critical topics are being generated.

Anything new under the sun?

On the whole, it seems that most researchers studying cyberspace avail themselves of methods known to them from traditional fieldwork. It seems that Hine was right in saying that 'as yet there is little radical methodological innovation to point to' (2008: 268). This, in spite of claims to the contrary by De Paoli and Teli (2011), editors of a special issue of *Etnografia e ricerca qualitativa*, with the title 'New groups and new methods? The ethnography and qualitative research of online groups'. Yet, Hine hastened to add that changes would probably appear. The examples quoted in this chapter and those included in the special issue (Comber, 2011; Demazière et al., 2011; Mack, 2011) suggest, in fact, that innovation may be the result of trying old methods in new settings, as many innovations do. In the meantime, fictive models that capture blending of the online with the offline continue to appear – Neal Stephenson's *Reamde* (2011), for example.

Cyberstudies

List the ways in which you could use (or could have used) virtual material in your dissertation.

EXERCISE 9

FURTHER READING

Hine, Christine (2000) *Virtual ethnography*. London: Sage.
Kozinets, Robert V. (2009) *Netnography: Doing ethnographic research online*. London: Sage.
Markham, Annette N. (1998) *Life online: Researching real experience in virtual space*. Lanham, MD: AltaMira Press.

10
Analyzing Field Material

In this chapter, I review ways of analyzing field material in which text analysis is not the goal: grounded theory approach, content analysis, discourse and conversation analyses, and visual analyses. The necessary brevity of various descriptions is compensated by a longer list of further reading.

Within a broad definition – the famous one by Barthes (1977), for example – every kind of field material can be interpreted as text. A more conventional definition would distinguish between texts and pictures, although scholars have recently become interested in sound, tactility, and taste (see e.g. Mann et al., 2011). I decided to dedicate the next chapter specifically to text analyses; in this chapter I discuss the analysis of field material that may consist of or include texts, but was collected with the aim of analyzing something else: public discourses, conversations, interactions, or pictures.

GROUNDED THEORY REVISITED

As mentioned in Chapter 5, 'the linguistic turn' (Rorty, 1967) did not reach the social sciences until the late 1970s, long after the original book on grounded theory was written. Therefore the original prescription for the analysis of material collected in the field, although indebted to both narrative and rhetorical analysis, focused on 'coding' and 'emerging categories', or what can be called a *thematic analysis*. This focus remains with the contemporary grounded theoreticians, such as Charmaz (2006/2014) and Seale (2012), who still omit literary aspects of coding and categorizing.

In this section I follow their example, noting, however, that it is definitely possible to apply narrative analysis to the material collected within the grounded theory approach. But the original idea was that the analysis consisted of classification (coding), apportioning material to categories (themes) that, in the researcher's view, best represented the contents of the field material – fieldnotes included. Unlike in text analyses, the form of the text is of no importance here.

The main concept of a grounded theory type of analysis is *constant comparative analysis* (Glaser and Strauss, 1967), which means that the collection of field material, its classification and interpretation are conducted simultaneously. The researcher begins by comparing the first sample of field material collected (an interview transcript, observation notes, a document) with the second one (not necessarily all of the same type, either). Obviously, the purpose is to look for similarities: Are these people, these documents, and my notes, saying the same thing? If so, what should it be called? (a category, a label, a theme). Equally obvious, one looks for differences: Are these people or documents saying the same thing, but in a slightly different manner? (a property of a category); or are they saying something else? (a new category).

In the next step, the researcher compares the first two samples to the third, and so on, looking for new properties of old categories and for new categories. Finding a new category does not necessitate a return to the previously analyzed material. If the category is relevant, it will become 'saturated' (Glaser and Strauss, 1967) with the material to come.

As coding and categorizing proceeds, the time comes to look for *connections among categories*. It can be said that a grounded theory of a phenomenon under study is ready (at least in the first version), to be 'tested' on the next case when the researcher can explain the phenomenon with a coherent map of connections between categories and their properties (where the connections need to be explicated, not merely signaled by arrows on a simplified model).[1]

Various adepts of grounded theory formulated several practical recommendations for the newcomers. Here are mine:

- Analyze your material as soon as possible; do not wait till it accumulates. Remember, this is abduction, not induction! (see Chapter 3)[2]

- Use what you have learned from your earlier material in your next visit to the field (remove irrelevant questions, improve ill formulated ones, stop collecting useless documents, add new questions if needed, etc.).

- Write down everything that comes to your mind; do not rely on your memory. Code carefully every piece of your field material, so that you can easily return to your work.

- Start writing your theory as soon as you have the first idea of how it may look; it does not matter that it will change many times.

If you can (and if the material is properly anonymized), work in a team or discuss your ideas (categories, properties, connections) with someone else (colleagues, friends, practitioners from the field). They will help you to kill your darlings, if necessary.

CONTENT ANALYSIS

Some researchers advocating grounded theory recommend the use of computerized content analysis to facilitate coding. This is a mistake, in that the reason for using quantitative content analysis is to establish the frequency of certain words, which may or may not denote themes or categories. The words used most often are usually those in fashion, or they may simply signal linguistic mannerisms. Thus content analysis is actually, and in spite of its name, a type of discourse analysis, but as it is older, I dedicate this separate section to it.

Traditional content analysis followed the sequence opposite to grounded theory, beginning with the formulation of categories and hypotheses concerning their frequency and connections between them (for an early example, see Donald Auster's analysis of the comic strip 'Little Orphan Annie', 1961; for a critical review of later usages, see Biernacki, 2012).

David Silverman's (1993) severe judgment of the uses of content analysis in any context other than mass communication studies (in his opinion, content analysis had unclear theoretical premises and tended to lead to trite conclusions), became somewhat softened in the latest edition of his book (2011). Still, he did not see much use for it in qualitative studies. An experience of one of my doctoral students (Vironmäki, 2007) convinced me that content analysis could actually play a critical role – that of testing the relative weight of categories generated within the grounded theory approach. Having processed her field material with QSR NVivo,[3] she noticed that a category that for her was central was actually visible only in a minor part of her material.

Certainly, as noted by many authors, no software can yet interpret the field material, say 'what it means', and especially 'what it may mean', allowing for several competing or complementary interpretations. This task remains the main responsibility of the researcher.

DISCOURSE ANALYSIS

I would like to begin with a brief comment on the difference between discourse analysis and conversation analysis, which tends to baffle my students. They are quite justified in their puzzlement, however, as there is an established tradition (e.g. Ricoeur, 1973)[4] that treats them as synonymous; another tradition which includes conversation analysis in discourse analysis (Potter and Wetherell, 1987); and a third one, which sees discourse analysis as conversation analysis with less detailed transcripts of conversations (Silverman, 1983/2011). I tend to agree with Potter and Wetherell and with Silverman insofar as it concerns the type of discourse analysis known as DA. Here, however, I focus on the type of discourse analysis propagated by the writings of Foucault (of which Fairclough, 2003, is the best known example) and by the linguists (e.g. Grimshaw, 2003). In general terms, the differences may be presented as follows (Table 10.1):

Table 10.1   Differences between discourse and conversation analysis

Discourse analysis	Conversation analysis
Discourse, from *discurrere* (to run about): formal and orderly, usually an extended expression of thought on a subject	Conversation, from *conversare* (to live, to keep company with; obsolete usage: conduct, behavior): oral exchange of sentiments, observations, opinions, or ideas
Discourse analysis: (Foucault) discourse is impersonal; no actors (talkers) visible or needed	Ethnomethodology: (Sachs) actors (talkers) are visible and central

Thus conversation analysis treats talk as action, whereas discourse analysis treats talk as talk (in fact, before Foucault was translated into English, the French *discours* was translated as 'speech'). Conversation analysis captures and analyzes a concrete speech situation that is located at a point in time and space. Discourse analysis addresses many conversations which take place over time, in different locations, and yet seem to be connected. Whereas conversation analysis uses transcripts or videotapes of a concrete interaction, discourse analysis collects various genres of inscriptions of 'conversations' which may never have been enacted in the ordinary meaning of the word. From the narrative perspective, the two analyses are complementary. The institutionalized discourse serves as a repertoire for actual conversations; these in turn reproduce and change the discourse.

It has been noted that there are no set rules or procedures for conducting Foucauldian-inspired analyses of discourse. One reason may be that Foucault himself suggested that it could be applied not only to linguistic utterances, but to practices and artifacts as well:

> I am supposing that in every society the production of discourse is at once controlled, selected, organized and redistributed according to a certain number of procedures, whose role is to avert its powers and its dangers, to cope with chance event, to evade its ponderous, awesome materiality. (Foucault, 1972: 216)

So speech, yes, but not any speech, and especially not vanishing, local speech acts, not inscribed in some material form. Here, the emphasis on 'procedures' that govern the production of discourse serves to define the materiality of knowledge as an instance of power. Arribas-Ayllon and Walkerdine (2008: 91) therefore suggested ways of using this approach in psychology to study 'discursive practices' on three dimensions:

> Firstly, the analysis of discourse entails *historical* inquiry, otherwise known as 'genealogy'. Secondly, analysis attends to mechanisms of *power* and offers a description of their functioning. And lastly, analysis is directed to *subjectification* – the material/signifying practices in which subjects are made up.

It must be added that the authors ended up with language analysis; the ambition of including nonlinguistic elements into discourse analysis is not easy to realize, although there have been many attempts to do so. Here are some of Fairclough's (2005: 924–925) suggestions for using discourse analysis:

> *Orders of discourse* are social structuring of linguistic/semiotic variation or difference. … An order of discourse can more specifically be seen as a particular combination of different discourses, different genres and different styles, which are articulated together in a distinctive way.

> *A discourse* is a particular way of representing certain parts or aspects of the (physical, social, psychological) world; for instance, there are different political discourses (liberal, conservative, social-democratic, etc.) which represent social groups and relations between social groups in a society in different ways. A *genre* is a particular way of acting socially, which means acting together, i.e. interacting; for instance, there are different genres for consulting, discussing or interviewing. A *style* is a particular way of being, i.e. a particular identity; for instance, there are distinguishable ways of managing or 'leading' in organizations which can be characterized as different styles.

I believe it is fair to say that Foucauldian discourse analysis is an attempt to make a sociological analysis with terms and tools borrowed from linguistics;[5] similar attempts to borrow them from narratology are described in the next chapter. It needs to be added that Foucauldian discourse analysis is usually conducted from a critical perspective.

CONVERSATION ANALYSIS

Conversation analysis has its roots in ethnomethodology, especially in works of Harold Garfinkel and Harvey Sacks (Heritage, 1988; Silverman, 2010). There are many formulations of 'basic tenets' of conversation analysis; here, I combine those listed by Heritage (2010) and Silverman (1983/2011).

Talk is action, and, like any other action, is organized; its organization reflects wider orders of organization of society. Because of their sequential character, it is easier to study conversations than to study other types of interaction:

> The basic idea is that the most elementary context in which a turn at talk occurs is the immediately preceding turn at talk. It is a default assumption in human conduct that a current action should be, and normally will be, responsive to the immediately prior one. Indeed persons have to engage in special procedures (e.g., 'Oh by the way...') to show that a next action is not responsive to the prior. The inherent turn-by-turn contextuality of conversation is a vital resource for the construction of understanding in interaction. Since each action will be understood as responsive to the previous one, the understanding that it displays is open for inspection. (Heritage, 2010: 210–211)

Sequences can be somewhat accidental; they are given special attention and the label of 'practice' (of interaction construction) when they have a distinctive character and noticeable consequences for the meaning of the conversation. Apart from practices consisting of *turn-taking*, other practices central to the management of an interaction are practices of *repair* (when the conversation halts or is broken; to these belongs what Goffman, 1959, called 'impression management'), and practices of *referencing* people and objects outside the conversation.

Students presented for the first time with the transcription rules for conversation analysis tend to judge that the technical transcription it requires is too complicated and too laborious to use. Once having tried it, they discover that it is, in fact, quite easy to learn, that transcribing an interview in a CA way[6] does not take more time than undertaking a conventional transcription, and that it gives richer material for analysis. As mentioned in Chapter 4, Charlotte Linde's 'A note on transcription conventions' (1993: xi–xiv) is extremely helpful in this matter.

It is not only the fact that transcription rules seem difficult that prevents a wider use of conversation analysis. Being of Anglo-Saxon origins, conversation analysis does not account for the fact that different cultures have different ways of turn-taking, making or not making confirming noises, and the like. It is possible to analyze a conversation conducted in a language other than English, of course, as Giolo Fele's (2007) long and systematic application of conversation analysis to Italian material shows. Not only research interviews, however, but also a great many naturally occurring conversations take place between strangers, who are speaking in languages other than their own, and enriching them with interaction structures alien to their interlocutors. Is a long pause between two words an indicator of a sensitive topic, or does it mean that the speaker cannot remember the correct English word? Analyzing such misunderstandings and unrecognized repair can open new venues for conversation analysis.

During his seminar at the University of Gothenburg (5 June 1996), Thomas Luckmann showed the audience a transcript of a conversation between two German missionaries in China and their Chinese interlocutor (made by his collaborator, Susanne Günthner; see Bergmann and Luckmann, 1999). Both sides did their best to demonstrate how well they had learned the other culture – with the result that the conversation turned into a chain of misunderstandings. These misunderstandings, and the effects of 'cross-culturation', were made visible, however, exactly via this transcript. Luckmann uses conversation analysis himself (see e.g. Luckmann, 2002),[7] quoting transcripts translated into English.

Here is another difficulty – related to the current need to present the results and even the analyzed texts in English. Even such reflective authors as Silverman and Torode (1980) assumed that translation is unproblematic. But it is highly problematic; especially with conversation analysis. One solution is to quote a literal translation first, and an understandable translation later, but it requires many annotations, which may render the text difficult to read. Another solution is to translate only the result of the analysis, hoping for the reader's trust. The third is to put the originals in an appendix. Yet there is no doubt that conversation analysis is a valuable tool for analyzing field material.

VISUAL ANALYSES

> Visual materials are articulations of human experience in specific times and places and represent a significant materialisation of the norms and concerns of people. (Brinkmann, 2012: 131)

Still images

As Howard S. Becker (1974) noted, photography and sociology were born at approximately the same time – Auguste Comte coined the term 'sociology' in 1838, and Daguerre showed his daguerreotype in 1839. Both were interested in exploring society, and both mixed science with art. In time, however, sociology moved closer to the sciences, and photography toward art.

It can certainly be claimed that present times witness a new rapprochement, not least because technology has become so much easier to use.[8] At present, as Marcus Banks (2007: 7) rightly observed, images are used either to study societies (when taken or elicited by researchers) or to study society via the images it produces. The first function has already been described in Chapters 4 and 5, but in the present context the distinction is no longer important. As 'author's intentions' have vanished from the horizon banished by New Criticism, images need to be analyzed and interpreted, no matter who produced them. All photographs – those taken by researchers and by people studied – have been framed, and in this context, Goffmanian terms must be taken both literally and metaphorically. What has been included, and what excluded? What is the focus and what is the background?

Dona Schwartz (1989) took these considerations seriously, assuming that her photographs of a rural Iowa farm community were 'inherently ambiguous, their specifiable meanings emergent in the viewing process' (Schwartz, 1989: 122). She used them for 'photo eliciting': showing photographs to middle-class families and asking for their comments, which she then recorded and transcribed. In a sense, it was the viewers who analyzed the pictures, although their comments as to the formal aspects were typically limited to ' "These pictures are so clear! You must have used a good camera!" ' (Schwartz, 1989: 127).

Collier Jr. (Collier and Collier, 1967/1986) was enthusiastic about photo eliciting, claiming that photographs stimulate deeper and sharper memories. Douglas Harper (2012) inherited this enthusiasm, but soon discovered − as did I − that the technique was not easy to apply. It is not enough to show people a photo and ask what comes to their minds (unless they themselves took the picture, like the people participating in experiments described in Chapter 7). Studying a mechanic shop in a rural neighborhood, Harper took pictures, and then asked the owner four questions: 'Who is this?', indicating persons in the photo; 'What is this?', indicating objects; 'What are you doing in this photo?'; and 'How do you work for neighbors and others?', thus moving from specific to general questions (Harper, 2012: 157).

The taking of photographs has a long history in social science research; asking people to take photos is newer, but what is truly overwhelming is the number of pictures surrounding us everywhere. It is not surprising, therefore, that marketing researchers have a strong interest in both field research and image analysis. Jonathan Schroeder, a proponent of a critical visual analysis, made a plea for interdisciplinary analysis, in which '*[h]umanities* provide theoretical tools to understand image genres, content, and narrative, whereas *social science* affords methods for discussing context, effects, and strategic implications' (2006: 304; italics in the original). He obviously forgot to add *art critique*, which plays a significant role in his list of main analytical categories for such critical visual analysis.

A visual analysis begins with *description*, highlighting the formal properties of an image, then placing it in a genre, and finally setting it in a wider context − both spatial and temporal.

More specifically, the first step consists of deciding what is the *subject matter of the image*: Which persons, objects, places, and/or events are represented in the image? The analysis then moves to *form*, in which the subject matter is presented, followed by a characteristic of the *medium*. A recognition of *style* and a classification of *genre* end the description, both obviously requiring a *comparison* with other images.

Within marketing research the aim of the analysis is to answer questions. What does the image communicate (where critical analysts use such categories as gender, race, and class)? How and where does the image circulate? How is it understood by consumers? And which consumer groups? 'Consumers' can be replaced by any category of spectators, making the analysis useful for other disciplines. Similarly, the interpretation of the interactions among identity, consumption, and image may have relevance for groups beyond critical marketers.

Moving pictures

The interdisciplinarity recommended by Schroeder (2006) is equally necessary – and practiced – in the analysis of moving pictures. Researchers analyzing films, videos, and TV series follow the lead of humanities and cultural studies, specifying categories to fit their interests (see e.g. Brinkmann, 2012). It is possible, however, to use more detailed tools in analyzing such material. Diana Rose (2000) offered examples of transcription templates for TV programs, in which both visual and verbal elements can be documented (Rose, 2000: 253) (see Table 10.2):

Table 10.2   Example of a transcription template

'The Bill', ITV, 28 May 1992 Visual	Verbal
Front of hotel, forensics, PO, DI comes out, another DI enters frame, both MW	DI1: Ian.
	DI2: Hello, Jack, how are you? Fill me in.
	DI1: Morgan's at the hospital now.
	He looks fit for all three killings.
	He's an alcoholic with a history of psychiatric disorder, no previous for violent offences.
	DI2: How did you get onto him?
	DI1: Your Sergeant R found personal possessions belonging to the victim, PH. I suppose he could have found her body by the railway line and then robbed it. Much more likely he killed her before dumping her there.
	DI2: And our girl AA is very nearly his latest victim.
	DI1: Yeah. Must have put up one heck of a fight. Otherwise.

This template was accompanied by a set of codes for camera angles (Table 10.3), allowing the visual notations to be simplified (Rose, 2000: 257):

Table 10.3   Camera angle codes accompanying transcription template

ECU	Extreme close-up
CU	Close-up
MCU	Medium close-up
MW	Medium wide
WA	Wide angle
Tracking	Camera follows action
Environment	Shot other than a person

Rose recommended a statistical analysis, just like the Colliers' in their by-now-classic book (Collier and Collier, 1967/1986). This is one possible, but not the only way to use transcripts of this type. They can be used in a similar way as in conversation analysis, but the visual element widens the area of their application.

Sten Jönsson (2005), a scholar of management, used video recording in his study of international project development teams at Volvo. Inspired by ethnomethodology, he transcribed the conversation during recorded meetings, but also used video elicit-ing, showing clips to the participants and asking for comments and explanations. When it came to the analysis, Jönsson framed it with help of the concept of Practical Reason, that is, a reasoning guided by the logic of appropriateness (March, 1994). According to this logic, actors do not ask themselves 'What is the best way of achieving my goal?' (Pure Reason), but simply 'What should a person like me do in a situation like this?' The answer requires (a) self-diagnosis (What kind of a person am I?), (b) diagnosis of the situation (What kind of situation is this?), and (c) the choice of an appropri-ate action from the accessible repertoire (What should I do?). This is an interesting take, but it must be emphasized that it applies best to the analysis of video-elicited accounts (one cannot see answers to those question on the screen).

All in all, I believe that analyses of visual material will become more and more popular in social sciences. Several developments point in this direction. The reprint-ing of photographs is becoming cheaper and of better quality (I am not sure that any of the readers of Dona Schwartz's article in 1989 thought, like her interlocutors, that her photographs were very clear, though she is an accomplished photographer). Alternative forms for doctoral dissertations (video films in ethnology and anthropol-ogy, for example) are becoming more common. And images play a more and more dominant role in contemporary life.

Douglas Harper (2012), although paying tribute to Becker's early interest in pho-tography, does not share Becker's pessimism about the future of visual sociology. I believe that his arguments can be extended to all social sciences. Visual material can be used in studying a variety of topics – from family life through city life to life online. Like sociologists, other social scientists, too, are 'visually hungry and a little weary of nuanced statistics and abstracted arguments' (Harper, 2012: 244). And, as examples in his book and in this section show, other analytical approaches men-tioned in this chapter – from grounded theory to conversation analysis – can be applied to visual material. Even techniques for analyzing texts, the subject of the next chapter, can be applied to images, as Barthes had suggested.

EXERCISE 10

Analyzing field material

Record two TV talk programs on the same topic, transcribe the talk, and analyze them (1) as two samples for a grounded theory construction, (2) as samples of public discourse, (3) as conversations, and (4) as visual messages.

FURTHER READING

Banks, Marcus (2007) *Using visual data in qualitative research (qualitative research kit)*. London: Sage.

Bell, Emma; Warren, Samantha; and Schroeder, Jonathan (eds.) (2014) *The Routledge companion to visual organization*. Abingdon: Routledge.

Biernacki, Richard (2012) *Reinventing evidence in social inquiry: Decoding facts and variables*. New York: Palgrave Macmillan.

Charmaz, Kathy (2006/2014) *Constructing grounded theory*, 2nd edn. London: Sage.

Collier, John Jr. and Collier, Malcolm (1967/1986) *Visual anthropology: Photography as a research method*. Albuquerque, NM: University of New Mexico Press.

Emmison, Michael and Smith, Philip (2000/2012) *Researching the visual*. London: Sage.

Fairclough, Norman (2003) *Analyzing discourse: Textual analysis for social research*. London: Routledge.

Harper, Douglas (2012) *Visual sociology*. Abingdon: Routledge.

Haw, Kaye and Hadfield, Mark (2011) *Video in social science research: Functions and forms*. Abingdon: Routledge.

Heath, Christian, Hindmarsh, Jon and Luff, Paul (2010) *Video in qualitative research: Analysing social interaction in everyday life*. London: Sage.

Sidnell, Jack and Stivers, Tanya (eds.) (2013) *The handbook of conversation analysis*. Chichester: Wiley-Blackwell.

Silverman, David (2010) *A very short, fairly interesting and reasonably cheap book about qualitative research*. London: Sage.

Notes

1. For a more structured version of a way to proceed, see Charmaz (2006/2014).
2. A way out for those who are forced to accumulate by external constraints (no time for analysis): Read your field material in the same order as you collected it.
3. Other frequently used softwares are ETHNOGRAPH and NUD★IST.
4. This article has been reprinted in many anthologies.
5. An instructive discussion of linguistic uses of discourse analysis can be found in Grimshaw (2003).
6. It needs to be added that CA experts favor naturally occurring conversations to elicited ones such as interviews.
7. Observe, however, that he put the transcripts into an appendix.
8. Becker was skeptical on this point. 'Sociologists are probably like anthropologists. As they become more photographically sophisticated they will produce more interesting images, but not necessarily ones that have sociological content' (Becker, 1974: 12).

11

Text Analyses

There is a host of options for anyone who wants to undertake a close reading of texts from the field. I mention only the most common in this chapter: rhetorical analysis, two versions of structuralist analysis, semiology-inspired analysis, and poststructuralist analysis. One option can be chosen or they can be combined, the choice fitting the research problem and the researcher's preferences. Because excellent instructions on how to proceed exist elsewhere, this chapter contains but a short introduction to each approach, complemented by an extended list of further readings.

RHETORICAL ANALYSIS

Rhetoricians (e.g. McCloskey, 1985/1998) will tell you that narrative analysis is but a part of rhetorical analysis; indeed, *narratio* is the second part of a six-part classical oration. Narratologists will tell you that rhetorical analysis is one step in an analysis of a narrative. I am a narratologist, but in the name of fairness, I am presenting some elements of rhetorical analysis first (more in Chapter 12, on writing the thesis). In this section I focus only on *tropes* (figures of speech), or the texture of the text (Lanham, 1991).

The best known tropes are metaphor, simile, metonymy, synecdoche, irony, personification, and hyperbole. Of these seven, metaphors have attracted the most attention from social scientists who, after having adopted the linguistic turn, started to examine their own rhetoric in the 1980s (Edmondson, 1984; McCloskey, 1985/1998; Nelson et al., 1987; Klamer et al., 1988; Simons, 1988). In organization theory, it was Gareth Morgan who first suggested that research paradigms were situated in master-metaphors of organization (Morgan, 1980, 1986). After that, the question of rhetoric was raised unsystematically in various works inspired by Kenneth Burke (1945/1969) (the best known of which is perhaps Mangham and Overington's *Organizations as Theatre*, 1987) and more systematically, in works originating in communication studies (Cheney, 1991).

Organization researchers were also among the first to analyze the rhetoric of their own field of practice. Early on, it was suggested that 'metaphors of the field' can become tools for a comparative analysis of different organizations (Manning, 1979), and that social policy formulation is guided by what Schön (1979) called 'generative metaphors'. It was postulated that metaphors were much more than symbols. They did serve the function of symbolic expression, but they were also instrumental – used for control purposes – and therefore bridged expressive and practical orders in organizations (Harré, 1981).

Here, too, metaphors were tropes that were primarily treated favorably in rhetorical analyses (see e.g. Grant and Oswick, 1996; Lennie, 1999). It has been noted that metaphors were an invaluable tool of organizing (Czarniawska-Joerges and Joerges, 1988). For one thing, they provided ambiguity, indispensable for people with a variety of interests to unite in a collective endeavor without necessarily uniting their points of view. Another, opposite reason was that by familiarizing the unknown, they reduced the immobilizing uncertainty caused by new or surprising situations, abundant in organizing efforts. In addition, they provided color and entertainment to the sometimes dreary everyday life in work organizations.

It needs to be added that more often than not, the term *metaphor* was used in social science texts as a synonym for *trope*, or any figurative speech. Similes (comparing two things: You look like a rose), metonymies (substituting a closely related concept: 'Hollywood' for the US cinema industry), and synecdoches (substituting a part for the whole: 'crown' for the kingdom) were all subsumed under metaphors proper ('market tigers' for young and ambitious entrepreneurs).

Irony is treated with distance by social scientists, some of whom strongly advise against its use, evoking as argument the well-known metaphor, 'Irony is a double-edged sword'. They claim that readers may not be aware of a writer's ironic intentions, and may read the text literally, attributing it a literal meaning, which in the case of irony is opposite to the one intended. It can also be difficult to detect irony in texts from the field; it is necessary to undertake a consultation with practitioners or competent members.

Personification (attributing human characteristics: societies remember) and hyperbole (exaggeration: I am so hungry I could eat a horse) are considered inappropriate in academic writing, although personification, as the example indicates, is commonly used.[1] When found in texts from the field, they are of great interest (had I said 'enormous interest', it would constitute hyperbole). CEOs' introductions to corporate annual reports and university websites compete in their use of hyperbole. Advertisers use it more carefully ('Carlsberg is probably the best beer in the world'), as its overuse may have legal consequences. All in all, more rhetorical analyses of public discourses would be a valuable addition to the research literature.

Yet it is narrative analyses that seem to be in fashion recently in the social sciences, as indicated by the growing number of textbooks and handbooks dedicated to them (see e.g. Clandinin and Connelly, 2000; Clandinin, 2006) and by the ongoing debate about their status (see e.g. Woods, 2011). Apart from the 'narrative turn',[2] the reason for it could be that there is a variety of narrative analyses to choose from, offering researchers some freedom. I am presenting some of the most popular here.

STRUCTURALISM: THE ORIGINS

Structural analysis is the traditional way of analyzing a narrative, constituting an enterprise close to semiology and formalism (Propp, 1928/1968). This enterprise was adopted and developed in anthropology by Claude Lévi-Strauss (1968). Even earlier, sociolinguists William Labov and Joshua Waletzky (1967) espoused and improved upon Propp's formalist analysis, suggesting that sociolinguistics should occupy itself with a syntagmatic analysis of simple narratives, which will eventually provide a key to understanding structure and functions in complex narratives. Their appeal has been implemented by several social scientists (Mishler, 1986/1991; Boje, 1991; Riessman, 1993).

Vladimir Propp (1895–1970) was a member of the Russian formalist group. Having analyzed 100 fairy tales out of a collection of 449, Propp noticed that the same character can perform different actions, and that different characters may perform the same action. Some actions can have various meanings, depending on when and where they occur in the tale; others always have the same meaning. From this discovery, Propp concluded that the key component of the tale is the *function* that the character's action plays in the whole of the story. Consequently, he distilled a list of functions, and described function as 'an act of a character, defined from the point of view of its significance for the course of events' (Propp, 1928/1968: 21). I quote a part of this list of functions here, in my own translation from the original of *Morphology of the Folktale* (1928):

1. One of the family members leaves home (Leave) p. 36

2. The hero encounters a prohibition (Prohibition) p. 36.

3. Prohibition is ignored (Transgression) p. 37

4. The villain attempts an investigation (Investigation) p.38

5. The villain obtains information about his victim (Betrayal) p.38

6. The villain attempts to mislead his victim in order to appropriate his or her property (Ruse) p. 39

7. The victim is misled and unwillingly helps the enemy (Collaboration) p. 40

8. The villain damages or harms a member of the family (Harm) p. 40

9. Misfortune or want is stated; the hero is asked or ordered to help, and starts his journey (Mediation) p. 46, etc.

Propp discerned additional elements of the tale, the most noteworthy of which is the division of the sphere of action among various characters: the Villain, the Donor, the Helper, a Princess (there could be several), a Princess's Father, the Dispatcher, the Hero and the False Hero. It is not difficult to see how these functions and characters can be (and were) translated into modern terms: a CEO, the Hero, gets the Princess (a company) after having defended it from an attempt of an aggressive takeover by a Villain, and so on.

Paleoanthropologist Misia Landau (1984, 1991) has undertaken an unusual application of Propp's categories, observing that the various theories of human evolution can be interpreted as versions of the hero tale in folk tales. Analyzing both classic and modern tales about evolution, Landau not only revealed their common narrative form, but also showed how this form accommodates differences in meaning – widely varying sequences of events, heroes, and donors. Consequently, the interpretations of fossil record differed according to what the paleontologist believed was the donor or primary evolutionary agent.

Landau's use of Propp's analysis is instructive, because its purpose is abundantly clear. As she said, '[t]he main purpose in fitting theories of human evolution into a common frame-work is *not* to demonstrate that they fit' (1991: 11–12; my italics, BC). One of two purposes can apply: either to show that they fit in spite of their diversity, thus upholding traditional cultural values (the case of paleontology); or to show how texts deviate from a generic scheme, thus subverting given cultural values (the case of such experimental novels as Jonathan Safran Foer's *Extremely Loud and Incredibly Close*, 2005). Merely showing that Propp's analysis can be applied to a text reveals little.

STRUCTURALISM IN PSYCHOLOGY

Psychologists' interest in stories, or at least in storytelling, goes back to Frederick C. Bartlett and his studies of remembering (1932). Whereas Jerome Bruner and Donald E. Polkinghorne brought narrative back into psychology in its literary version, cognitive psychologists were developing the notion of *scripts and schemas* (Mandler, 1984).

Jean Matter Mandler suggested that it is important to distinguish between a story grammar and a story schema and to study both:

A story grammar is a rule system devised for the purpose of describing the regularities found in one kind of text. The rules describe the units of which stories are composed, that is, their constituent structure, and the ordering of the units, that is, the sequences in which the constituents appear. A story schema, on the other hand, is a mental structure consisting of sets of expectations about the way in which stories proceed. (Mandler, 1984: 18)

According to my reading, a story grammar is a structure of the text; a story schema is the location of its plot in a repertoire of plots typical for a certain interpretive community.

In analyzing story grammars, Mandler extended and reformulated Propp's categories (1984: 22–30). Like other 'proper' structuralists, Mandler assumed that all stories have a basic structure that remains relatively unchanged in spite of differences in the content of various stories:

- A setting, which introduces a protagonist and other characters, and statements about the time and place of the story.

- One or more episodes that form a plot of the story. Such episodes have a similar structure:

  o a beginning (one or more events)

  o a development:

    o the reaction of a protagonist: simple (anger, fear) or complex. If complex, it is followed by

    o the setting of a goal (what to do about the beginning event(s)),

    o a goal path,

    o an outcome (success or failure)

  o the ending, often including a commentary concerning the consequences of the episode, or the protagonist's or the narrator's reflection. The ending of the final episode becomes

- The ending of the story, which may also contain a moral lesson.

Episodes can be temporally or causally connected (the two rules of association). There are two kinds of causal connections. One is called *ending-embedded*: The end reveals the substitution, or the transformation – a new protagonist–goal combination, for example (after the suitor saves the heroine's life, she understands that she always loved him). The other is *outcome-embedded*: The structure of the story and the connections between episodes depend on the episode's outcome, and they can therefore change during the narrative (a hero who failed starts a different chain of episodes, or an anti-program).

Mandler and her collaborators then started a series of experiments aimed at testing both cognitive structures and recall. For one of the experiments, they constructed three types of stories (chronological, ending–embedded, and outcome–embedded), but presented the elements as unconnected (omitting 'and', 'then', and even punctuation marks). The people who read the texts connected the stories, sometimes following standard grammar (a 'canonical' version) and sometimes providing alternative structures. In another experiment, one version of the story was schematic and chronological; in the other version, the episodes were interleaved ('...meanwhile'). In recalling the interleaved story, many people (and especially children) reconstructed a schematic story, rather than the story they had actually heard (both stories were perfectly understandable). Please bear this experiment in mind when reading the section on poststructuralism.

INSPIRATION FROM SEMIOLOGY: ACTOR–NETWORK THEORY

Many social scientists who use structuralist analysis,[3] particularly in science and technology studies (STS), use the actant model suggested by the French semiologist of Lithuanian origin, Algirdas Greimas (see e.g. Greimas and Courtés, 1982), rather than Propp's model. Greimas took Propp's work as a point of departure for developing a model for understanding the organizing principles of all narrative discourses.

Greimas introduced the notion of a *narrative program*, a change of state produced by any subject affecting any other subject or object. This (grammatical) subject may or may not reveal itself as a person. Therefore Greimas replaced the term 'character' with the term 'actant' – 'that which accomplishes or undergoes an act' (Greimas and Courtés, 1982: 5) because 'it applies not only to human beings but also to animals, objects, or concepts'. The introduction of this category highlights the ways actants change roles throughout a narrative: An actant may become an actor (acquire a character) or remain an object of someone else's action. 'Thus the hero will be the hero only in certain parts of the narrative – s/he was not the hero before and s/he may well not he the hero afterwards' (p. 6). 'So defined, the actant is not a concept which is fixed once and for all, but is virtually subsuming an entire narrative trajectory' (p. 207).

These elements of Greimas's version of structuralism made it attractive to STS scholars, who intended to give the central place in their narrative to machines and artifacts, and felt encumbered by the notions of 'actor' and 'action', so clearly based on the assumption of a human character and an intentional conduct. 'Actant' and 'narrative program' would do much better, they thought, even if the universalistic ambitions of Greimas were alien to them.

Accordingly, Bruno Latour not so much *applied* Greimas's model as *used* it, to employ Richard Rorty's distinction (Rorty, 1989). In this way, Latour claimed, science and technology studies can gain a new narrative resource. In 'Technology is society made durable', Latour (1992) presented the history of the Kodak camera's invention and the simultaneous emergence of a mass market for amateur photography as a sequence of programs and anti-programs (from the point of view of Eastman). Here is an example (where capitals denote actants):

> *Program*: professional-amateur (A)/ wet collodion (C) **1850**/ paper manufacturing (D) *anti-program*: doing everything oneself right away. (Latour, 1992: 111)

As the narrative proceeds, it is marked by two operations: association (called *syntagm* in narratology) and substitution (*paradigm*). 'The film is substituted to the plates, and the dry collodion is substituted to the wet collodion, capitalists replace other capitalists, and above all, average consumers replace professional-amateurs' (1992: 113). But the question of greatest interest to Latour, and the reason he conducted this Greimasian analysis, was the question of power:

> Is the final consumer forced to buy a Kodak camera? In a sense, yes, since the whole landscape is now built in such a way that there is no course of action left but to rush to the Eastman company store. However, this domination is visible only at the end of the story. At many other steps in the story the innovation was highly flexible, negotiable, at the mercy of a contingent event. (1992: 113)

There is a crucial difference between Latour's analysis and the conventional analysis of social science. Latour's reading constructed the story as outcome-embedded: Each episode is determined by the outcome of the previous one (see also next section). Conventional social science is ending-embedded, or teleological (Landau, 1991, quoted paleontology as a typical example).

Latour concluded that an innovation is but a syntagmatic line (connecting programs to further programs) containing human and nonhuman actants that were recruited to counter the anti-programs. Each time an anti-program emerged or was introduced (e.g. by competitors), Eastman Kodak managed to recruit new actants to their next program. In this way, the company became a major actor – but only at the end of the story. There was nothing in the 'character' of Eastman Kodak at the beginning of the story that could help the observer foresee its final success. It was an actant like any other; and it became an actor because it succeeded in recruiting many other actants to its cause, thus becoming an actor-network. But at many times during the course of the story, Eastman Kodak could have shared the fate of many other entrepreneurs who ended up bankrupt and unknown.

The Latourian/Greimasian procedure could therefore be summarized as follows. It begins with the identification of *actants* (those who act and are acted upon). Thereupon the researcher follows the actants through a *trajectory* – a series of *programs* and *anti-programs* – until some of them become actors, until they acquire a distinct and relatively stable character. Which actants, then, have the opportunity to become actors? Those whose programs succeeded in combating anti-programs (alternatively, those whose anti-programs won, as in the stories of opposition and resistance). This success, according to Latour, is due to *association* – to the formation and stabilization of networks of actants, who can then present themselves as actor-networks.

Latour used many more Greimasian concepts in his analysis, which is longer and more complex than I presented it here. I wish to call attention to two aspects of his analysis. First, Latour did not endeavor to demonstrate his knowledge or skill in using the Greimasian model.[4] He used it because the model permitted him to say things about his chosen topic – innovation and power – that he would not have been able to say otherwise. Second, he never claimed to have 'found' a structure in the texts he analyzed; it is obvious that he chose to impose a certain structure on a variety of texts from the field. His approach could just as well be called poststructuralist, if the label was of any importance here.

POSTSTRUCTURALISM

Almost before structuralism acquired legitimacy in the social sciences, it was swept away by poststructuralism, or so it seemed for a good while during the 1990s. The move from structuralism to poststructuralism was not as dramatic as it may seem, however. It meant, above all, abandoning the depth for the surface: If deep structures are demonstrable, they must be observable. Structures could no longer be 'found', as they were obviously inserted into the text – by those who read the text, including the author (after all, reading is writing anew). This meant abandoning the idea of the universal structure of language, or of mind, and accepting the idea of a common repertoire of textual strategies, which are recognizable to both the writer and the reader. This relaxation of basic assumptions led also to the relaxation of the technique; as there is no one true deep structure to be discovered, various techniques can be applied in order to structure a text and therefore permit its novel reading. Additionally, poststructuralism was invented by ex-structuralists – Ronald Barthes (1977), for example.

Although several scholars experimented with *interruption* (Silverman and Torode, 1980; Czarniawska-Joerges, 1994) and even deconstruction (e.g. Barbara Johnson, 1980; Joanne Martin, 1990; Martha Feldman, 1995), such provocative readings have not spread widely in the social sciences, In what follows, I describe a use of poststructuralism that I find highly instructive.

Australian sociologist Bronwyn Davies was interested in the way people discover their gender, and her starting point was the assumption that children learn to become male or female by becoming skilled in discursive practices in which all people are positioned as either male or female. She adopted the vocabulary of poststructuralism because it provided her with the conceptual tools – devices – to make sense of her material. She chose it because it is a radical discourse, which 'allows us to think beyond the male–female dualism as inevitable, to the constitutive processes through which we position ourselves as male or female and which we can change if we so choose' (Davies, 1989: xi).

One part of Davies's inquiry (I do not report the whole of it here) consisted of her reading a variety of feminist revisions of well-known fairy tales to seven four- and five-year-old children. She spent many hours with each child over a period of one year, reading the stories and discussing the children's thoughts about each story. One of the stories, *The Paper Bag Princess* (Munsch, 1980), was a variation of the well-known 'princess rescued from the dragon by the prince' storyline:

At the beginning of the story, Princess Elizabeth and Prince Ronald are planning to get married, but then the dragon comes along, burns Elizabeth's castle and clothes and flies off into the distance carrying Prince Ronald by the seat of his pants. Elizabeth is very angry. She finds a paper bag to wear and follows the dragon. She tricks him into displaying all of his magic powers until he falls asleep from exhaustion. She rushes into the dragon's cave to save Ronald only to find that he does not want to be saved by a princess who is covered in soot and only has an old paper bag to wear. Elizabeth is quite taken aback by this turn of events, and she says: 'Ronald, your clothes are really pretty and your hair is very neat. You look like a real prince, but you are a bum.' The last pages show her skipping off into the sunset alone and the story ends with the words: 'They didn't get married after all.' (Davies, 1989: viii)

In the discussions that followed, the three girls placed themselves in the position of the princess, whom they saw as nice and beautiful. They all understood Elizabeth's plan and concluded that Ronald was not nice. One of them, however, believed that Elizabeth should have done as Ronald told her – to go away, get changed, and come back when she looked more like a real princess.

Three of the four boys wanted to be in the position of the prince. Two of them believed the prince was clever; the third boy did not think the prince was nice, but still wanted to be like him. The fourth boy recognized the prince as 'not very good' and 'stupid', and wanted to be the dragon. Although the boys understood Elizabeth's plan, they all refused her the position as the central character, attributing it to Ronald or the dragon. The two boys who saw Ronald as clever, argued, for example, that 'Ronald very cleverly holds on to his tennis racquet tightly which is why he stays up in the air' (Davies, 1989: 61), or that 'He's got a tennis jumper and he won the tennis gold medal' (p. 62). All the boys were concerned with Elizabeth's looks: she was 'messy', 'messy and dirty', 'yucky'. 'I'd tell her "You look dumb with your old paper bag on"' (p. 62). There were many clues, Davies noticed, that it was not dirt but Elizabeth's temporary nakedness that was the central problem, although it remained unspoken.

Davies regrouped the children, not according to gender, but according to whether they understood the feminist interpretation of the story: That Elizabeth is the hero and that Ronald is not nice. It turned out that the four children who adopted the feminist interpretation had employed mothers, and their fathers assumed a greater than average share of domestic duties. The three children who saw Elizabeth's actions as a ploy to get her prince back and save her future marriage had mothers who were housewives, although two of them had a university degree.

Davies pointed out that it would be a mistake to see a causal connection between mother's employment and her children's ability to imagine women as active agents in the public world. If it were as simple as mother's employment creating children who see women and men as social equals, the solution to gender inequality would simply be sending all women to work. 'But going out to work is not necessarily accompanied by discursive practices in which the work the woman undertakes is seen as giving her agency or power' (p. 64). Indeed, being able to compare an all-female and all-male team working in basically the same position in city administration in Warsaw and Stockholm, I was struck by the difference in their conversations during their job and about their job. Whereas men were obviously convinced of both the difficulty and the importance of their work, women talked in the same way about their professional tasks and about their last summer holidays or knitting.

Davies concluded that '[t]he power of the pre-existing structure of the traditional narrative to prevent a new form of narrative from being heard is ever-present' (1989: 69). And, as Jean Matter Mandler demonstrated, the traditional (schematic) narratives are easier to recall.

At the end of this chapter it is appropriate to highlight the fact that both structural and poststructural analyses required a crucial change from the assumptions of traditional hermeneutics. They turned the central question in interpretation from 'What does a text say?' to 'How does a text say it?' Although explanation, as posited in Chapter 2, is a stage of all attempts at interpretation, the recent text analyses are all inspired by the assumption so well summarized in the title of the book by historian Hayden White: *The Content of the Form* (1987). The form of a text also carries a message, sometimes louder and more explicit, and sometimes even contradicting the missive of the content.

Finally, it needs to be remembered that social scientists (and semioticians, literary critics, and linguists) are not the only ones who interpret, interrogate, or interrupt texts. Everyone does it, some of us more often, some of us less often; the world is full of semiotic readers.[5] Such semiotic reading is a somewhat dizzying challenge, requiring a great deal of caution, but nevertheless extremely satisfying. The caution concerns the necessity of a symmetrical stance, that is, the awareness that the authors of the text that social scientists analyze may be even more skillful analysts themselves. The dizziness comes from an attempt to maintain a balance between standing under, over, and for the analyzed text. The 'natural attitude' of a social scientist is to stand over, to explain (as I did in this chapter), but an admiring explication is an attitude that should be applied more often.

Text analyses

Find a story in your daily or weekly newspaper (or choose a story you found in one of your interviews) and analyze it, first in a structuralist and then in a poststructuralist mode.

EXERCISE 11

FURTHER READING

Boje, David (2001) *Narrative methods for organizational and communication research.* London: Sage.

Cooren, François (2000) *The organizing property of communication.* Amsterdam: John Benjamins.

Czarniawska, Barbara (2004) *Narratives in social science research.* London: Sage.

Gabriel, Yiannis (2000) *Storytelling in organizations: Facts, fictions, and fantasies.* Oxford: Oxford University Press.

Mandler, Jean Matter (1984) *Stories, scripts, and scenes: Aspects of schema theory.* Hillsdale, NJ: Lawrence Erlbaum.

Mishler, Elliot G. (1986) *Research interviewing: Context and narrative.* Cambridge, MA: Harvard University Press.

Riessman, Catherine Kohler (2008) *Narrative methods for the human sciences.* Thousand Oaks, CA: Sage.

Silverman, David and Torode, Brian (1980) *The material word: Some theories about language and their limits.* London: Routledge and Kegan Paul.

Notes

1. Daniel Kahneman (2011) claimed that personification greatly contributes to successful communication. Perhaps the way out is to personify, but to warn the reader that it is done, like Latour did in *Aramis, or the Love of Technology* (1996).
2. Usually dated back to W.J.T. Mitchell's *On Narrative* (1981).
3. For example, Donna Haraway (1992), Catherine Hayles (1993), François Cooren (2000), Daniel Robichaud (2003), and Anne-Marie Søderberg (2003). See also Timothy Lenoir (1994) for a cautionary voice.
4. He did not even quote Greimas; it is known from his other texts that he used him as an inspiration (see e.g. Latour, 1988, 1993). This move is not recommended, but further indicates that a use of a specific model is not the point.
5. A term introduced by Umberto Eco (1990) to indicate critical readers, as opposed to semantic – naive – readers.

12
Writing it Up

Writing is seen as craft in this chapter, and the advice on how to improve one's craftsmanship is extracted from both rhetoric (how to structure a convincing argument) and literary theory (how to construct representations, characters, and plots). The final examples of excellent writing styles are to serve as models for beginners.

HOW FIELDWORK IS WRITTEN

Textwork is suturing together of two words meant to convey that writing is a labor-intensive craft. (Van Maanen, 2006: 13)

In an article titled 'Ethnography then and now', John Van Maanen examined two decades of ethnographic writing. His observations have relevance beyond ethnography, however, and can be applied to all types of writing studies based on fieldwork.

The changes that occurred in ethnographic writing were not dramatic, but they are noticeable, and the models propagated in method courses and method books do not always catch up with them. The writer, for example, is still presented as a hard-working, lonely scholar who writes all day long in a quiet corner. In reality, social science writers rarely write alone – they are forever in conversation with other authors, their colleagues, and people in the field, who have changed from innocent 'informants' practically into co-authors. In reality, too, academics teach, have dual-career families, pets, chums, and sports – so those perfect days of quiet writing happen, possibly 'once every two or three months' (Van Maanen, 2006: 14). But they do happen, and the craft is practiced.

As to textual strategies, the three distinguished by Van Maanen in 1988 – realism, confessional tale, and impressionism – still exist. Realism has become more inventive, though, and the examples I have been quoting in this book corroborate this opinion. Confessional tales are fewer, but they have graduated from appendices to the main text. Impressionism has been fragmented into many experimental techniques encouraged by and in cultural studies. But they have also diminished in proportion, giving way to a new type of text, which Van Maanen called 'advocacy texts', with a strong normative message.

Changes or not, 'the appeal of any single work remains tied to the specific arguments made within a given text and referenced to particular, not general, substantive, methodological and narrative matters' (Van Maanen, 2006: 16). This is why I begin with the most traditional approach to the issues of writing: conventional and less conventional structures of the text.

A STRUCTURE OF A THESIS

The most common structure of a scientific text, be it an article or a monograph, is still based on the formal oration in Greek rhetoric, which looked as follows:

1. Exordium: catches the audience's interest while introducing the subject.

2. Narration: sets forth the facts.

3. Proposition (or Division): sets forth points stipulated and points to be contested (states the case).

4. Proof: sets forth the arguments in support of the case.

5. Refutation: refutes opponents' arguments.

6. Peroration: sums up arguments and stirs audience (Lanham, 1991).

This structure was considered to work best for persuasion in the court of law. In time, however, it was elaborated into a conventional structure of a thesis, with added elements, and, in its positivist version, a changed order of Steps 2 and 3:

1. Problem/Issue/Aims (Exordium)

2. Literature Review

3. Hypotheses (Proposition)

4. Method

5. Results (Narration)

6. Discussion (Proof)

7. Conclusion (Peroration).

The similarity is obvious, but a thesis is written rather than spoken (the traditional structure is worth remembering when preparing a PowerPoint presentation!), and this partly explains the differences. A contemporary thesis is grounded in the forensic (judicial) rhetoric which originated in the courtroom, but with the addition of the so-called praise-and-blame (epideictic) rhetoric: thus a 'Literature Review'. What was written before is important in a way that differs from the way precedents are important in court. The truly modern addition is the 'Method' – positivism's contribution to classical rhetoric.

Not all dissertations, or even all articles, copy this structure. A thesis written in a spirit of grounded theory approach (Glaser and Strauss, 1967), for example, may be structured in this way:

1. There is something strange going on in the world ... (Exordium)

2. Has somebody else explained it? (Literature Review). If not:

3. I'd better go and learn more about it. But how? (Method)

4. Now that I have understood it, I will try to explain it to the others. So, let me tell you a story ... (Narration)

5. Now, what does it remind me of? Is there somebody else who thinks similarly? (Proof)

6. This is the end (and the point) of my story (Peroration) (Czarniawska, 2004: 124).

Like their classic predecessors, these structures are meant to persuade. Like their classic predecessors, they often follow chronology as well – not the chronology of oration, but of research itself.

Yet chronological structuring produces as many problems as it solves. For one thing, novices in the craft of research (Booth et al., 1995) often suffer from its insincerity. It is well known that research seldom goes as planned. What to do? Report all moves back and forth, all hesitations and mistakes? When well done, it is an achievement in itself, but not easy to accomplish. What, then? Hide the truth?

Research is a search for truth, but not the truth of all the embarrassing details from the life of the researcher (though such details can become a valuable part of a method paper). The main question to be asked before deciding the form of a research report is: Will it persuade? Additional questions may differentiate between audiences: Will it persuade grant givers? My adviser? My colleagues? The people I studied? The general educated reader? And although such questions can never be answered in advance with certainty, experience shows that mechanical structuring is usually inferior to a successful emplotment.

What, then, is a successful emplotment? I suggest that plot can be considered to be the theory of the work (Czarniawska, 2013b). There must first be something to emplot however – a description or a re-presentation of the field and the phenomenon under study. Academic writers share with fiction writers two basic challenges: how to represent (that which is called *mimesis*, an imitation of the 'real' world) and how to make sense of this representation – how to theorize (emplotment). The next two sections address these two challenges.

DESCRIPTION, OR HOW TO RE-PRESENT THE WORLD

To paint with words

How to represent? The traditional answer within academia was a simple one: 'Faithfully'. Reality should be recreated in the text. A scientific text should reflect what it describes, hopefully in one-to-one correspondence. This should not be a problem, as 'facts speak for themselves', and texts can be rendered loyally to the intentions of the authors. That this is even possible was questioned in both art and in social sciences (see e.g. Levine, 1993; Brown, 1995; Van Maanen, 1995b). This questioning addressed many problems, two of which are crucial.

The first problem is the incompatibility of worlds and words (Rorty, 1980). How can words be compared to that which they (purportedly) describe? A one-to-one correspondence is impossible if the media differ. The word 'cat' does not look like a cat or sound like a cat. It is therefore sensible to think of representation of an object as involving the production of another object, which is indeed related to the first, but only by a *coding convention*. Coding conventions of a given time and place determine 'what counts as similar in the right way' (Van Fraassen and Sigman, 1993: 74).

The second problem concerns the *politics of representation* (Latour, 1999). Considering that there are always competing versions of the world in circulation, who, and by what criteria, has the right to judge them? Even within the same coding convention, there will always be several representations of the same phenomenon: those of management and of unions, of school administrators and parents, and even those of psychologists and of sociologists. Whom to believe? If facts do not speak for themselves, who has the right to speak on their behalf? How do coding conventions arise? And who has the right to determine the right way?

As these are complex queries, I begin from the opposite end, by discussing what has counted as a skillful representation in social science texts. The general opinion is that, in the case of field material, it is a representation that makes readers feel as if they were there, in the field. But how to achieve that effect, if facts refuse to speak for themselves?

All descriptions are necessarily *figurative* (White, 1999). In order to evoke in readers an image of something they have not seen, this image must be connected to something they have already seen, and *tropes* – figures of speech – are the linguistic means to achieve just this effect. The word *metaphor*, which in Greek means a transport from one place to another, means exactly that in authorial practice: the reader is moved from here to there, whether 'there' is another physical setting or another book. And not for nothing are tropes *figures* of speech; they are the means to visualize, to paint with words.

Painting with words is a task to be fulfilled throughout the thesis, but it is in the description of the setting that it comes to the fore. The most frequent description of a setting for a social science study follows the theatrical convention: *stage instructions* plus the *cast of characters* (often collective rather than individual – a group of employees, a profession, a social stratum). The influence of serialized novels, and later radio and TV series popularized another descriptive element: *'the story-so-far'* (an historical background).

Another type of introduction to a setting is typical to sociological ethnographies, Chicago style. The authors borrow from naturalist fiction, introducing the reader 'as if a stranger or an outsider, in the fashion of a guidebook' (Atkinson, 1990: 32), but with a difference – with a hint of something that needs to be explained:

> In the winter, summer becomes inescapably visible. Walking through a vacation-land in January feels rather like an archeological expedition through the remains of an alien culture. I am the only inhabitant of this wintry landscape out at the coast, moving freely between the abandoned houses, crossing lawns, and glancing through windows.

> The barren bushes and threadbare winter grass mercilessly expose frost-bitten leftovers from summer: lost toys, tennis balls, a Martini bottle cap, faded confetti from end-of-season parties. (Löfgren, 1999: 1)

A great many details, but not a complete list. Neither fictive accounts nor ethnographic reports aim at 'a literal description or transcription of people, places or events' (Atkinson, 1990: 40). A skillful description depends heavily upon metonymy and synecdoche – on deleting some information – in the hope that readers will fill in the blanks, which should also increase their engagement in the reproduction of the text (Atkinson, 1990: 52). Löfgren attempted to recreate an atmosphere, not to make an inventory of things to be found on a Swedish beach in winter, and he assumed that the readers know what Martini is. But the main effect is the question the readers are to ask themselves: What is he doing there, and why?

Yet another literary device used to describe the setting is to throw the reader into the midst of the events while simultaneously creating a puzzle to be solved:

> Just after 11.00 a.m., every weekday that is not a bank holiday, an apparently mundane calculation is performed at a couple of desks in an unremarkable open-plan office in London's Docklands. Small sets of numbers arrive electronically or by telephone. The two people orchestrating the calculation correct obvious typing mistakes and check less clear-cut discrepancies by telephone calls: 'Hello, it's [X]. Just want to check the one week on the Danish [Krone]. You guys are quoting 2.51. You want to keep it around that?' (MacKenzie, 2009: 1)

Again, a host of questions arise. Is what they are doing 'normal'? Why are they doing it? What consequences does it have? These are questions to be answered by adding more material, and by the subsequent analysis.

Both guide-like instructions and putting the reader in the midst of the story anecdotes aim at a rich, abundant, and colorful description – a 'thick description', in Gilbert Ryle's words, made popular by Geertz (1973). Mimesis aims at a description that is both vivid and credible (the two aid one another) – a persuasive description.

The stage is set, the backdrop has been painted, but re-presentation is not only visual, but also auditory. Somebody must tell the story.

Voices from the field

Whereas choosing the tropes is a matter of skill or art, choosing the voice or voices is a political choice. Should the author tell the story? Or should field voices be allowed in, and if so, to what extent? Merely by using excerpts from interviews? Or can they speak for themselves?

The difficulty in representing multiple voices in field studies was perhaps most sharply focused in anthropology. After decades of all-knowing anthropological texts that explained the 'native ways of being' to the 'more developed civilization', a wave of political and ethical doubts pervaded the discipline, best summarized in the volumes edited by Clifford and Marcus (1986) and Marcus and Fischer (1986). Many contributors to these volumes opted for a different, polyphonic (multi-voiced) ethnography, in which people could speak in their own voices. This approach led to a great deal of discussion about whether it was, in fact, possible to make non-researchers speak in their own voices.

It is worth recalling that these anthropologists took inspiration from literary theoretician Mikhail Bakhtin (1981), who had in mind not a polyphony in which many people are speaking (after all, they may be saying the same thing), but something called *heteroglossia* or 'variegated speech'. This is a textual strategy whereby the author uses different languages (dialects, slangs, vocabularies) in the text. There is no need for the illusion that 'these people' are speaking for themselves; indeed they are not. But the author pays them a compliment by making the reader clearly aware of the fact that different languages *are* being spoken within one and the same linguistic tradition.

From this perspective, it is easier to approach a suggestion coming from science and technology studies – giving voice even to nonhumans. Latour (1996) put this suggestion into action in his case study of the failed introduction of an automated train, in which 'Aramis' (an automated train system) was given a voice of its own. At a certain point in this story, Master and Pupil (who both studied Aramis's 'life') have a heated exchange on the legitimacy of that move: 'Do you think I don't know', barks the Master at the doubting Pupil, 'that giving Aramis a voice is but an anthro-pomorphization, creating a puppet with a voice?' (p. 59).

Thus social sciences may end up with a staged conversation, in which the goal of political representation must live side-by-side with an awareness that the scholars are in fact performing an act of ventriloquism. This amounts to relinquishing the goal of speaking on behalf of the Other in any literal sense – the goal of being 'a tribune for the unheard, a representer of the unseen, a kenner of the misconstrued', as Geertz ironically put it (1988: 133). Social scientists do most harm when they impose their interpretations on what they claim are 'authentic voices from the field'. If rendering these voices is the purpose, the way to go about it is to quit social science (silence one's own voice) and to engage in the political activity of creating speaking plat-forms for those who are not heard. Otherwise, a variegated speech in social science texts is a sensible solution to the problems of correct representation.

EMPLOTMENT, OR HOW TO THEORIZE

In the rhetorical tradition, there is a distinction between mimesis (a description) and emplotment (an arrangement) in a text. But this distinction makes sense only in a method book. In the practice of writing, it is obvious that each description must be arranged. The arrangement of descriptions can be coherent with the arrangement of the whole thesis, or incoherent with it. In other words, mimesis can corroborate the plot, or oppose it. Although it is possible to think of a mimesis opposing the plot and therefore contributing to some kind of a meta-plot, it is safe to assume that, in a social science text, coherence is still a virtue. I further suggest that description should be subordinated to the requirements of the plot. The descriptive material that does not directly support the plot (the theory) can be put in an appendix (or saved for other uses, see Chapter 14). Emplotment is the crucial part of writing a social science text – and the most difficult.

The term *emplotment* was introduced in 1973 by Hayden White, who ventured to say that historians do not *find* plot in history but *put it in* themselves. The word refers to the introduction of a structure that allows one to make sense of the events reported. Traditionally, it answers the question 'Why?' From a positivist view, the answer should be formulated in terms of causal laws; in a romantic view, in terms of motives; in a post-positivist, post-romantic discourse (R. H. Brown, 1989), it assumes the form of showing 'How come?' where laws of nature, human intentions, and random events form a hybrid. This is why a social science theory can be seen as a plot of a story, and why it is worthwhile to learn more about the possible ways of emplotting a text.

The plot

The easiest way of emplotting is by chronology, or what Mandler (1984; see also Chapter 11 in this book) called a temporal connection. This is what Aristotle in *Poetics* called a simple story ('a narrative of events arranged in their time-sequence'), contrasting it with a plot that arranges the events according to some kind of causality.

Psychologist Donald Polkinghorne thus translated the literary notion of plot and its function to be used in the social sciences: 'The plot functions to transform a chronicle or listing of events into a schematic whole by highlighting and recognizing the contribution that certain events make to the development of the whole' (1987: 18–19). But not only that; a plot can weave the historical and social context into the story, along with information about physical laws and thoughts and feelings reported by people. 'A plot has the capacity to articulate and consolidate complex threads of multiple activities by means of the overlay of subplots' (p. 19). This is a valuable property from the point of view of social scientists, who are often faced with the fact that, as many things happen simultaneously, a simple chronology is not sufficient to tell a story. Even here, the assumptions resembling those of grounded theory turn out to be relevant: 'The recognition or construction of a plot employs the kind of reasoning that Charles Peirce called "abduction", the process of suggesting an hypothesis that can serve to explain some puzzling phenomenon. Abduction produces a conjecture that is tested by fitting it over the "facts" ' (p. 19). Last, but most important, '[m]ore than one plot can provide a meaningful constellation and integration for the same set of events, and different plot organizations change the meaning of the individual events as their roles are reinterpreted according to their functions in different plots' (p. 19). A lavish party has a different meaning in the story of a success than it does in a story of bankruptcy.

The most quoted contemporary explanation of a basic plot is Tzvetan Todorov's (1977/1995: 11):

> The minimal complete plot consists in the passage from one equilibrium to another. An 'ideal' narrative begins with a stable situation which is disturbed by some power or force. There results a state of disequilibrium; by the action or a force directed in the opposite direction, the equilibrium is re-established; the second equilibrium is similar to the first, but the two are never identical.

Most stories contain more than one plot, which must be connected to one another. According to Todorov (1977/1995), this combination of plots is usually achieved through one of two strategies: *linking* (coordination – adding simple plots to one another so they fit) and *embedding* (subordination – setting one plot inside the other).

One can add, after Hayden White (1973), that, like an historian, a social scientist usually confronts 'a veritable chaos of events *already constituted*, out of which he must choose the elements of the story he would tell' (p. 6, footnote 5). Thus the necessity for two additional tactics: *exclusion* and *emphasis* (deciding which plot is to be the main one). Outcome-embedded stories have plots subordinated to one another in a sequence (the outcome of one episode determines the plot of the next), whereas the ending-embedded stories have all plots subordinated to the one that is revealed at the end (Mandler, 1984), or, as in many academic texts, announced at the beginning as the end-to-be-expected.

Marie-Laure Ryan (1993) created a useful list of steps to be taken in the work of emplotment:

- Constructing *characters* (which, in social science texts, often begin as nonhuman actants: a newspaper article, new unemployment statistics, a new computer technology);

- Attributing *functions* to single events and actions (a crisis in the newspaper industry *led to a search* for spectacular scoops, which *resulted in dramatizing* the mistakes of the city council, and so on); and

- Finding an *interpretative theme* (global financial crisis? loss of trust in elective democracy?).

The ordering of the steps in this list is somewhat convoluted. Whereas an interpretative theme is found via the construction of characters and by attributing functions to events and actions, once found, it rules over the other two. In other words, an interpretative theme emerges while the writer is trying out characters and functions, but once it has been decided upon, the text requires a tighter adjustment. Thus commonsense wisdom says that, after having written the last chapter, one must go back and rewrite the rest.

There is, as mentioned in Chapter 11, a tendency in social science texts for ending-embedded plots. The whole text is supposed to be geared toward 'the conclusions'. Yet there is a possibility that the outcome of one episode will change the structure – of the next episode or of the whole text. The writer may admit to readers that the first hypothesis did not work, and that the entire study had to change accordingly. This does not have to be an admission of error; to the contrary, as in Latour's story of Aramis, this is the basic structure of the text that is outcome-embedded. At each turn, the previous turn of events turns out to be misleading (not for nothing is the classic example of abduction found in the deeds of Sherlock Holmes, though he calls it 'deduction'; Sebeok and Sebeok, 1981). This is not a common way of emplotting a scientific text, but certainly makes for a fascinating story.

In what follows I quote three relatively unusual but striking examples of writing: a case study, a praxiography, and an ethnography.

FIRST STORY: A CASE

To illustrate case writing, I have chosen a work that focused on an unusual case of a well-studied phenomenon: industrialization. There are a great many case studies of industrialization, beginning with the industrialization of entire countries, as in Karl Polanyi's classical work, *The Great Transformation* (1944/2001), and extending to cases of industrialization of economic sectors, of certain professions, and of small family companies. Ruth Schwartz Cowan (1983) chose to focus on the industrialization of housework. The title of her book signals the plot: *More Work for Mother: The Ironies of Household Technology from the Open Hearth to the Microwave*. The plot, or the theory, can be easily summarized. The industrialization of housework, traceable through the continuous introduction of new technologies, was intended to free housewives from their burden. As it turned out, it did free men and children, who had been heavily involved in housework, while increasing the burden of women, as the standards of housework were raised with each new technology. Cowan won the 1984 Dexter Prize given by the US Society for the History of Technology, and no work could deserve it more.

The book begins with a sketch of an historical background, describing house-hold work and tools in the pre-industrial era. The chapters that follow are ordered chronologically, from the early stages of industrialization in the USA to the postwar years, all confirming the theory of the book. But Cowan's work also contains some less conventional elements.

One is a chapter on counterfactuals – a device used primarily by historians (McCloskey, 1987). In Chapter 5 of her book, Cowan pondered over such 'roads not taken' as failed commercial options and failed machines – and concluded that neither capitalism nor patriarchy can explain those failures and the success of other commercial undertakings. Cowan's story is outcome-embedded. A subordinate plot suggests that 'when the choices were available ... , the majority of people – whether rich or poor, owners or workers, male or female – chose to preserve in both the realm of symbol and the realm of fact, those activities that they deemed crucial to the creation and the maintenance of family life' (Cowan, 1983: 149).

Another original trait is 'Picture Essays': thematically grouped pictures and repro-ductions, such as 'From housewifery to housework', 'The transportation system', 'Washday', and 'The rich and the poor'. I suspect that here a vice has been turned into a virtue; many publishers still allow pictures only if grouped on the same plate, and the quality of reproduction is not very good. Still, Cowan made them into 'essays', adding a story that ties the pictures together.

At the end of the book, there are 'Bibliographic Essays', introduced by a letter to the reader:

Each chapter of this book is based upon very different kinds of primary and secondary source materials. Rather than overburden the text with didactic notes, I have decided to provide, in the bibliographic essays that follow, some sense of the sources from which each chapter was drawn. Many of the works cited here are not specifically referred to in the text, but they were essential in my own research, and I hope that they will provide a useful guide for those who might like to explore further this fascinating subject. (Cowan, 1983: 220)

My 'Further reading' list is but a feeble imitation of Cowan's, whose bibliographic essays are followed by notes that together would form at least a paper, if not a thin book. This care for the reader's convenience and the attempts to make reading easier are as rare as they are truly laudable. To show her own engagement, Cowan ended her story with a postscript describing her futile efforts to liberate herself from housework. The last paragraph is truly optimistic:

> Many of the rules that tyrannize housewives are unconscious and therefore potent. However manufacturers and advertisers may exploit these unconscious rules, they do not create them. By exploring their history we can bring these rules into consciousness and thereby dilute their potency. (Cowan, 1983: 219)

I have chosen this example because I, too, find the subject fascinating, but mostly because I admire Cowan's writing. It shows that it is indeed possible to keep a chronological structure of the presentation of field material, without replacing plot with chronology. The emerging theory is clear and convincing. Innovative elements, such as those listed previously, make Cowan's work attractive to the reader and well grounded in the material. I realize that her example may be difficult for a beginning researcher to follow, but this comment applies to all three works I am presenting here. Reach for the stars, and you may reach the moon.

SECOND STORY: A PRAXIOGRAPHY

In *The Body Multiple: Ontology in Medical Practice* (2002), Dutch philosopher Annemarie Mol described the diagnosis and treatment of atherosclerosis, drawing on her fieldwork in a Dutch university hospital. Thus a praxiography: Mol's neologism, which seems to me to provide a correct description of a great many field studies in contemporary societies.

At a first glance, Mol did what many other researchers currently try to do; she depicted a local practice in the health sector and drew some abstract conclusions from her study. But her book is far from ordinary. As mentioned in Chapter 1, she separated her text into two parts on each page. The upper part is her praxiography: She followed, or 'shadowed' patients' bodies, thus enabling her to show how, moving from one hospital department to another, the body, the patient, and the disease transform into different ontological entities. As in Cowan's book, the plot is signaled in the title, and then used throughout to emplot Mol's report from the field, so that it reads as a fascinating story – not because there are great heroes or dramatic events in it, but because it is so well plotted.

The lower part of the page contains a developing theoretical reasoning on various stances in medicine, philosophy, and social sciences. It follows the divisions in chapters of the upper part, and each theoretical part is relevant for the praxiography part it underpins. The reader can choose to read the theory first and the praxiography afterwards, or the other way around. One could also say that the praxiography part contains the plot of the story being told, whereas the theory part contains a meta-plot; it is, in fact, a theory about changes and developments in theories. Mol's is an example of a most ingenious way of combining a theoretical reflection with an attention-getting rendition of the field material.

Two of Annemarie Mol's other innovations are noteworthy. Apart from observation, she also used 'ethnographic interviews', but not in the sense given to the term by US anthropologist James Spradley (1979), who coined the expression. For him, the purpose of such interviews was 'to describe a culture'. In contrast, Mol suggested that the term 'ethnographic interviews' should mean that the interviewees themselves become ethnographers (2002: 15). Furthermore, she replaced the well-known concept of 'tacit knowledge' with 'imbedded knowledge' in her analysis – to denote knowledge accumulated in various parts of an action net created by the actions of producers, their suppliers, and their clients. Such an action net is activated by each of them for the purpose at hand, without the necessity of anyone mastering the whole of it.

The result is truly impressive. Mol managed to make the practice she described fascinating – and not only to readers interested in health care. What is more, she managed to make a local practice globally appealing (as the reader learns from the lower part of the text, a critical US reviewer actually provoked her to highlight the 'Dutchness' of her study, to make it more interesting for a non-Dutch reader). Her claim is that health practices travel globally, and that the imitation of practices is common; on the other hand, each translation is local. Thus bodies multiply in most hospitals in the world, but certain aspects of the transformation are more 'Dutch' than others. So here is a text written by a philosopher that reads like a story – a text in which the writer uses a local example to inform the reader about a crucial phenomenon in the contemporary world, medical intervention – a text that never ceases to be concrete and constantly produces insightful abstractions.

THIRD STORY: AN ETHNOGRAPHY

Bruno Latour's study of the French Council of State (2010) fully deserves the label of ethnography; the 'tribe' is small but distinct. Administrative law can be seen as a set of practices, but although the diagnosis and treatment of atherosclerosis can also be seen as several practices, they are more subparts of one more general. That which is practiced in the Council of State is more diversified. Indeed, although the English title is *The Making of Law*, the French was *La fabrique du droit*: the law factory.

It starts with an historical sketch, explaining the origins of this French institution, invented by Napoleon Bonaparte to protect citizens against the state. The Council deals exclusively with the administrative law (its equivalent in the UK is the Law Lords). It advises the government if the government so wishes, and assumes the causes brought by citizens against the administration.

The character of the book is clearly announced in the first paragraph of the first chapter:

> In which we introduce the readers into the bicentennial celebrations in order to get them warmed up – In which larcenous pigeons allow us to meet the commissioner of the law, who is a main character in the story – In which we discover the importance of a missing signature to a decree … (Latour, 2010: 1)

Yes, this is how fairy tales begin, and this beginning serves Latour to announce that the main analytical tool in the ethnography has been borrowed from Greimas again. The field material takes the form of small window studies, mini-praxiographies, and nine cases – the forms often found in anthropological ethnographies. But the analysis consists of following the passage of law ('the movement'), told as a story of circulations of the *objects of value*. There are ten objects that circulate, and their ontology differs – from those that are actually material (the files sent around) to such quasi-objects as the arguments used and such symbolic objects as the authority of a Councilor in the eyes of his or her colleagues (which may vary).

Some more explanation of the meaning of value objects is needed at this point:

> Narrative discourse is often seen in the form of a circulation of objects of value. Its organization can then be described as a series of **transfers of values**. A particular and complex mode of transfer is that of the exchange of values. (Greimas and Courtés, 1982: 365–366; bold in the original)

The factory of law, when functioning, works by supporting the constant circulation of the objects of value, thus permitting a series of transfers of values. But *cui bono*? Why does the factory exist? What good does all this circulation bring? And to whom?

Latour considered three possible interpretations, amounting to three theories. One, which can be called 'critical', postulates that the production of administrative law is a dissimulation intended to hide power relationships. Another theory, which can be called 'formalist', would claim that the Council of State, like any other unit of the law, applies the rules of law to particular cases. Anything else can count as 'human error'. A third theory, which is Latour's, claims that law is being performed via its practices:

> … the reason why we represent justice as blind, and holding scales in her hands, is precisely because she hesitates, and proceeds feeling her way forward. … In moving blindly from left to right in this way, justice uses only ordinary reasoning, the kind of interrupted syllogism that we all use to organize our daily lives, the heterogeneous totality of which is rather like a taste, a sense of smell, a nose,

a thing of habit, of culture, of experience and common sense. ... Justice only writes law through winding paths. In other words, if she had refused to make mistakes, if she had applied a rule, if she had summed pieces of information, we could not identify her as being either just or indeed legal. *For her to speak justly, she must have hesitated.* (Latour, 2010: 151–152; italics in the original)

This unorthodox theory of how law is made is not the end of the study. Latour compared his ethnography of the Council of State with a great many ethnographies and cases of science and technology that he had written previously. There are quite a few similarities – indeed, science has forensic ideals – but in Latour's opinion, the two should be differentiated. The solidity of the scientific facts could be compared to the rigor of the law. But are they made of the same stuff? True, lawyers and scientists begin with an exegesis of existing texts and end up producing a new one, or several new ones. But whereas the law hesitates for a long time and then announces the sentence, science aspires to certainty at the outset, but this certainty is in time demolished by the tribunal of history. Science is a chain of references; law is a chain of obligations. 'Scientists speak vaguely about precise objects, lawyers speak in precise terms about vague objects' (2010: 237).

One conclusion is that law is, and must be, superficial.

If it holds everything, if it makes it possible to link all people and all acts, ... it is also because it extracts only a tiny part of their essence from all situations. Its fabric resembles that of a delicately knitted lace. This is what common sense retains of its movement when it qualifies it as cold, formal, meticulous, abstract, empty. Indeed, empty it should be! (2010: 264)

Like Mol's fieldwork on the site of a Dutch hospital, Latour's fieldwork on the site of a French institution tells his readers about far more than a set of local mores; it offers original insight into the functioning of contemporary institutions.

I end this chapter with yet another quote from John Van Maanen, who postulated that,

... all ethnographies owe a good deal of their persuasive power and wonder to contingent social, historical and institutional conditions. And no meta-argument, reflexive turn or navel-gazing can effectively question these contingencies. Yet, ... this sublime contingency matters little when it comes to putting ink to paper because any particular ethnography must still make its points by the same means that were available before the contingency was recognized and absorbed. These means are of course the old ones that include the hard work of putting forth evidence, providing interpretations, inventing and elaborating analogies, invoking authorities, working through examples, marshalling one's tropes, and so on (and on). (2006: 16)

In other words, a well-written text may persuade or not, depending on the time and place it is read. But one of the duties of a social scientist is to try to persuade – and to write well.

The craft of writing

Select a dissertation (an article or a book) that you find particularly well written, and try to analyze its formal properties.

FURTHER READING

Atkinson, Paul (1990) *The ethnographic imagination: Textual construction of reality*. London: Routledge.

Becker, Howard (1986) *Writing for social scientists: How to start and finish your thesis, book, or article*. Chicago, IL: The University of Chicago Press.

Billig, Michael (2013) *Learn to write badly: How to succeed in the social sciences*. Cambridge: Cambridge University Press.

Czarniawska, Barbara (1999) *Writing management: Organization theory as a literary genre*. Oxford: Oxford University Press.

Rhodes, Carl (2001) *Writing organization: (Re)presentation and control in narratives at work*. Amsterdam: John Benjamins.

Styhre, Alexander (2013) *How to write academic texts: A practical guide*. Lund: Studentlitteratur.

Van Maanen, John (1988) *Tales of the field: On writing ethnography*. Chicago, IL: University of Chicago Press.

13

Good Academic Writing: Beauty and Credibility

This chapter is a plea for changing the criteria of 'good scientific writing', based on the assumption that social science texts should be readable for a wider audience. This goal can be achieved by a skillful blending of literary and scientific styles, as illustrated by examples of texts written by renowned authors.

BLURRING GENRES

I am not sure that this book qualifies as a work of social science. It is so directly concerned with change and upheaval, both individual and social, that at times I had the feeling that I was writing the conceptual outline of a *Bildungsroman* (with, as always in novels, a number of autobiographical touches mixed in here and there).

This blurring of genres does not bother me, but it exacts a price. I have tried to make the various turns and transitions, which stand in the center of the essay, as compelling as possible. But they admittedly fall short of carrying the conviction and of achieving the generality which social science likes to claim for its propositions. Then again, as many of these claims have proven excessive, perhaps I need not worry. (Hirschman, 1982/2002: xv–xvi)

This is what Albert O. Hirschman, master of hybrid genres and the crossing of disciplinary borders, wrote in the introduction to his book *Shifting Involvements*. Perhaps a world celebrity need not worry over matters that a doctoral student worries about, but there are at least two messages in this introduction that are worth taking to heart. First, every scientific work is a product of a writer, a person in a specific point on the timeline of life. This fact can be an explicit point in the work (a 'confessional tale', Van Maanen, 1988) or merely reflected upon and incorporated into the text. But a more important message concerns the secret of an absorbing story: its pivots, its various 'turns and transitions', as Hirschman called them. When nothing happens, boredom descends upon the writer and the reader, but skillful writers can turn even a lack of events into an event. As to generality, I return to it later. At this point, I am considering the eternal question: What is 'good academic writing'?

An author tries to anticipate readers' reactions, in part by projecting the past criteria of the 'goodness' of a scientific text onto the future. I say 'in part' because all innovative writers hope to establish new criteria by defying earlier ones. To be followed or to be broken, evaluation criteria seem to be helpful to a writer. Experience teaches us that it is impossible to establish those criteria once and for all, or even to predict the success or failure of a given text. There is only a pattern of conventional readers' responses – and those known only retrospectively – and a bunch of institutionalized norms for writing that may be observed or broken in practice.

TRADITIONAL CRITERIA OF GOODNESS

One traditional set of such norms refers to *validity*, the correspondence between the text and the world; and to *reliability*, the guarantee of repeated results with the use of the same method. These are supposedly ostensive traits; they characterize (or not) the study, and can therefore be demonstrated.

Validity as a correspondence criterion has attracted its greatest criticism from recent theories of knowledge. Whether one claims to speak of a reality or a fantasy, the value of utterances cannot be established by comparing them to their object, but only by comparing them to other utterances. Words cannot be compared to worlds, only to other words. A look into actual validation practices reveals that they always require texts to be checked against other texts. Thus when Ricoeur (1991) spoke of 'validation of guesses', he hastened to add that he was not referring to an application of the logic of empirical verification. 'To show that an interpretation is more probable in the light of what is known is something other than showing that a conclusion is true. … Validation is an argumentative discipline comparable to the juridical procedures of legal interpretation' (p. 159). And, as one could learn from Latour's ethnography of the factory of law in Chapter 12 (Latour, 2010), following these procedures involves a great deal of doubt and hesitation.

Reliability, in turn, was usually understood as a replication of results. It could be claimed, however, that results are repeated not because the correct method has been repeatedly applied to the same object of study, but because institutionalized research practices tend to produce similar results. One can go even further and claim that results are as much a part of research practice as methods are. An excellent illustration of this phenomenon is the 1990s debate within AIDS research, wherein it was possible to show that studies that did not arrive at what was seen as the legitimate conclusion were not funded (Horton, 1996). Silverman (2010) quoted an example of the violent reaction of medical researchers to a field study that produced results casting doubt upon their standard findings. It is perhaps more accurate to speak of 'conformity' rather than of reliability. It is not the results that are reliable or unreliable, but the researchers – by conforming to dominant rules.

Dissatisfaction with positivist criteria for 'good scientific texts' and a wish for alternative guidelines have led to a search for a new set of criteria within the interpretive tradition. Thus Guba (1981) spoke of the trustworthiness of naturalist studies (truth value, applicability, consistency, and neutrality); Fisher (1987) spoke of narrative probability (coherence) and narrative fidelity (truth value), constituting narrative rationality; and Golden-Biddle and Locke (1993) suggested authenticity, plausibility, and criticality as the ways in which ethnographic texts convince their audiences. Unfortunately, like the positivist criteria they criticize, these are again *ostensive* criteria of a text's success – the attributes of a text that can be demonstrated and therefore applied *a priori* to determine a text's success.

Authors under the influence of poststructuralism looked for other solutions, on the assumption that properties of a text are attributed by the readers rather than found in the text. Patty Lather, after having suggested four new ways of defining validity (Lather, 1993), concluded that 'validity is a "limit question" of research, one that repeatedly resurfaces, one that can neither be avoided nor resolved' (Lather, 2006: 52). Norman Denzin (1995) proposed to borrow a more complex notion of *verisimilitude* from literary theory (Todorov, 1977/1995), in the sense of the degree to which a text fulfills the rules of correct representation established within a given genre of writing.

Another possible loan could be from literary theoretician Wolfgang Iser's *reader-response theory*, which states that '[e]ffects and responses are properties neither of the text nor of the reader; the text represents a potential effect that is realized in the reading process' (Iser, 1978/1980: ix). Iser rejected the traditional hermeneutics by which scholars looked for the intentions of the author, and distanced himself from reception theory as well: 'A theory of response has its roots in the text; a theory of reception arises from the history of readers' judgments' (Iser, 1978/1980: x). Reading and the production of meaning arise in a triangle: the text, the reader, and the situation of the reading. A text read twice will be interpreted differently the second time: The context is not the same and the reader is an older person, but the text has also changed. This is so, Iser explained (1989: 7), because any literary text is full of indeterminacies – gaps filled in by the reader (in fact, enthymeme, an argument that proceeds from unstated premises, is popular in social scientific texts; see Feldman and Sköldberg, 2002). The subsequent reading uses the memory of previous filling-in operations, and the text seems different.

Readings are therefore subjective, but rarely idiosyncratic. Other readings influence a given reading as an aspect of situation; at any time and place there are professional readings and lay readings; dominant readings, but also novel readings (DeVault, 1990). Marjorie DeVault postulated that the traditional picture of a lonely reader lost in the world of her book needs to be replaced, like that of a lonely writer (Van Maanen, 2006), by seeing writing and reading as collective activities. Writers must take the opinions of their pre-publishing reviewers into account; readers read reviews and talk to other readers.

Reader-response theory is close to the pragmatist stance (Rorty, 1992), which gives preference to *performative* criteria. These are not rules which, when observed by writers, will guarantee the positive reception of their works, but descriptions that summarize the typical justifications given when a positive reception occurs. Such descriptions concern not the text, but the responses of the readers as reported in the legitimate vocabulary of the day.

Social science writers who craved success in the 1990s might, for example, have chosen postmodernism as their mantle. Although some of these texts survived well (perhaps in spite of the mantle taken), others soon became obsolete. Texts written at the peak of fashion may become classical or outmoded, and no 'objective' properties of the text can help to determine which is to be their fate. In sociology, Durkheim and Weber held for a century, but now they seem to be losing out to their previously less successful competitors, Tarde and Simmel.

Aspiring authors cannot count on readers to tell them what they are going to like next, but may try to remember how they justified their past judgments, hoping that their preferences will hold for a while.

There are two common types of justifications: the *pragmatic* and the *aesthetic*. It is even possible to claim that the aesthetic is included in the pragmatic and vice versa, if treated broadly enough. Something 'works' because it touches me, because it is beautiful, because it is a powerful metaphor, but one can also hear engineers say of a machine, 'Look how beautifully it works!' Rorty (1992) said that although usefulness is decided according to the *purpose at hand* (the term coined by phenomenologist Alfred Schütz, 1946/1964), the best readings are not those that serve that purpose, but those that have changed it. He called such a text an *edifying* discourse – a discourse with the power 'to take us out of our old selves by the power of strangeness, to aid us in becoming new beings' (Rorty, 1980: 360). Edifying discourse, therefore, is one that is both useful and beautiful – in the eyes of the reader.

ARGUMENTS THAT HAVE WORKED

Objectivity, that high praise when addressed to scientific texts, can be seen as no more and no less than conformity to the norms of justification common in a relevant community (Rorty, 1980: 36) – praiseworthy because it is a difficult achievement. Conforming to the norms accepted by an academic community, however, does not guarantee a readership beyond that community; and yet that is, or should be, the aim of the social sciences. The way to go is first to look at the norms that are actually observed in the practice of writing (rather than declared as those that ought to be observed), and then decide which guidelines to follow.

The received belief is that scientific texts contain facts and use formal logic (appeals to *logos*, in rhetorical terms) to form their arguments. I scrutinized four texts written by sociologists and organization theorists (Czarniawska, 1999) and discovered that the only place in these books containing facts and facts alone was the copyright page. As Latour (1988) pointed out, scientific realism differs from fictional realism by the textual strategy of inviting readers to inspect the source of the facts, which likely contains other references of the same kind. The final loop in the chain, then, consists of interview transcriptions or some other 'hard data', whereas names and addresses on the copyright page can be verified against original sources. Tzvetan Todorov (1978/1990: 26) has observed that novelists strike a fictional contract with their readers: 'Suspend your disbelief, and I will entertain you'. Social scientists, on the other hand, offer a *referential contract*: 'Suspend your disbelief, and I will show you my references'.

One explanation for this surprising lack of facts can be found in the introduction to one of the texts analyzed: a book by Knorr Cetina (1981), in which she claimed that etymologically 'facts' (from *facere*) are basically fabrications and that their production is a specialty of certain places, such as natural science laboratories. Social scientists seem to be only marginally engaged in fact production; their attention is focused on *how* the facts and the important societal fictions are produced (Knorr Cetina, 1994). 'Stories' and 'facts' are both made, but according to different recipes.

If that is the case, social science would move closer to literature, in which the status of facts is not high: 'Once accepted as true, the factual judgment ... dies as such in order to generate a stipulation of a code. ... Successful judgments are remembered as such only when they become famous ("the famous discovery of Copernicus"...)' (Eco, 1979/1983: 86). Facts, once known/fabricated, are used in the production of further facts; their repetition brings no added value into a discourse. Metaphors, on the other hand, 'tend to resist acquisition. If they are inventive (and thus original) they cannot be easily accepted; the system tends not to absorb them' (Eco, 1979/1983: 86). Once accepted, they become redundant and lose their attraction. Stories, on the other hand, are allowed redundancy. A narrative of a redundant nature – said semiotician and novelist Umberto Eco, in defending detective stories – offers a fastidious reader (often a scientist) an opportunity to relax. Thus the combination of stories and metaphors seems to be irresistible; yet that combination seemingly presents a threat to the genre of social science studies, which may vanish into literature. It seems, however, that this danger does not loom strongly, and many social scientists agree with Silverman's (1997: 240) caution: 'the craft of writing fiction or verse is quite different from the craft of social science'.[1]

Still, the craft of social science is a craft of writing, and aesthetic criteria apply to it, as to any other writing. The preferences may differ (Silverman voted for 'a minimalist aesthetic'), but social sciences are simply too big to hold to one standard form of writing. And as different authors tap inspiration from different sources, Clifford Geertz's (1980) observation is more accurate now than then: ' in recent years there has been an enormous amount of genre mixing in social science, as in intellectual life generally, and such blurring of kinds is continuing apace' (p. 165).

This blurring of genres is also visible in the kind of argumentation used in social science texts. My scrutiny of sociology and organization theory also revealed that the authors whose texts I had been reading rarely, if at all, used formal logic – in the sense of the particular mode of reasoning – because all of them used logic in the sense of syntactic rules. Indeed, logical fallacies – such as the assumption that correlation equals causality or that the opposite of a true statement is also true – are common in academic texts (although not in those I examined). What is noteworthy, however, is that instead of limiting themselves to *logos*, social scientists often appeal to *ethos* and *pathos*. Appeals to ethos – to authority – are supposed to have vanished, together with the authority of Fathers of the Church or great leaders, but they are actually abundant in social sciences – under the guise of references.

Surely, however, arguments using *pathos* or emotional appeals are not allowed? Perhaps not, but they are used, not the least by economists, and with good reason. The findings of social science research are supposed to be generalizable. Traditionally, this goal was achieved by following a proper procedure of sampling, guaranteeing representativeness of the results. As many researchers who sampled correctly know from bitter experience, however, no statistical sampling will survive a protest from a member of the audience who says 'I have an uncle working in the company you studied, and he says it's not like that at all'. Here again, literature theoreticians can help. It is readers, not authors, who generalize when convinced by an argument; and, the rhetoricians say, pathos is usually more convincing than logos.

Do I recommend giving up logos? No, merely supporting it with ethos and pathos, in proportions suiting the author. The exact proportions are the matter of style.

STYLE

... even within the constraints of disciplinary norms, most academics enjoy a far wider range of stylistic choices than they realize. (Sword, 2012: vii)

Among many definitions offered by the *New Shorter Oxford English Dictionary*, one is especially relevant: '**III11b** A particular or characteristic way, form, or technique of making or producing a thing, esp. a work of art; a way of executing a task; a manner of performance' (*NS OED*, 1993: 3112). The notion of style points toward a personal character of a text – in a political sense ('style as voice', Megill and McCloskey, 1987) and in an emotional sense. Indeed, 'style is the man', as literary theorists used to say, unchecked for a good while (see Lepenies, 1988).

A feminist perspective is not the only innovation in ways of understanding style. Another innovation is the collapse of the traditional distinction between style and content or form and content (especially by historian Hayden White, 1987). This change encouraged John Van Maanen to speak of 'style as theory' (1995a). I still insist that it is the plot that is the theory, but I understand his intention as pointing to the personal nature of theories.

Indeed, Umberto Eco said that style was

> … a very personal, unrepeatable, characteristic 'way of forming' – the recognizable trace that every artist leaves in his[2] work and which coincides with the way the work is formed. Thus, the artist gives himself form in the work. (Eco, 1989: 165)

An additional explanation came from French literary theoretical Philippe Lejeune:

> I call here 'style', for lack of a better term, everything that disturbs the transparency of written language, … and makes the *work on the words* apparent whether we are dealing with parody, plays on meaning, or versification. (Lejeune, 1989: 127; my italics, BC)

Is it too much to expect from a researcher writing a first article or a first book to know how to work on the words, how to do 'textwork'? It depends on the amount of writing the person has done in the past; some people have already acquired a distinct style before they entered university. Others do not need to waste time in stylistic exercises if they do not want to (if they choose to, they can be inspired by Raymond Queneau, 1947/1981, who wrote 99 versions of the same anecdote). My recommendation would be to read a text of a writer that you admire and would like to imitate just before you start writing your own text.

SOCIAL SCIENCES AS A BLURRED GENRE

But can an academic imitate a novelist or a literature scholar? Does academic writing not differ from any other, with its own criteria of what is good and what is bad writing?

Judgments about goodness or badness, objectivity and edification, not to mention beauty, are rarely unanimous, even within a community, and they change over time. One can at best speak of a type of writing or, rather, types of writing that are considered legitimate and that are read in a specific time and place. In the 1960s it was absolutely forbidden to use the first person in scholarly writing. It was considered better to have long, unwieldy sentences in order to avoid bringing a personal touch into the picture. The debate on what is good and bad writing can thus be replaced or at least aided by a discussion of genres – institutionalized forms of writing. Achieving an inventory and a description of genres not only allows for probabilistic estimates of success, but also allows for the understanding of deviations. Every avant-garde, every vibrant fringe, every edifying discourse feeds on the mainstream, on normal science, on systematizing discourse. By the same token, the 'canonical tradition' (MacIntyre, 1988) depends on deviations for its survival, and also owes them its eventual demise.

As long as a tradition can incorporate innovations, they vitalize it; when it cannot do it anymore, the tradition dies. This paradoxical relationship between the mainstream and the margin is well known but rarely recognized, as it threatens the grounds of legitimacy of both the mainstream and the margin. The legitimate vision of the relationships between the two is an agonistic relationship; as in a traditional science, the best man (yes) wins.

This reasoning can be applied to itself: It is possible to imagine a non-agonistic science, and an explicit awareness of the mutual dependence between the avant-garde and the retro-garde. Such views, although marginal at present, may repay in reflection and sophistication what they cost in legitimacy. And it is such a view that prompted me to suggest that social sciences should favor one (blurred) genre – the one that combines insights from literary theory with an anthropological frame of mind.

Social science texts, as a genre, or perhaps a family of subgenres (case studies, praxiographies, ethnographies), should therefore make skillful use of tropes and narratives; they should also use the insights of literary theory to assist in self-reflection. Such insights can assist in the escape from an inherited image of the social sciences as a (still) defective natural science.

I do not suggest that it should become a defective fiction instead. I argue for a conscious and reflective creation of a family of genres that recognizes its tradition without being paralyzed by it, that seeks inspiration in other genres without imitating them, and that derives confidence from the importance of its topic and from its own growing skills. Then, perhaps, 'we could write texts which would at once be craftily written, scrupulously true, which would not make the readers believe that what is reported is exact and which would still be interesting' (Latour, 1988: 166). And the dominating genre could be that of 'a subtle realism which maintains a view of language both as constructing new worlds and as referring to a reality outside the text, a means of communicating past experience as well as imagining new experiences' (Seale, 1999: 15).

This stance is grounded in a belief that social science, in order to matter more in the life of contemporary societies, needs to reach readers from outside its circles. Although the texts of disciplinary self-reflection will remain interesting and relevant only for social scientists (which does not mean that the writers of such texts should abandon literary pretentions – social scientists love beautiful texts, too), the bulk of social science needs to be skillfully crafted. And the questions – from inside and outside – questions like 'Is it valid? Is it reliable? Is it Science?' should be replaced by 'Is it relevant (useful)? Is it beautiful (aesthetic)? Is it moving (edifying)? And if yes, for whom and to whom?'

A caveat on experimental writing would not be out of place here. Like all other experiments, experiments in writing may succeed – or fail. As in entrepreneurship, the majority of new undertakings do fail, and the rejection of an experimental piece of writing does not have to be a proof of editors' and publishers' obsolete mindsets. Here the arts provide a good example: for one Damian Hirst, there are thousands of other artists who crossed conventions but failed to gain acclaim. And yet they continue trying. So, although not always rewarded by success, trying out new forms may be more gratifying than copying the old ones (although copying is also a skill).

EXERCISE 13

The art of writing

Write a review of a doctoral dissertation that you consider excellent, following a format of book reviews in the journal you read most.

FURTHER READING

Billig, Michael (2013) *Learn to write badly: How to succeed in the social sciences.* Cambridge: Cambridge University Press.

Brown, Richard Harvey (ed.) (1995) *Postmodern representations: Truth, power, and mimesis in the human sciences and public culture.* Chicago, IL: University of Illinois Press.

Seale, Clive (1999) *The quality of qualitative research.* London: Sage.

Sword, Helen (2012) *Stylish academic writing.* Cambridge, MA: Harvard University Press.

Notes

1. Not that it is impossible for some writers to do both; Umberto Eco is the best known example, but also sociologist Fabrizio Battistelli and ethnologist Mariusz Czubaj write excellent fiction.

2. Eco wrote that male pronoun in 1989, the same year that Richard Rorty dared to write for the first time a general text using female pronouns (Rorty, 1989). Could be, though, that it was Eco's translator who did it.

14

When to Stop, and What to do Next

The two parts of this title must be further separated into various sub-questions, and, to complicate the matter still further, the answers cannot be uniform. Situations vary, but so do researchers. This chapter begins, therefore, with a famous taxonomy of intellectuals – the foxes and the hedgehogs – which can be a good starting point for self-diagnosis, which, in turn, should facilitate a selective reading of the remaining text.

ON FOXES AND HEDGEHOGS

In 1953, Isaiah Berlin, a British social and political theorist of Russian-Jewish origin, wrote an essay on Tolstoy, with the title *The Hedgehog and the Fox*. The title alluded to a cryptic saying by Greek poet Archilochus: 'The fox knows many things, but the hedgehog knows one big thing'. Berlin suggested that this dichotomy could be applied to all writers and thinkers, and perhaps to all human beings. Hedgehog types 'relate everything to a single central vision, one system, less or more coherent and articulate, in terms of which they understand, think and feel – a single, universal, organising principle in terms of which alone all that they are and say has significance' (1953/1997: 436). Foxes, on the other hand, 'pursue many ends, often unrelated and even contradictory, connected, if at all, only in some *de facto* way, for some psychological or aesthetic principle' (p. 436). Hedgehogs 'lead lives, perform acts and entertain ideas' that are centripetal. Foxes are centrifugal: 'their thought is scattered or diffused, moving on many levels' (pp. 436–437). Among hedgehogs he counted Plato, Lucretius, Dante, Pascal, Hegel, Dostoyevsky, Nietzsche, Ibsen, and Proust; among foxes were Herodotus, Aristotle, Montaigne, Erasmus, Shakespeare, Molière, Goethe, Pushkin, Balzac, and Joyce. Luminous, albeit exclusively male company in both cases.

It has been noted that Berlin saw himself as a fox, which made him slightly prejudiced against hedgehogs. In defense, US lawyer and philosopher Ronald Dworkin wrote the highly acclaimed book, *Justice for Hedgehogs* (2011), in which he loquaciously supported the hedgehog's point of view on morality and justice.

I am a fox, but I am acutely aware of the dangers of projecting one's own point of view onto others. I tried to check this bias in this book; after all, as Thomas Nagel (1986) has noted, there is no view from nowhere, but human beings are capable of distancing themselves from their own interests. Readers will judge the extent to which I have succeeded in this task.

Still, I claim that the hedgehog–fox dichotomy is a useful self-diagnostic device for any researcher, even given the possibility that one can be a fox believing oneself to be a hedgehog (or forced into this belief by a hedgehog adviser or employer) or even change perspectives during a scientific career. My observation of myself and other foxes, and many conversations (including heated debates) with various hedgehogs have revealed a great many differences in research style between the two groups. Apart from the main difference – that of portraying the world as heterogeneous and fragmented (foxes) versus homogenous and unified (hedgehogs) – there is also a difference of obvious importance for the topic of this chapter. Foxes jump easily from one topic to another, and are quickly bored by the same or similar issues; hedgehogs believe that the further one delves into something, the more fascinating it becomes.

WHEN TO STOP?

First stop: When to stop reading?

Embarking on a research project, one needs first to establish if it has already been done, and if not, if a theory exists that may explain the phenomenon of interest, to be applied straightforwardly or at least tested on new ground (see Chapter 2). This procedure seems to be easy in the days of the Internet, yet even the virtual library has its complications. You may miss relevant texts because they have not been properly classified (on the role of classification in science, I highly recommend Bowker, 2006) or you may amass texts that only loosely relate to your topic of interest, if at all. Check them all carefully, by all means, but do not throw away those that seem interesting but loosely coupled to your project. They may become useful later.

As you continue your project, your colleagues, advisers, and reviewers will be suggesting additional items that you must read. Be firm. Ask, if you dare, what it is that makes them necessary for you to read? One of the perils awaiting doctoral students in particular, is the probability of reading too much. Think that German philosopher Gottfried Leibniz, who lived between 1646 and 1716, had already complained that there was too much written for a person to read. By now, writings have multiplied so incredibly that it is possible to become lost in literature. So, read only what you really need to read, but do not throw away the surplus suggestions – add them to the list that you have already created for further use.

Second stop: When to stop collecting field material?

At the second stop, the difference is not so much between foxes and hedgehogs as between quantitative and qualitative researchers. Researchers who plan to test an hypothesis on a selected population choose an appropriate sample to analyze. Qualitative researchers enter the field with their eyes and ears open, even if they have sketched the direction in which to proceed. But even this direction may change, when a visit to the field discloses phenomena that appear to be of greater interest than the one originally chosen. Hedgehogs will probably maintain the chosen direction, whereas foxes will be tempted to continue collecting. A guide that prevents a researcher from getting lost in the richness of field material can be found in the precepts of grounded theory (see Chapter 3). The advice is simple, perhaps deceptively so: When your field material (interviews, observations, documents collected) becomes repetitive, it is time to stop. Not immediately, of course – repetition may prove to be misleading. The interviews could have been made with people who are close to one another; observations could have focused on routine activities; documents might have come from the same source or the same period. But when there is no doubt that the material has become repetitive, it is time to stop and move on – to the next case or the next site.

Nevertheless, when the time for analysis does arrive, it is likely that too much field material has been collected. Amusing scenes, captivating insights, fascinating texts seem always to be too precious to abandon. A common reaction is to put everything of interest into the text, only to be met with harsh reactions from advisers, reviewers, or critics. Remove them from the text; but, once again, do not throw them away. This advice concerns all field material collected during the study. Even when the analysis has been completed and the text is ready for publication, do not throw anything away. See to it that the field material is preserved according to the ethical requirements of proper research – hidden from the eyes of a curious onlooker, but safe. It, also, can be of later use.

Third stop: When to stop writing?

Here the perils for foxes and hedgehogs differ somewhat: Foxes will tend to add more and more topics, insights, and threads, whereas hedgehogs may go into too many details to elaborate and strengthen their all-encompassing theory. Tolstoy, a fox who, according to Berlin, wanted to be a hedgehog, did both. Thus the complaints that his *War and Peace* is far too long – complaints from readers who wanted to know more about Pierre Bezukhov and André Bolkonsky, and from readers who wanted to know more about the history and about Tolstoy's philosophy. I doubt that any current publisher would accept his manuscript in its original version; certainly no scientific publisher would accept a monograph of that length. Thus the necessity to stop when the main theme has been explicated and illustrated convincingly. Once again, additional plots and themes need not be sacrificed – merely saved for later use.

Another problem concerns revisions. Here the foxes and the hedgehogs differ significantly. When reviews come, the fox has usually found many new topics of interest, and can hardly be bothered returning to what seems to have been done so long ago. Actually, a long time between the first draft and a revision is optimal, although rarely possible in the case of a dissertation and bitterly complained about in cases of journal reviews. The best revisions are made when the time of writing is so distant that the text seems to have been written by somebody else. The flow of thought has been forgotten, the ready expressions are not so ready anymore, and the task of revising has become simpler.

The hedgehog, however, may have a tendency to strive for perfection, and engage in ceaseless revisions, until the adviser or the journal editor loses patience. One way out of this dilemma is to set a personal deadline and decide that the text must be ready by a given date, no matter what. And then it is time to move on.

WHERE TO GO NEXT?

It is likely that by the time the monograph or the article is ready for print, the fox has already found many new and different interests, while the hedgehog has decided that work with the all-encompassing theory has only begun: time to move on, in a different direction or the same direction! But both of them can feel burnout, tiredness, or emptiness. What to do next? Here are some possible sources of inspiration.

Discarded literature

Remember all those texts that you found on Google, and those recommended by your colleagues and reviewers? Now is the time to examine them – not in the light of the previous project, but as products in their own right. Is there something provocative? Something boring or false that needs correction? Something inspirational?

But it is not only the previously unused texts that may contain grains of gold. When you were reading the texts in light of your problem and with the purpose of preparing a literature overview, you were reading them selectively. Reread any of these previous texts, and you will see that there is much you did not notice or attend to. Of course, there is no need to reread everything – just those items you considered exceptionally good, no matter how relevant to your previous interests. As literary theorist Wolfgang Iser pointed out, even if the text in the sense of the physical object remains the same at rereading, the reader and the situation is no longer the same, and therefore this triangular 'act of reading' is not the same, either (Iser, 1978/1980; see Chapter 13 in this book). Reading the same story again may be more attractive to hedgehogs than to foxes, but both should remember that on a second reading, 'additional information will affect and condition the meaning projection, so that now the gaps between the different segments as well as the spectrum of their possible connections can be applied in a different, or perhaps more intense, way' (Iser, 1989: 10).

Previous field material

Now may also be a good time to return to all those fascinating scenes you observed but did not use in your final reports; snippets of interviews concerning issues that did not directly relate to your previous research problem; and fascinating documents that pointed toward issues that were not in focus during your original study. It is like going to a bric-a-brac shop: Perhaps these items are just useless bits and pieces, but there could be real gems hidden there as well. After all, you are not the same reader as you were earlier. The situation is different, at least in the sense that stress of the necessity of reporting is (temporarily) over, so it is likely that you will see the old material with new eyes.

But there is another point in preserving old field material. Social sciences suffer primarily from a lack of historical, or at least longitudinal studies. Repeating a study after ten years may bring results that are unique and of general interest. Changes do not happen when researchers decide to study a change; even a planned change tends to bring many unexpected consequences long after its formal evaluation. Sometimes the most striking discovery is that of stability and repetition; thus New Zealand British anthropologist Raymond Firth repeated his 1929 study of Tikopia in 1952 and found, to his surprise, that in spite of dramatic changes (such as the islanders' conversion to Christianity), the basic social structure and such elements as chieftainship remained intact over a generation (Firth, 1959). Your field material collected in quiet times may later acquire a dramatic character.

Unused topics and themes

Although each field study produces too much material to be used in the first report or reports, it is bound to contain themes that can be developed further in subsequent research. Hedgehogs will probably decide that they did not dig deeply or widely enough in the first effort, and will therefore continue along the line already sketched. Foxes might have often been distracted in preparing their original report by promising topics and themes that did not fit the text they were preparing. It is easy, therefore, to return to those unused topics and themes for the next study. Sometimes it is merely a matter of changing perspective or adopting a specific aspect of the previous work. Other times the results might have introduced new questions, the answering of which requires a new study.

Melville Dalton's *Men Who Manage* (1959) is a classic study. Five years later after its publication, Dalton published an article entitled 'Preconceptions and method in *Men Who Manage*' (1964) – an often-reprinted method article, in which he not only reflected on his study from a methodological point of view, but also revealed details that he was unable to incorporate in his original book. In 1968, he contributed a chapter, 'Reorganization and accommodation: A case in industry', to the Festschrift, *Institutions and the Person*, in honor of Everett C. Hughes. The chapter explores yet other aspects of his previous studies – not only *Men Who Manage*, but also his earlier work on union–management conflicts and incentive systems.

One could protest that Dalton's later works did not acquire the fame of his 1959 work, but it may well work in the opposite direction: A topic from an earlier, less well known work can become a bestseller, because it will be an idea 'whose time has come', to borrow an expression from Victor Hugo.

Ideas whose time have come are sometimes disparaged as 'simply fashionable', because of the negative clang of the term *fashion* when applied to scientific work (as discussed in Chapter 1). Yet fashions and trends in research tend to mirror current societal concerns, with some delay.

Mass media

One field that provides a constant list of current societal concerns is the mass media. There is no doubt, either, that the mass media play an enormous role in selecting, formulating, and interpreting current societal problems – and solutions. Gaye Tuchman ended her famous study, *Making News: A Study in the Construction of Reality* (1978), by claiming that the 'news media set the frame in which citizens discuss public events' (p. ix). It can be disputed whether or not they do so: Does not the public influence the media's frame as well, and are the media alone in trying to frame citizens' discussion? But here I would like to concentrate on similarities and differences between mass media and scholarly research. There is no doubt that the two fields compete within this activity of framing public events, and it may seem, as Tuchman suggested, that mass media are the winners.

I believe that social scientists have a serious advantage over journalists. True, the media do set, or at least try to set, the frame for interpreting current events. As Niklas Luhmann emphasized in his analysis of the mass media, however, both researchers and journalists look for 'things that are true', but journalists do it under limiting conditions that differ from the limiting conditions of the scientist (Luhmann, 2000). Both professions reduce and simplify – a map cannot be identical to the territory – but in a different manner.

A crucial limiting condition for journalists is the absolute demand for speed (Czarniawska, 2012). As a result, the mass media are forced to use old frames and existing interpretive templates in interpreting and framing new events and phenomena. They are the first to list events and phenomena, but their interpretations are, by default, obsolete – unless the event or the phenomenon is but a variation on a well-known theme. Scholars have time – never as much as they wish, but compared to journalists, near-eternities – so they can discern new topics and themes and reframe them in a new, hopefully intriguing or useful way.

Erving Goffman and Karl Weick are two well-known scholars who used the news media for this very purpose. Their works reveal their uncanny talent for turning everyday anecdotes from the media – 'strips of everyday activity', as Goffman (1974) called them – into evidence for their theories. 'A true reader is an armchair ethnographer, able to catch the significance of the accident scene and to use that significance to reanimate a floundering project' (Weick, 2004: 197).

I understand well that this is not an easy feat, even for foxes, for whom the approach should be simple. Every day when I open my newspaper, I promise myself that I will follow the example of those two great scholars and collect amazing events from everyday life that are stranger than fiction. But, alas, I fail to see their relevance at the time. Only much later do I vaguely remember having read about something or someone that seemed to illustrate precisely the phenomenon that interests me. Yet it is a skill that needs to be taught and learned because, even if systematic fieldwork remains our main source of material, the world of today is too rich, too fragmented, and too fast moving to be grasped by a prolonged visit to one site. Moving on with the media leads to a type of work that Weick (2004) called 'bricolage'; but perhaps bricolage is the most fitting technique for depicting the social life of today. So, clip those articles that seem vaguely interesting and keep them safely stored!

Social media

Here I would like to suggest a move that may seem even more peculiar than my encouragement to follow research fashions or to sift through the media: checking the interests reported by your friends on Facebook. A counterargument could be that such a move leads to inbreeding and the creation of digital ivory towers, my counter-counterargument is that university departments offer even more opportunities for inbreeding and insulation. Facebook friends are usually a mixed group; their interests differ, and so do the directions that can be pursued. Although it seems on the surface to be a technique for foxes only, hedgehogs should not neglect it. Hedgehog friends might have excavated something by going further and helping to develop the theory that needs to be developed. What is more, unlike university departments, where not everyone is happy when somebody else takes up 'their' research topic, Facebook and other social media encourage the sharing of interests, connections, and directions.

Fiction

The idea that the social sciences can be enriched through close contact with literary fiction can be traced to the very beginnings of social sciences.[1] It has probably been most fruitfully explored by the Chicago School of Sociology (Capetti, 1993). A good guide to these encounters can be found in Lewis A. Coser's (1963) *Sociology Through Literature*. Fiction, Coser claimed, is social evidence and testimony, a commentary on events and morals, and more likely to be a source of sociological insights than are the random comments of untrained informants. Recourse to literature cannot replace systematically collected scientific knowledge, but can complement and enhance it. After all, the social sciences stem from the humanities. Although Coser did not state it explicitly, quotes from literary theorists show that they were his guides in his search for excerpts to illustrate central sociological topics.

In 1968, Dwight Waldo published *The Novelist on Organization and Administration*. His argument was similar to Coser's, in the sense that he considered fiction to be complementary to science, but he was more interested in a psychological complement. Fiction can add to scientific writing that which was removed in the first place: the concrete, the sensual, the emotional, and the idiosyncratic. He also called attention to the gains emphasized later by narratologists: Novels are a source of vicarious experience. Similarly, he was the first to indicate the possibility of genre analysis conducted from the point of view of organizational knowledge.

In 1989, *Harvard Business Review* published an article entitled 'Reading fiction to the bottom line', by literary theorist Benjamin DeMott. DeMott chose a story by Lionel Trilling from 1945 and another by Donald Barthelme from 1980 to show how they captured the social character of their times and how they presaged metaphors and concepts that emerged much later in the social sciences. He was not the first to make this claim. Russian post-Formalist Mikhail Bakhtin, whose works have become posthumously influential, claimed that novelists had a keen sense for emerging processes, partly because they did not have to be cautious like scientists. Novelist and literary theoretician Milan Kundera noted that the novel dealt with the unconscious before Freud did, discussed class struggle before Marx did, and practiced phenomenology before the term had been invented (Kundera, 1988). Neither is the event of scholars reaching for fiction a passing trend. In the aftermath of the financial crisis of 2007–2010, Melville's novella of some 150 years ago, *Bartleby the Scrivener: A Story of Wall Street* (1853/2004), was brought to the attention of intellectuals commenting on the crisis.

Novels are obviously a source of inspiration, and should be among the texts to be considered when scientific texts are being produced. They are versions of the world, relevant and valid – not because they match the world exactly, but because they could contain appealing categories. It is the power of creative insight rather than documentary precision that makes novels potential competitors to and dialogue partners for social sciences. Again, like journalists, both novelists and social scientists reduce and simplify – but in a different way. One could say that novelists have even fewer limiting conditions than social scientists do. Not only do they have more time, but their contract with their readers (Todorov, 1978/1990) is much more generous, as it allows for both fiction and fantasy.

Fictional texts are always – although not always simply – reflective of societies in which their authors have been raised (Irons, 1995). They are part of the contemporary discourse, which means that they not only reflect the experience of life at a given time and a given place, but they also form it and are part of it. They present work environments and situations that few of their readers would know from experience. Additionally, certain genres – detective novels, for example – have a special place among fiction texts (Czarniawska, 1999). Due to their long tradition of realism, they set high standards of credibility for their detail, as their long list of acknowledgments clearly indicates. The authors may invent the course of events and the psychology of the characters, but their descriptions are truly ethnographical in detail, as there are, and always have been, a great many pedantic readers checking the details. Thus Sara Paretsky, for example, attacks one current social problem in the USA in each of her detective novels. Similarly, although not in a detective story format, Sebastian Faulks's *A Week in December* (2009) contains an almost-complete list of current problems troubling the UK.

Yet unlike the mass media, literature can offer more than a list of current topics; it can also help the researcher to change the ways in which field material is analyzed and scholarly reports are written. A scientific text is assumed to differ from a literary text in its avoidance of indeterminacies: Everything should be spelled out. 'Multiplicity of meaning, subtle and complex ambiguity, is frequently a positive and vital feature of literary, as opposed to scientific discourse' (Goodman and Elgin, 1988: 55). *Frequently* is perhaps the key word here, however. Scientific texts, though undoubtedly different, are closer to literary texts than one might expect. Genres are indeed blurred.

Another connecting point is the similar way that scholars read their field material and literary critics read literary products – thus, as suggested in Chapter 11, the possibility of borrowing and imitating techniques used in text analysis. There is a strong similarity between a researcher reading an annual report and a literary critic reading a novel – especially now, when annual reports and legal documents have become objects of discourse and text analysis, both quantitative and qualitative (see e.g. Cummins and Bawden, 2010; Tengblad and Ohlsson, 2010). Thus it is not merely fiction, but also literature theory that can be used as inspiration in the search for methods that do not imitate natural sciences. Social sciences is, and should remain, a literary genre of its own, even if blurred.

EXERCISE 14

When to stop

Try to diagnose the stage you have reached in your research project and make a list of actions necessary to finish the project.

FURTHER READING

Berlin, Isaiah (1953/1997) The hedgehog and the fox. In: Berlin, Isaiah, *The proper study of mankind*. New York: Farrar, Strauss and Giroux, 436–498.

Shaffir, William B. and Stebbins, Robert A. (eds.) (1991) *Experiencing fieldwork: An inside view of qualitative research*. (Part IV). Newbury Park, CA: Sage.

Notes

1. At present, this statement can be extended to movies and TV series. I do not dedicate a separate section to those, as many points are the same as in the case of literary fiction. The latter, however, can be additionally considered a useful analogy in terms of the 'textwork'.

References

Abdelsalam, Omneya H. and Street, Donna L. (2007) Corporate governance and the timeliness of corporate internet reporting by U.K. listed companies. *Journal of International Accounting, Auditing and Taxation*, 16(2): 111–130.

Abolafia, Mitchell Y. (1996) *Making markets: Opportunism and restraint on Wall Street.* Cambridge, MA: Harvard University Press.

Abu-Lughod, Lila (1991) Writing against culture. In: Fox, Richard G. (ed.) *Recapturing anthropology: Working in the present.* Santa Fe, NM: School of American Research Press, 137–162.

Adolfsson, Petra (2005a) Environment's many faces: On organizing and translating objects in Stockholm. In: Czarniawska, Barbara and Sevón, Guje (eds.) *Global ideas: How ideas, objects and practices travel in the global economy.* Malmö/Copenhagen: Liber/CBS Press, 94–105.

Adolfsson, Petra (2005b) Obelisks of Stockholm. In: Latour, Bruno and Weibel, Peter (eds.) *Making things public: Atmospheres of democracy.* Karlsruhe/Cambridge, MA: ZKM/MIT Press, 396–397.

Agger, Ben (1990) *The decline of discourse: Reading, writing and resistance in postmodern capitalism.* New York: The Falmer Press.

André, Elisabeth and Rist, Thomas (2001) Controlling the behavior of animated presentation agents in the interface – scripting versus instructing. *AI Magazine*, 22(4): 53–66.

Arribas-Ayllon, Michael and Walkerdine, Valerie (2008) Foucauldian discourse analysis. In: Willig, Carla and Stainton-Rogers, Wendy (eds.) *The Sage handbook of qualitative research in psychology.* London: Sage, 91–109.

Atkinson, J. Maxwell and Heritage, John (1984) *Structures of social action: Studies in conversation analysis.* Cambridge: Cambridge University Press.

Atkinson, Paul (1990) *The ethnographic imagination: Textual constructions of reality.* London: Routledge.

Atkinson, Paul and Silverman, David (1997) Kundera's *Immortality*: The interview society and the invention of self. *Qualitative Inquiry*, 3(3): 304–325.

Auster, Donald (1961) A content analysis of 'Little Orphan Annie'. In: Lipset, Seymour Martin and Smelser, Neil J. (eds.) *Sociology: The progress of a decade.* Englewood Cliffs, NJ: Prentice-Hall, 241–247.

Baker, Carolyn (1997) Membership categorization and interview accounts. In: Silverman, David (ed.) *Qualitative research: Theory, method and practice.* London: Sage, 130–143.

Bakhtin, Mikhail M. (1981) Discourse in the novel. In: Bakhtin, Mikhail M., *The dialogic imagination: Four essays.* Austin, TX: University of Texas Press, 259–422.

Bales, Robert F. (1950) *Interaction process analysis*. Cambridge, MA: Addison-Wesley.

Banks, Marcus (2007) *Using visual data in qualitative research (qualitative research kit)*. London: Sage.

Barley, Nigel (1983) *The innocent anthropologist: Notes from a mud hut*. London: Penguin.

Barley, Nigel (1995) *Dancing on the grave: Encounters with death*. London: John Murray.

Barley, Stephen R. and Kunda, Gideon (2001) Bringing work back in. *Organization Science*, 12(1): 76–95.

Barrett, Lisa Feldman and Barrett, Daniel J. (2001) An introduction to computerized experience sampling in psychology. *Social Science Computer Review*, 19(22): 175–185.

Barthes, Roland (1977) *Image-music-text*. Glasgow: William Collins.

Bartlett, Frederick C. (1932) *Remembering: A study in experimental and social psychology*. Cambridge: Cambridge University Press.

Bate, S. Paul (1997) Whatever happened to organizational anthropology? A review of organizational ethnography and anthropological studies. *Human Relations*, 50(9): 1147–1175.

Bauman, Zygmunt (1995) *Life in fragments: Essays in postmodern morality*. Oxford: Blackwell.

Becker, Howard S. (1970) *Sociological work: Method and substance*. Chicago, IL: Aldine.

Becker, Howard S. (1974) Photography and sociology. *Studies in the Anthropology of Visual Communication*, 1(1): 3–26.

Becker, Howard S. (1986) *Writing for social scientists: How to start and finish your thesis, book, or article*. Chicago, IL: The University of Chicago Press.

Bell, Emma, Warren, Samantha and Schroeder, Jonathan (eds.) (2014) *The Routledge companion to visual organization*. Abingdon: Routledge.

Bergmann, Jörg R. and Luckmann, Thomas (eds.) (1999) *Kommunikative konstruktion von Moral*. Opladen, Wiesbaden: Westdeutscher Verlag.

Berlin, Isaiah (1953/1997) The hedgehog and the fox. In: Berlin, Isaiah, *The proper study of mankind*. New York: Farrar, Strauss and Giroux, 436–498.

Bernheimer, Charles and Kahane, Claire (1990) *In Dora's case: Freud-hysteria-feminism*. New York: Columbia University Press.

Beunza, Daniel and Stark, David (2005) How to recognize opportunities: Heterarchical search in a trading room. In: Knorr Cetina, Karin and Preda, Alex (eds.) *The sociology of financial markets*. Oxford: Oxford University Press, 84–101.

Biernacki, Richard (2012) *Reinventing evidence in social inquiry: Decoding facts and variables*. New York: Palgrave Macmillan.

Billig, Michael (2013) *Learn to write badly: How to succeed in the social sciences*. Cambridge: Cambridge University Press.

Blumer, Herbert (1954) What is wrong with social theory. *American Sociological Review*, 18: 3–10.

Boje, David (1991) The story-telling organization: A study of story performance in an office-supply firm. *Administrative Science Quarterly*, 36(1): 106–126.

Boje, David (2001) *Narrative methods for organizational and communication research*. London: Sage.

Boltanski, Luc and Thévenot, Laurent (2006) *On justification: The economies of worth*. Princeton, NJ: Princeton University Press.

Bonazzi, Giuseppe (1998) Between shock absorption and continuous improvement: Supervisors and technicians in a Fiat 'integrated factory'. *Work, Employment and Society*, 12(2): 219–243.

Booth, Wayne C., Colomb, Gregory G. and Williams, Joseph M. (1995) *The craft of research*. Chicago, IL: University of Chicago Press.

Bowker, Geoffrey C. (2006) *Memory practices in the sciences*. Cambridge, MA: The MIT Press.

Brandt, Joel, Weiss, Noah and Klemmer, Scott R. (2007) txt 4 l8r: Lowering the burden for diary studies. *Extended Abstracts of ACM-CHI Conference on Human Factors in Computing Systems*, San Jose, CA, 28 April–3 May.

Brinkmann, Svend (2012) *Qualitative inquiry in everyday life*. London: Sage.

Brose, Hanns-Georg (2004) Introduction. Towards a culture of non-simultaneity? *Time and Society*, 13(1): 5–26.

Brown, Barry A.T., Sellen, Abigail J. and O'Hara, Kenton P. (2000) A diary study of information capture in working life. *Proceedings of ACM-CHI Conference on Human Factors in Computing Systems*, The Hague, 1–6 April. New York: ACM Press, 438–445.

Brown, Colin, Guillet de Monthoux, Pierre and McCullough, Arthur (1976) *The access-casebook*. Stockholm: Teknisk Högskolelitteratur.

Brown, Richard Harrey (1989) *Social science as civic discourse: Essays on the invention, legitimation and uses of social theory*. Chicago, IL: The University of Chicago Press.

Brown, Richard Harvey (ed.) (1995) *Postmodern representations: Truth, power, and mimesis in the human sciences and public culture*. Chicago, IL: University of Illinois Press.

Bruner, Jerome (1986) *Actual minds, possible worlds*. Cambridge, MA: Harvard University Press.

Bruner, Jerome (1990) *Acts of meaning*. Cambridge, MA: Harvard University Press.

Bruni, Attila (2005) Shadowing software and clinical records: On the ethnography of non-humans and heterogeneous contexts. *Organization*, 12(3): 357–378.

Bruni, Attila, and Gherardi, Silvia (2001) Omega's story. The heterogenous engineering of a gendered professional self. In: Dent, Mike and Whitehead, Stephen (eds.) *Managing professional identities*. London: Routledge, 174–198.

Bruni, Attila and Gherardi, Silvia (2002) En-gendering differences, transgressing the boundaries, coping with the dual presence. In: Aaltio, Iiris and Mills, Albert J. (eds.) *Gender, identity and the culture of organizations*. London: Routledge, 21–38.

Bruyn, Severyn (1966) *The human perspective in sociology: The methodology of participant observation*. Englewood Cliffs, NJ: Prentice-Hall.

Bruyn, Severyn (2002) Studies of the mundane by participant observation. *Journal of Mundane Behavior*, 3(2): 1–9.

Burawoy, Michael (1979) *Manufacturing consent*. Chicago, IL: University of Chicago Press.

Burawoy, Michael (1991) *Ethnography unbound: Power and resistance in the modern metropolis*. Berkeley, CA: University of California Press.

Burawoy, Michael (1998) The extended case method. *Sociological Theory*, 16(1): 4–33.

Burgess, Robert G. (1991) Sponsors, gatekeepers, members and friends: Access in educational settings. In: Shaffir, William B. and Stebbins, Robert A. (eds.) *Experiencing fieldwork: An inside view of qualitative research*. Newbury Park, CA: Sage, 43–52.

Burke, Kenneth (1945/1969) *A grammar of motives.* Berkeley, CA: University of California Press.
Capetti, Carla (1993) *Writing Chicago: Modernism, ethnography and novel.* New York: Columbia University Press.
Carson, David, Gilmore, Audrey, Perry, Chad and Gronhaug, Kjell (2001) *Qualitative marketing research.* London: Sage.
Carter, Scott and Mankoff, Jennifer (2005) When participants do the capturing: The role of media in diary studies. *Proceedings of ACM-CHI Conference on Human Factors in Computing Systems,* Portland, OR, 2–7 April, 899–908.
Cassinger, Cecilia (2010) *Retailing retold: Unfolding the process of image construction in every-day practice.* Lund: Institute of Economic Research, Lund Business Press.
Castaneda, Carlos (1968) *The teachings of Don Juan.* Berkeley, CA: University of California Press.
Chandler, Alfred D. Jr. (1977) *The visible hand: The managerial revolution in American business.* Cambridge, MA: Harvard University Press.
Charmaz, Kathy (2006/2014) *Constructing grounded theory,* 2nd edn. London: Sage.
Cheney, George (1991) *Rhetoric in organizational society: Managing multiple identities.* Columbia, SC: University of South Carolina Press.
Cicourel, Aaron V. (1964) *Method and measurement in sociology.* New York: Free Press.
Clandinin, D. Jean (ed.) (2006) *Handbook of narrative inquiry.* Thousand Oaks, CA: Sage.
Clandinin, D. Jean and Connelly, F. Michael (2000) *Narrative inquiry: Experience and story in qualitative research.* San Francisco, CA: Jossey-Bass.
Clarke, Alison and Miller, Daniel (2002) Fashion and anxiety. *Fashion Theory,* 6(2): 191–214.
Clegg, Stewart R., Kornberger, Martin and Rhodes, Carl (2004) Noise, parasites and translation: Theory and practice in management consulting. *Management Learning,* 35(1): 31–44.
Clifford, James and Marcus, George E. (eds.) (1986) *Writing culture: The poetics and politics of ethnography.* Berkeley, CA: University of California Press.
Collier, John Jr. and Collier, Malcolm (1967/1986) *Visual anthropology: Photography as a research method.* Albuquerque, NM: University of New Mexico Press.
Comber, Rob (2011) Negotiating access with known and unknown others. *Etnografia e ricerca qualitativa,* IV(2): 189–209.
Cooren, François (2000) *The organizing property of communication.* Amsterdam: John Benjamins.
Coser, Lewis A. (1963) *Sociology through literature.* Englewood Cliffs, NJ: Prentice-Hall.
Cowan, Ruth Schwartz (1983) *More work for mother: The ironies of household technology from the open hearth to the microwave.* New York: Basic Books.
Cozzi, Donatella (2004) Specchio delle mie brame. Problemi metodologici dello shadowing nei servizi socio-sanitari. *Antropologia della salute,* 50: October. http://www.noinos.it/azioni_sez.asp?idcat=8&idsez=27, accessed 25 March 2007.
Cummins, Joanna and Bawden, David (2010) Accounting for information: Information and knowledge in the annual reports of FTSE 100 companies. *Journal of Information Science,* 36(3): 283–305.

Czarniawska, Barbara (1985) *Controlling top management in large organisations.* Aldershot: Gower.

Czarniawska-Joerges, Barbara (1994) Gender, power, organizations. In: Hassard, John and Parker, Martin (eds.) *The new organization theory revisited.* London: Routledge, 227–247.

Czarniawska, Barbara (1997) *Narrating the organization: Dramas of institutional identity.* Chicago, IL: University of Chicago Press.

Czarniawska, Barbara (1999) *Writing management: Organization theory as a literary genre.* Oxford: Oxford University Press.

Czarniawska, Barbara (2000) *A city reframed. Managing Warsaw in the 1990s.* Reading: Harwood Academic Publishers.

Czarniawska, Barbara (2001) Is it possible to be a constructionist consultant? *Management Learning,* 32(2): 253–272.

Czarniawska, Barbara (2002) *A tale of three cities, or the glocalization of city management.* Oxford: Oxford University Press.

Czarniawska, Barbara (2004) *Narratives in social science research.* London: Sage.

Czarniawska, Barbara (2007) *Shadowing, and other techniques for doing fieldwork in modern societies.* Malmö/Copenhagen: Liber/CBS Press.

Czarniawska, Barbara (ed.) (2009) *Organizing in the face of threat and risk.* Cheltenham: Edward Elgar.

Czarniawska, Barbara (2012) *Cyberfactories: How news agencies produce news.* Cheltenham: Edward Elgar.

Czarniawska, Barbara (2013a) The uncertainties of consulting. *International Studies of Management and Organization,* 43(3): 11–21.

Czarniawska, Barbara (2013b) What social science theory is, and what it is not. In: Corvellec, Hervé (ed.) *What is theory? Answers from the social and cultural sciences.* Malmö: Liber, 99–118.

Czarniawska, Barbara (2013c) Negotiating selves: Gender at work. *Tamara Journal for Critical Organization Inquiry,* 11(1): 59–72.

Czarniawska, Barbara and Hernes, Tor (2005) Constructing macro actors according to ANT. In: Czarniawska, Barbara and Hernes, Tor (eds.) *Actor-network theory and organizing.* Malmö/Copenhagen: Liber/CBS Press, 7–13.

Czarniawska-Joerges, Barbara and Joerges, Bernward (1988) How to control things with words: On organizational talk and organizational control. *Management Communication Quarterly,* 2(2): 170–193.

Czarniawska, Barbara and Löfgren, Orvar (eds.) (2012) *Managing overflow in affluent societies.* New York: Routledge.

Czarniawska, Barbara and Rhodes, Carl (2006) Strong plots: Popular culture in management practice and theory. In: Gagliardi, Pasquale and Czarniawska, Barbara (eds.) *Management education and humanities.* Cheltenham: Edward Elgar, 195–218.

Czerwinski, Mary, Horwitz, Eric and Wilhite, Susan (2004) A diary study of task switching and interruptions. *Proceedings of ACM-CHI Conference on Human Factors in Computing Systems,* Vienna, April, 175–182.

Dalton, Melville (1959) *Men who manage.* New York: John Wiley and Sons.

Dalton, Melville (1964) Preconceptions in method in *Men who manage*. In: Hammond, Phillip E. (ed.) *Sociologists at work*. New York: Basic Books, 50–95.

Dalton, Melville (1968) Reorganization and accommodation: A case in industry. In: Becker, Howard S., Riesman, David and Weiss, Robert (eds.) *Institutions and the person: Festschrift in honor of Everett C. Hughes*. Piscataway, NJ: Transaction Books, 14–21.

Davis, Barbara L. and MacNeilage, Peter F. (1990) Acquisition of correct vowel production: A quantitative case study. *Journal of Speech, Language and Hearing Research*, 33(March): 16–27.

Davies, Bronwyn (1989) *Frogs and snails and feminist tales*. North Sydney: Allen and Unwin.

Davies, Bronwyn and Harré, Rom (1991) Positioning: The discursive production of selves. *Journal for the Theory of Social Behaviour*, 20(1): 43–63.

De Certeau, Michel (1984/1988) *The practice of everyday life*. Berkeley, CA: University of California Press.

Demazière, Didier, Horn, François and Zune, Marc (2011) Distant observation and in-depth ethnography in the study of free software 'communities'. *Etnografia e ricerca qualitativa*, IV(2): 211–232.

DeMott, Benjamin (1989) Reading fiction to the bottom line. *Harvard Business Review*, May–June: 128–134.

Denzin, Norman K. (1995) Poststructural crisis in the social sciences. In: Brown, Richard Harvey (ed.) *Postmodern representations: Truth, power, and mimesis in the human sciences and public culture*. Chicago, IL: University of Illinois Press, 38–59.

Derrida, Jacques (1967/1976) *Of grammatology*. Baltimore, MD: Johns Hopkins University Press.

De Paoli, Stefano and Teli, Maurizio (2011) New groups and new methods? The ethnography and qualitative research of online groups. *Etnografia e ricerca qualitativa*, IV(2): 183–188.

DeVault, Marjorie L. (1990) Novel readings: The social organization of interpretation. *American Journal of Sociology*, 95(4): 887–921.

Dworkin, Ronald (2011) *Justice for hedgehogs*. Cambridge, MA: Harvard University Press.

Eco, Umberto (1979/1983) *The role of the reader: Explorations in the semiotics of texts*. London: Hutchinson.

Eco, Umberto (1989) *The open work*. Cambridge, MA: Harvard University Press.

Eco, Umberto (1990) *The limits of interpretation*. Bloomington, IN: Indiana University Press.

Edmondson, Ricca (1984) *Rhetoric in sociology*. London: Macmillan.

Emmison, Michael and Smith, Philip (2000/2012) *Researching the visual*. London: Sage.

Eriksson, Päivi and Kovalainen, Anne (2008) *Qualitative methods in business research*. London: Sage.

Eriksson-Zetterquist, Ulla (2009) Risk and organizing – the growth of a research field. In: Czarniawska, Barbara (ed.) *Organizing in the face of risk and threat*. Cheltenham: Edward Elgar, 9–24.

Fabian, Johannes (1983) *Time and the other: How anthropology makes its object.* New York: Columbia University Press.

Fairclough, Norman (2003) *Analyzing discourse: Textual analysis for social research.* London: Routledge.

Fairclough, Norman (2005) Discourse analysis in organization studies: The case for critical realism. *Organization Studies,* 26(6): 915–939.

Feldman, Martha S. (1995) *Strategies for interpreting qualitative data.* Newbury Park, CA: Sage.

Feldman, Martha S. and Sköldberg, Kaj (2002) Stories and the rhetoric of contrariety: Subtexts of organizing (change). *Culture and Organization,* 8(4): 275–292.

Feldman, Martha S., Bell, Jeannine and Berger, Michele Tracy (2003) *Gaining access: A practical and theoretical guide for qualitative researchers.* Walnut Creek, CA: AltaMira Press.

Fele, Giolo (2007) *L'analisi della conversazione.* Bologna: Il Mulino.

Fetterman, David M. (2010) *Ethnography: Step by step.* London: Sage.

Firth, Raymond (1959) *Social change in Tikopia.* London: George Allen and Unwin.

Fischer, Ann (1970/1986) Field work in five cultures. In: Golde, Peggy (ed.) *Women in the field.* Chicago, IL: Aldine, 267–292.

Fisher, Walter R. (1987) *Human communication as narration: Toward a philosophy of reason, value, and action.* Columbia, SC: The University of South Carolina Press.

Fletcher, Joyce K. (1999) *Disappearing acts: Gender, power and relational practice at work.* Cambridge, MA: MIT Press.

Flyvbjerg, Bent (1998) *Rationality and power: Democracy in practice.* Chicago, IL: University of Chicago Press.

Flyvbjerg, Bent (2006) Five misunderstandings about case-study research. *Qualitative Inquiry,* 12(2): 219–245.

Flyvbjerg, Bent (2011) Case study. In: Denzin, Norman K. and Lincoln, Yvonna S. (eds.) *The Sage book of qualitative research,* 4th edn. Thousand Oaks, CA: Sage, 301–316.

Foucault, Michel (1972) *The archeology of knowledge.* New York: Harper and Row.

Frandsen, Ann-Christine (2009) From psoriasis to numbers and back. *Information and Organization,* 19(2): 103–128.

Frye, Northrop (1957/1990) *The anatomy of criticism.* London: Penguin.

Gabriel, Yiannis (2000) *Storytelling in organizations: Facts, fictions and fantasies.* Oxford: Oxford University Press.

Gauntlett, David (2004) Web studies: What's new. In: Gauntlett, David and Horsley, Ross (eds.) *Web.studies.* London: Arnold, 3–23.

Geertz, Clifford (1967) Under the mosquito net. *The New York Review of Books,* 14 September.

Geertz, Clifford (1973) *The interpretation of cultures.* New York: Basic Books.

Geertz, Clifford (1980) Blurred genres. The refiguration of social thought. *American Scholar,* 29(2): 165–179.

Geertz, Clifford (1988) *Works and lives: The anthropologist as author.* Stanford, CA: Stanford University Press.

Gergen, Kenneth (1999/2009) *An invitation to social construction.* London: Sage.

Ginzburg, Carlo (1966/1983) *The night battles: Witchcraft and agrarian cults in the sixteenth and seventeenth centuries.* Baltimore, MD: Johns Hopkins University Press.

Ginzburg, Carlo (2011) Qualche domanda a me stesso. In: *Premi Balzan 2010.* Milan: Fondazione Internazionale Balzan, 9–17.

Glaser, Barney G. (1978) *Theoretical sensitivity: Advances in the methodology of grounded theory.* Mill Valley, CA: Sociology Press.

Glaser, Barney G. and Strauss, Anselm (1967) *The discovery of grounded theory: Strategies for qualitative research.* Chicago, IL: Aldine.

Gobo, Giampietro (2005) Personal communication (e-mail), 8 July.

Gobo, Giampietro (2008) *Doing ethnography.* London: Sage.

Goffman, Erving (1959) *The presentation of self in everyday life.* New York: Doubleday.

Goffman, Erving (1974) *Frame analysis: An essay on the organization of experience.* Boston, MA: Northeastern University Press.

Golde, Peggy (ed.) (1970/1986) *Women in the field: Anthropological experiences.* Berkeley, CA: University of California Press.

Golden-Biddle, Karin and Locke, Karin (1993) Appealing work: An investigation of how ethnographic texts convince. *Organization Science,* 4(4): 595–616.

Goode, William J. and Hatt, Paul K. (1952) *Methods in social research.* New York: McGraw-Hill Book Company.

Goodman, Nelson and Elgin, Catherine Z. (1988) *Reconceptions in philosophy and other arts and sciences.* London: Routledge.

Goody, Jack (1986) *The logic of writing and the organization of society.* Cambridge: Cambridge University Press.

Grant, David and Oswick, Cliff (eds.) (1996) *Metaphor and organizations.* London: Sage.

Green, Judith and Thorogood, Nicki (2004) *Qualitative methods for health research.* London: Sage.

Greimas, Algirdas Julien and Joseph Courtés (1982) *Semiotics and language: An analytical dictionary.* Bloomington, IN: Indiana University Press.

Grimshaw, Allen D. (2003) Genres, registers, and contexts of discourse. In: Graesser, Arthur C., Gernsbacher, Ann Morton and Goldman, Susan R. (eds.) *Handbook of discourse processes.* Mahwah, NJ: Lawrence Erlbaum, 25–82.

Grint, Keith and Woolgar, Steve (1997) *The machine at work: Technology, work and organization.* Cambridge: Polity Press.

Guba, Edwin G. (1981) Criteria for assessing truthworthiness of naturalistic inquiries. *Educational Communication and Technology Journal,* 29(2): 75–91.

Gubrium, Jaber F. and Holstein, James A. (2002) From the individual interview to the interview society. In: Gubrium, Jaber F. and Holstein, James A. (eds.) *Handbook of interview research: Context and method.* Thousand Oaks, CA: Sage, 3–32.

Gubrium, Jaber F., Holstein, James A., Marvasti, Amir B. and McKinney, Karyn (eds.) (2012) *The Sage handbook of interview research: The complexity of the craft.* Thousand Oaks, CA: Sage.

Gustavsson, Eva (2005) Virtual servants: Stereotyping female front-office employees on the Internet. *Gender, Work and Organization,* 12(5): 400–419.

Gustavsson, Eva and Czarniawska, Barbara (2004) Web woman: The on-line construction of corporate and gender images. *Organization,* 11(5): 651–670.

Hammersley, Martyn and Atkinson, Paul (1983/2007) *Ethnography: Principles in practice.* London: Routledge.

Hannaway, Jane (1989) *Managers managing: The workings of an administrative system.* New York: Oxford University Press.

Haraway, Donna (1992) The promises of monsters: A regenerative politics for inappropriate/d others. In: Grosberg, Lawrence, Nelson, Cary and Treichler, Paula (eds.) *Cultural studies.* London: Routledge, 295–337.

Harper, Douglas (2012) *Visual sociology.* Abingdon: Routledge.

Harré, Rom (1981) Philosophical aspects of the micro-macro problem. In: Knorr Cetina, Karen and Cicourel, Aaron (eds.) *Advances in social theory and methodology.* Boston, MA: Routledge and Kegan Paul, 3–18.

Hart, Chris (1998) *Doing a literature review: Releasing the social science research imagination.* London: Sage.

Haw, Kaye and Hadfield, Mark (2011) *Video in social science research: Functions and forms.* Abingdon: Routledge.

Hayles, Catherine (1993) Constrained constructivism: Locating scientific inquiry in the theater of representation. In: Levine, George (ed.) *Realism and representation: Essays on the problem of realism in relation to science, literature and culture.* Madison, WI: University of Wisconsin Press, 27–43.

Heath, Christian, Hindmarsh, Jon and Luff, Paul (2010) *Video in qualitative research: Analysing social interaction in everyday life.* London: Sage.

Heritage, John (1988) Explanations as accounts: A conversation analytic perspective. In: Antaki, Charles (ed.) *Analysing everyday conversation: A casebook of methods.* London: Sage, 127–144.

Heritage, John (2010) Conversation analysis: Practices and methods. In: Silverman, David (ed.) *Qualitative sociology.* London: Sage, 208–230.

Hernadi, Paul (1987) Literary interpretation and the rhetoric of the human sciences. In: Nelson, John S., Megill, Allan and McCloskey, D.N. (eds.) *The rhetoric of the human sciences.* Madison, WI: University of Wisconsin Press, 263–275.

Hine, Christine (2000) *Virtual ethnography.* London: Sage.

Hine, Christine (2008) Virtual ethnography: Modes, varieties, affordances. In: Fielding, Nigel, Lee, Raymond M. and Blank, Grant (eds.) *The Sage handbook of online research methods.* London: Sage, 257–271.

Hirschman, Albert O. (1982/2002) *Shifting involvements: Private interest and public action.* Princeton, NJ: Princeton University Press.

Horton, Richard (1996) Truth and heresy about AIDS. *New York Review of Books,* 23 May: 14–20.

Hunt, Jennifer (1984) The development of rapport through the negotiation of gender in field work among police. *Human Organization,* 43(4): 283–296.

Irons, Glenwood (1995) Introduction: Gender and genre: the woman detective and the diffusion of generic voices. In: Irons, Glenwood (ed.) *Feminism in women's detective fiction.* Toronto: University of Toronto Press, ix–xxiv.

Iser, Wolfgang (1978/1980) *The act of reading: A theory of aesthetic response.* Baltimore, MD: Johns Hopkins University Press.

Iser, Wolfgang (1989) *Prospecting: From reader response to literary anthropology*. Baltimore, MD: Johns Hopkins University Press.

Järviluoma, Helmi, Moisala, Pirkko and Vilkko, Anni (2003) *Gender and qualitative methods*. London: Sage.

Jemielniak, Dariusz and Kociatkiewicz, Jerzy (eds.) (2009) *Management practices in high-tech environments*. Hershey, PA: IGI Global.

Johnson, Barbara (1980) *The critical difference: Essays in the contemporary rhetoric of reading*. Baltimore, MD: Johns Hopkins University Press.

Jönsson, Sten (2005) Seeing is believing: On the use of video recording in research. In: Tengblad, Stefan, Solli, Rolf and Czarniawska, Barbara (eds.) *The art of science*. Malmö/Copenhagen: Liber/CBS Press, 236–261.

Kaelber, Lutz (2002) Max Weber's *Protestant Ethics* in the 21st century. *International Journal of Politics, Culture and Society*, 16(1): 133–146.

Kahneman, Daniel (2011) *Thinking, fast and slow*. New York: Farrar, Straus and Giroux.

Kaplan, Norman (1965) The norms of citation behavior: Prolegomena to the footnote. *Journal of the American Society for Information Science and Technology*, 16(3): 179–184.

Kelly, Aileen (1993) Revealing Bakhtin. *The New York Review of Books*, 10 June: 44–61.

Klamer, Arjo, McCloskey, D.N. and Solow, Robert M. (eds.) (1988) *The consequences of economic rhetoric*. Cambridge: Cambridge University Press.

Kleinman, Sherryl (1991) Field-workers' feelings: What we feel, who we are, how we analyze. In: Shaffir, William B. and Stebbins, Robert A. (eds.) *Experiencing fieldwork: An inside view of qualitative research*. Newbury Park, CA: Sage, 184–195.

Knorr Cetina, Karin (1981) *The manufacture of knowledge: An essay on the constructivist and contextual nature of science*. Oxford: Pergamon Press.

Knorr Cetina, Karin (1994) Primitive classification and postmodernity: Towards a socio-logical notion of fiction. *Theory, Culture and Society*, 11(1): 1–22.

Knorr Cetina, Karin and Bruegger, Urs (2002) Global microstructures: The virtual societies of financial markets. *American Journal of Sociology*, 107(4): 905–950.

Kociatkiewicz, Jerzy (2004) *Social construction of space in a computerized environment*. Warszawa: Polska Akademia Nauk.

Kokk, Gary and Jönsson, Sten (2013) Visual research methods and the importance of analytical spaces. *Management and Organizational History*, 8(2): 174–184.

Kostera, Monika (2007) *Organizational ethnography: Methods and inspirations*. Lund: Studentlitteratur.

Kozinets, Robert V. (2009) *Netnography: Doing ethnographic research online*. London: Sage.

Kuhn, Thomas S. (1962/2012) *The structure of scientific revolutions*. Chicago, IL: University of Chicago Press.

Kunda, Gideon (1992/2006) *Engineering culture: Control and commitment in a high-tech organization*. Philadelphia, PA: Temple University Press.

Kundera, Milan (1988) *The art of the novel*. London: Faber and Faber.

Kvale, Steinar (1996) *InterViews: An introduction to qualitative research interviewing*. Thousand Oaks, CA: Sage.

Labov, William and Waletzky, Joshua (1967) Narrative analysis: oral versions of personal experience. In: Helms, June (ed.) *Essays on the verbal and visual arts.* Seattle, WA: University of Washington Press, 12–44.

Laing, Ronald D. (1967) *The politics of experience and the bird of paradise.* Harmondsworth: Penguin.

Lakoff, Robin Tolmach and Coyne, James C. (1993) *Father knows best: The use and abuse of power in Freud's case of Dora.* New York: Teachers' College Press.

Lamont, Michèle (2009) *How professors think: Inside the curious world of academic thinking.* Cambridge, MA: Harvard University Press.

Landau, Misia (1984) Human evolution as narrative. *American Scientist*, 72(May–June): 262–268.

Landau, Misia (1991) *Narratives of human evolution.* New Haven, CT: Yale University Press.

Lanham, Richard A. (1991) *A handlist of rhetorical terms.* Los Angeles, CA: University of California Press.

Lather, Patty (1993) Fertile obsession: Validity after post-structuralism. *Sociological Quarterly*, 34(4): 673–693.

Lather, Patty (2006) Paradigm proliferation as a good thing to think with: Teaching research in education as a wild profusion. *International Journal of Qualitative Studies in Education*, 19(1): 35–57.

Latour, Bruno (1986) *The pasteurization of France.* Cambridge, MA: Harvard University Press.

Latour, Bruno (1988) The politics of explanation: An alternative. In: Woolgar, Steve (ed.) *Knowledge and reflexivity: New frontiers in the sociology of knowledge.* London: Sage, 155–176.

Latour, Bruno (1992) Technology is society made durable. In: Law, John (ed.) *A sociology of monsters: Essays on power, technology and domination.* London: Routledge, 103–131.

Latour, Bruno (1993) *We have never been modern.* Cambridge, MA: Harvard University Press.

Latour, Bruno (1995/1999) Circulating reference. In: Latour, Bruno, *Pandora's hope.* Cambridge, MA: Harvard University Press, 24–79.

Latour, Bruno (1996) *Aramis, or the love of technology.* Cambridge, MA: Harvard University Press.

Latour, Bruno (1999) *Pandora's hope.* Cambridge, MA: Harvard University Press.

Latour, Bruno (2004) *Politics of nature: How to bring the sciences into democracy.* Cambridge, MA: Harvard University Press.

Latour, Bruno (2005) *Reassembling the social: An introduction to Actor–Network Theory.* Oxford: Oxford University Press.

Latour, Bruno (2010) *The making of law: An ethnography of Conseil d'Etat.* Cambridge: Polity.

Latour, Bruno and Callon, Michel (1981) Unscrewing the big Leviathan or how actors macrostructure reality and how sociologists help them to do so. In: Knorr Cetina, Karin and Cicourel, Aaron (eds.) *Advances in social theory and methodology: Toward an integration of micro and macro sociologies.* London: Routledge and Kegan Paul, 277–303.

Latour, Bruno and Woolgar, Steve (1979/1986) *Laboratory life*. Princeton, NJ: Princeton University Press.

Leidner, Robin (1993) *Fast food, fast talk: Service work and the routinization of everyday life*. Berkeley, CA: University of California Press.

Lejeune, Philippe (1989) *On autobiography*. Minneapolis, MN: University of Minnesota Press.

Lennie, Ian (1999) Managing metaphorically. *Studies in Cultures, Organizations and Societies*, 5(1): 43–59.

Lenoir, Timothy (1994) Was the last turn the right turn? The semiotic turn and A.J. Greimas. *Configurations*, 2(1): 119–136.

Lepenies, Wolf (1988) *Between literature and science: The rise of sociology*. Cambridge: Cambridge University Press.

Lévi Strauss, Claude (1968) *Structural anthropology*. London: Allen Lane.

Levine, George (1993) Introduction. Looking for the real: Epistemology in science and culture. In: Levine, George (ed.) *Realism and representation*. Madison, WI: University of Wisconsin Press, 3–23.

Lindberg, Kajsa and Czarniawska, Barbara (2006) Knotting the action net, or organizing between organizations. *Scandinavian Journal of Management*, 22(4): 292–306.

Linde, Charlotte (1993) *Life stories: The creation of coherence*. New York: Oxford University Press.

Löfgren, Orvar (1999) *On holidays: A history of vacationing*. Berkeley, CA: University of California Press.

Löfgren, Orvar (2013) Selective knowledge: Learning to forget and ignore. In: Czarniawska, Barbara and Löfgren, Orvar (eds.) *Coping with excess: How organizations, communities and individuals manage overflows*. Cheltenham: Edward Elgar, 244–267.

Luckmann, Thomas (2002) Moral communication in modern societies. *Human Studies*, 25(1): 19–32.

Luhmann, Niklas (1989/2005) Communication barriers in management consulting. In: Seidl, David and Becker, Kai Helge (eds.) *Niklas Luhmann and organization studies*. Malmö/Copenhagen: Liber/CBS Press, 351–364.

Luhmann, Niklas (1995) *Social systems*. Stanford, CA: Stanford University Press.

Luhmann, Niklas (1998) *Observations on modernity*. Stanford, CA: Stanford University Press.

Luhmann, Niklas (2000) *The reality of the mass media*. Oxford: Polity Press.

MacIntyre, Alasdair (1988) *Whose justice? Which rationality?* London: Duckworth Press.

Mack, Alexandra (2011) Studying physical processes in the virtual world: Online forums and mail packages. *Etnografia e ricerca qualitativa*, IV(2): 233–252.

MacKenzie, Donald (2009) *Material markets: How economic agents are constructed*. Oxford: Oxford University Press.

Makoto Su, Norman and Mark, Gloria (2008) Designing for nomadic work. *DIS 2008 Proceedings*, Cape Town, South Africa, 25–27 February.

Malinowski, Bronisław (1967/1989) *A diary in the strict sense of the term*. Stanford, CA: Stanford University Press.

Mandler, Jean Matter (1984) *Stories, scripts and scenes: Aspects of schema theory.* Hillsdale, NJ: Lawrence Erlbaum.

Mangham, Iain L. and Overington, Michael A. (1987) *Organizations as theatre: A social psychology of dramatic appearances.* Chichester: John Wiley.

Mann, Anna M., Mol, Annemarie, Satalkar, Pruiya P., Savirani, Amalinda, Selim, Nasima and Yates-Doerr, Emily H. (2011) Mixing methods, tasting fingers: Notes on an ethnographic experiment. *HAU: Journal of Ethnographic Theory,* 1(1): 221–243.

Manning, Peter K. (1979) Metaphors of the field: Varieties of organizational discourse. *Administrative Science Quarterly,* 24(4): 660–671.

March, James G. (1994) *A primer in decision making: How decisions happen.* New York: Free Press.

March, James G. and Simon, Herbert A. (1958/1993) *Organizations.* Oxford: Blackwell.

Marcus, George E. and Fischer, Michael M.J. (1986) *Anthropology as cultural critique.* Chicago, IL: University of Chicago Press.

Markham, Annette N. (1998) *Life online: Researching real experience in virtual space.* Lanham, MD: AltaMira Press.

Martin, Joanne (1990) Deconstructing organizational taboos: The suppression of gender conflict in organizations. *Organization Science,* 1(4): 339–359.

Martin, Patricia Y. and Turner, Barry A. (1986) Grounded theory and organizational research. *The Journal of Applied Behavioral Science,* 22(2): 141–157.

McCloskey, D.N. (1985/1998) *The rhetoric of economics.* Madison, WI: The University of Wisconsin Press.

McCloskey, D.N. (1987) Counterfactuals. In: Eatwell, John, Millgate, Murray and Newman, Peter (eds.) *The New Palgrave: A dictionary of economics.* London: Macmillan, 95–97.

McDonald, Seonaidh (2005) Studying actions in context: A qualitative shadowing method for organizational research. *Qualitative Research,* 5(4): 455–473.

McDowell, Linda (1997) *Capital culture: Gender at work in the city.* Oxford: Blackwell.

Megens, Hellen and Martin, Brian (2003) Cybermethods: An assessment. *First Monday,* 8(2–3). http://firstmonday.org/issue/view/154, accessed 22 December 2012.

Megill, Allan and McCloskey, D.N. (1987) The rhetoric of history. In: Nelson, John S., Megill, Allan and McCloskey D.N. (eds.) *The rhetoric of the human sciences.* Madison, WI: University of Wisconsin Press, 221–238.

Meho, Lokman I. (2006) E-mail interviewing in qualitative research: A methodological discussion. *Journal of the American Society for Information Science and Technology,* 57(10): 1284–1295.

Mendieta, Eduardo (ed.) (2006) *Take care of freedom and truth will take care of itself: Interviews with Richard Rorty.* Stanford, CA: Stanford University Press.

Merton, Robert K. (1965/1985) *On the shoulders of giants: A Shandean postscript.* New York and London: Harcourt Brace Jovanovich.

Merton, Robert K. and Barber, Elinor (2004) *The travels and adventures of serendipity.* Princeton, NJ: Princeton University Press.

Meyer, John W. and Rowan, Brian (1977) Institutionalized organizations: Formal structure as myth and ceremony. *American Journal of Sociology,* 83(2): 340–363.

Miller, Daniel (1998) *A theory of shopping*. Cambridge: Polity Press.

Miller, Daniel (2007) Personal communication (e-mail), 4 March.

Mills, C. Wright (1959) *The sociological imagination*. New York: Oxford University Press.

Mintzberg, Henry (1970) Structured observation as a method to study managerial work. *The Journal of Management Studies*, 17(1): 87–104.

Mintzberg, Henry (1973) *The nature of managerial work*. Englewood Cliffs, NJ: Prentice-Hall.

Mishler, Elliot G. (1986/1991) *Research interviewing: Context and narrative*. Cambridge, MA: Harvard University Press.

Mitchell, W.J.T. (ed.) (1981) *On narrative*. Chicago, IL: The University of Chicago Press.

Mitchell, W.J.T. (1987) *Iconology*. Chicago, IL: The University of Chicago Press.

Mol, Annemarie (2002) *The body multiple: Ontology in medical practice*. Durham, NC: Duke University Press.

Morgan, Gareth (1980) Paradigms, metaphors and puzzle solving in organization theory. *Administrative Science Quarterly*, 25(4): 641–652.

Morgan, Gareth (1986) *Images of organization*. London: Sage.

Mulkay, Michael and Gilbert, G. Nigel (1982) Accounting for error: How scientists construct their social world when they account for correct and incorrect belief. *Sociology*, 16(2): 165–183.

Muniesa, Fabian (2012) A flank movement in understanding of valuation. *The Sociological Review*, 59(2): 24–38.

Munsch, Robert (1980) *The paper bag princess*. Toronto: Annick Press.

Nader, Laura (1974) Up the anthropologist – perspectives gained from studying up. In: Hymes, Dell (ed.) *Reinventing anthropology*. New York: Vintage Books, 284–311.

Nagel, Thomas (1986) *The view from nowhere*. New York: Oxford University Press.

Nelson, John S., Megill, Allan and McCloskey D.N. (eds.) (1987) *The rhetoric of the human sciences*. Madison, WI: University of Wisconsin Press.

New Shorter Oxford English Dictionary (1993) New York: Oxford University Press.

Neyland, Daniel (2007) *Organizational ethnography*. London: Sage.

Oakeshott, Michael (1959/1991) The voice of poetry in the conversation of mankind. In: *Rationalism in politics and other essays*. Indianapolis, IN: Liberty Press, 488–541.

Oliver, Paul (2012) *Succeeding with your literature review: A handbook for students*. Maidenhead: Open University Press.

Oxman, Andrew D., Sackett, David L., Chalmers, Iain and Prescott, Trine E. (2006) A surrealistic mega-analysis of redisorganization theories. *Healthcare Quarterly*, 9(3): 50–54.

Palen, Leysia and Salzman, Marilyn (2002) Voice-mail diary studies for naturalistic data capture under mobile conditions. *Proceedings of ACM-CHI Conference on Computer-Supported Cooperative Work*, New Orleans, LA, April, 87–95.

Peters, Tom and Waterman, Robert H. (1982) *In search of excellence*. New York: HarperCollins.

Polanyi, Karl (1944/2001) *The great transformation*. Boston, MA: Beacon Press.

Polkinghorne, Donald E. (1987) *Narrative knowing and the human sciences*. Albany, NY: State University of New York Press.

Potter, Jonathan and Wetherell, Margaret (1987) *Discourse and social psychology: Beyond attitudes and behaviour*. London: Sage.

Prasad, Pushkala and Prasad, Anshu (2002) Casting the native subject: Ethnographic practice and the (re)production of difference. In: Czarniawska, Barbara and Höpfl, Heather (eds.) *Casting the other: The production and maintenance of inequalities in work organizations*. London: Routledge, 185–204.

Propp, Vladimir (1928/1968) *Morphology of the folktale*. Austin, TX: University of Texas Press.

Quattrone, Paolo (2006) The possibility of testimony: A case for case study research. *Organization*, 13(1): 143–157.

Queneau, Raymond (1947/1981) *Exercises in style*. New York: New Directions.

Reichertz, Jo (2010) Abduction: The logic of discovery of grounded theory. *Forum: Qualitative Social Research*, 11(1). http://www.qualitative-research.net/index.php/fqs/article/view/1412/2902, accessed 10 December 2012.

Rhodes, Carl (2001) *Writing organization: (Re)presentation and control in narratives at work*. Amsterdam: John Benjamins.

Ricoeur, Paul (1973) The model of the text: Meaningful action considered as text. *New Literary History*, 5(1): 91–117.

Ricoeur, Paul (1991) *From text to action*. Evanston, IL: Northwestern University Press.

Riessman, Catherine Kohler (1993) *Narrative analysis*. Thousand Oaks, CA: Sage.

Riessman, Catherine Kohler (2008) *Narrative methods for the human sciences*. Thousand Oaks, CA: Sage.

Roan, Amanda and Rooney, David (2006) Shadowing experiences and the extension of communities of practice: A case study of women education managers. *Management Learning*, 37(4): 433–454.

Robichaud, Daniel (2003) Narrative institutions we organize by. In: Czarniawska, Barbara and Gagliardi, Pasquale (eds.) *Narratives we organize by*. Amsterdam: John Benjamins, 37–54.

Rorty, Richard (ed.) (1967) *The linguistic turn*. Chicago, IL: University of Chicago Press.

Rorty, Richard (1980) *Philosophy and the mirror of nature*. Oxford: Basil Blackwell.

Rorty, Richard (1982) *Consequences of pragmatism*. Minneapolis, MN: University of Minnesota Press.

Rorty, Richard (1989) *Contingency, irony and solidarity*. Cambridge: Cambridge University Press.

Rorty, Richard (1992) The pragmatist's progress. In: Eco, Umberto (ed.) *Interpretation and overinterpretation*. Cambridge: Cambridge University Press, 89–108.

Rose, Diana (2000) Analysis of moving images. In: Bauer, Martin W. and Gaskell, George (eds.) *Qualitative researching with text, image, and sound*. London: Sage, 247–263.

Rosen, Michael (2002) *Turning words, spinning worlds: Chapters in organizational ethnography*. Reading: Harwood Academic Publishers.

Ryan, Marie-Laure (1993) Narrative in real time: Chronicle, mimesis and plot in baseball broadcast. *Narrative*, 1(2): 138–155.

Ryan, Marie-Laure (2001) *Narrative as virtual reality*. Baltimore, MD: Johns Hopkins University Press.

Sacks, Harvey (1992) *Lectures on conversations.* Oxford: Blackwell.

Sacks, Harvey, Schegloff, Emanuel and Jefferson, Gail (1974) A simplest systematics of the organization of turn-taking in conversation. *Language,* 50(4): 696–735.

Sands, Ashley, Borgman, Christine L., Wynholds, Laura and Traweek, Sharon (2012) Follow the data: How astronomers use and reuse data. *ASIST 2012,* Baltimore, MD, 28–31 October.

Schacter, Daniel L., Wang, Paul L., Tulving, Endel and Freedman, Morris (1982) Functional retrograde amnesia: A quantitative case study. *Neuropsychologia,* 20(5): 523–532.

Schaffer, Frederic Charles (2006) Ordinary language interviewing. In: Yanow, Dvora and Schwartz-Shea, Peregrine (eds.) *Interpretation and method: Empirical research methods and the interpretive turn.* New York: M.E. Sharpe, 150–160.

Schama, Simon (1987) *The embarrassment of riches: An interpretation of Dutch culture in the Golden Age.* New York: Knopf.

Schatzki, Theodore R., Knorr Cetina, Karin and Von Savigny, Elke (eds.) (2001) *The practice turn in contemporary theory.* London: Routledge.

Schein, Edgar H. (1999) Kurt Lewin's change theory in the field and in the classroom: Notes toward a model of managed learning. *Reflections. The SoL Journal of Knowledge, Learning and Change,* 1(1): 59–72.

Schön, Donald A. (1979) Generative metaphor: A perspective on problem-setting in social policy. In: Ortony, Andrew (ed.) *Metaphor and thought.* Cambridge: Cambridge University Press.

Schrijvers, Joke (1991) Dialectics of a dialogical ideal: Studying down, studying sideways and studying up. In: Nencel, Lorraine and Pels, Peter (eds.) *Constructing knowledge: Authority and critique in social science.* Newbury Park, CA: Sage, 162–179.

Schroeder, Jonathan E. (2006) Critical visual analysis. In: Belk, Russell (ed.) *Handbook of qualitative research methods in marketing.* Cheltenham: Edward Elgar, 303–321.

Schultze, Ulrike (2011) The avatar as sociomaterial entanglement: A performative perspective on identity, agency and world-making in virtual worlds. *ICIS 2011 Proceedings,* Shanghai, 6 December. http://aisel.aisnet.org/icis2011/proceedings/hci/11, accessed 22 December 2012.

Schultze, Ulrike (2012) Using photo-diary interviews to study cyborgian identity performance in virtual worlds. In: Bhattacherjee, Anol and Fitzgerald, Brian (eds.) *Shaping the future of ICT research: Methods and approaches,* IFIP WG 8.2 Working Conference, Tampa, FL, 13–14 December, 79–88.

Schultze, Ulrike (2014) Performing embodied identity in virtual worlds. *European Journal of Information Systems,* 23(1): 84–95.

Schütz, Alfred (1946/1964) The well-informed citizen. In: *Collected papers II. The problem of social reality.* The Hague: Martinus Nijhoff, 120–134.

Schütz, Alfred (1953/1973) Common-sense and scientific interpretation of human action. In: *Collected papers I. The problem of social reality.* The Hague: Martinus Nijhoff, 3–47.

Schütz, Alfred and Luckmann, Thomas (1983) *The structures of the life-world.* Evanston, IL: Northeastern University Press.

Schwartz, Dona (1989) Visual ethnography: Using photography in qualitative research. *Qualitative Sociology*, 12(2): 119–154.

Schwartz-Shea, Peregrine and Yanow, Dvora (2002) 'Reading' 'methods' 'texts': How research method texts construct political science. *Political Research Quarterly*, 55(2): 457–486.

Schwartzman, Helen B. (1993) *Ethnography in organizations*. Newbury Park, CA: Sage.

Sclavi, Marianella (1989) *Ad una spanna da terra* [Six inches off the ground]. Milan: Feltrinelli.

Sclavi, Marianella (2007) *An Italian lady goes in the Bronx*. Milan: Italian Paths of Culture.

Scott, Martin B. and Lyman, Stanford M. (1968) Accounts. *American Sociological Review*, 33(1): 46–62.

Seale, Clive (1999) *The quality of qualitative research*. London: Sage.

Seale, Clive (2012) Generating grounded theory. In: Seale, Clive (ed.) *Researching society and culture*. London: Sage, 239–248.

Sebeok, Thomas A. and Sebeok, Jean Umiker (1981) 'You know my method'. In: Sebeok, Thomas A. (ed.) *The play of musement*. Bloomington, IN: Indiana University Press, 17–52.

Seidl, David and Becker, Kaj (eds.) (2005) *Niklas Luhmann and organization studies*. Malmö/Copenhagen: Liber/CBS Press.

Shaffir, William B. and Stebbins, Robert A. (eds.) (1991) *Experiencing fieldwork: An inside view of qualitative research*. Newbury Park, CA: Sage.

Shirky, Clay (2008) *Here comes everybody: The power of organizing without organizations*. London: Allen Lane.

Sidnell, Jack and Stivers, Tanya (eds.) (2013) *The handbook of conversation analysis*. Chichester: Wiley-Blackwell.

Sigona, Nando (2005) Locating 'the Gypsy problem'. The Roma in Italy: Stereotyping, labeling and 'nomad camps'. *Journal of Ethnic and Migration Studies*, 31(4): 741–756.

Silverman, David (1993/2011) *Interpreting qualitative data: Methods for analysing talk, text and interaction*. London: Sage.

Silverman, David (1997) Towards an aesthetics of research. In: Silverman, David (ed.) *Qualitative research: Theory, method and practice*. London: Sage, 239–253.

Silverman, David (2000/2013) *Doing qualitative research: A practical handbook*. London: Sage.

Silverman, David (2010) *A very short, fairly interesting and reasonably cheap book about qualitative research*. London: Sage.

Silverman, David and Torode, Brian (1980) *The material word: Some theories about language and their limits*. London: Routledge and Kegan Paul.

Simons, Herbert (ed.) (1988) *The rhetorical turn*. Chicago, IL: University of Chicago Press.

Smith, Dorothy E. (1987) *The everyday world as problematic: A feminist sociology*. Boston, MA: Northeastern University Press.

Smith, Warren (1998) Computers and representation: Organization in the virtual world. In: Hassard, John and Holliday, Ruth (eds.) *Organization representation – work and organizations in popular culture*. London: Sage, 229–245.

Søderberg, Anne-Marie (2003) Sensegiving and sensemaking in integration processes: A narrative approach to the study of an international acquisition. In: Czarniawska, Barbara and Gagliardi, Pasquale (eds.) *Narratives we organize by*. Amsterdam: John Benjamins, 3–36.

Sombart, Werner (1913/1967) *Luxury and capitalism*. Ann Arbor, MI: University of Michigan Press.

Sorokin, Pitirim (1956) *Fads and foibles in modern sociology*. Chicago, IL: Henry Regnery Company.

Spradley, James P. (1979) *The ethnographic interview*. New York: Holt, Rinehart and Winston.

Stewart, Rosemary (1967) *Managers and their jobs*. London: Macmillan.

Strannegård, Lars and Friberg, Maria (2001) *Already elsewhere: Play, identity and speed in the business world*. Stockholm: Raster.

Strawson, Galen (2004) Against narrativity. *Ratio*, 17(4): 428–452.

Sword, Helen (2012) *Stylish academic writing*. Cambridge, MA: Harvard University Press.

Tengblad, Stefan (2003) Classic, but not seminal: Revisiting the pioneering study of managerial work. *Scandinavian Journal of Management*, 19(1): 85–101.

Tengblad, Stefan (2006) Is there a 'new managerial work'? A comparison with Henry Mintzberg's classic study 30 years later. *Journal of Management Studies*, 43(7): 1437–1460.

Tengblad, Stefan and Ohlsson, Claes (2010) The framing of corporate social responsibility and the globalization of national business systems: A longitudinal case study. *Journal of Business Ethics*, 93(4): 653–669.

Todorov, Tzvetan (1977/1995) *The poetics of prose*. Oxford: Blackwell.

Todorov, Tzvetan (1978/1990) *Genres in discourse*. Cambridge: Cambridge University Press.

Traweek, Sharon (1992) Border crossings: Narrative strategies in science studies and among physicists in Tsukuba Science City, Japan. In: Pickering, Andrew (ed.) *Science as practice and culture*. Chicago, IL: University of Chicago Press, 429–466.

Tuchman, Gaye (1978) *Making news: A study in the construction of reality*. New York: Free Press.

Turkle, Sherry (1996) *Life on the screen: Identity in the age of the Internet*. London: Weidenfeld and Nicolson.

Van Fraassen, Bas C. and Sigman, Jill (1993) Interpretation in science and in the arts. In: Levine, George (ed.) *Realism and representation: Essays on the problem of realism in relation to science, literature and culture*. Madison, WI: University of Wisconsin Press, 73–99.

Van Maanen, John (1982) Fieldwork on the beat. In: Van Maanen, John, Dabber, James M. Jr. and Faulkner, Robert R. (eds.) *Varieties of qualitative research*. Beverly Hills, CA: Sage, 103–151.

Van Maanen, John (1988) *Tales of the field*. Chicago, IL: The University of Chicago Press.

Van Maanen, John (1991) Playing back the tape: Early days in the field. In: Shaffir, William B. and Stebbins, Robert A. (eds.) *Experiencing fieldwork: An inside view of qualitative research*. Newbury Park, CA: Sage, 31–42.

Van Maanen, John (1995a) Style as theory. *Organization Science*, 6(1): 133–143.

Van Maanen, John (1995b) An end to innocence. In: Van Maanen, John (ed.) *Representation in ethnography*. Thousand Oaks, CA: Sage, 1–35.

Van Maanen, John (2006) Ethnography then and now. *Qualitative Research in Organizations and Management: An International Journal*, 1(1): 13–21.

Vironmäki, Emma (2007) *Academic marketing in Finland: Living up to conflicting expectations.* Turku: Åbo Akademi School of Business.

Waldo, Dwight (1968) *The novelist on organization and administration.* Berkeley, CA: Institute of Government Studies.

Walker, Charles R. and Guest, Robert H. (1952) *The man on the assembly line.* Cambridge, MA: Harvard University Press.

Walker, Charles R., Guest, Robert H. and Turner, Arthur N. (1956) *The foreman on the assembly line.* Cambridge, MA: Harvard University Press.

Warren, Roland L., Rose, Stephen M. and Bergunder, Ann F. (1974) *The structure of urban reform: Community decision organizations in stability and change.* Lexington, MA: Lexington Books.

Wax, Rosalie (1971/1985) *Doing fieldwork: Warnings and advice.* Chicago, IL: University of Chicago Press.

Weick, Karl E. (2004) How projects lose meaning. In: Stablein, Ralph E. and Frost, Peter (eds.) *Renewing research practice.* Stanford, CA: Stanford University Press, 183–204.

White, Hayden (1973) *Metahistory: The historical imagination in nineteenth-century Europe.* Baltimore, MD: Johns Hopkins University Press.

White, Hayden (1987) *The content of the form: Narrative discourse and historical representation.* Baltimore, MD: Johns Hopkins University Press.

White, Hayden (1999) *Figural realism.* Baltimore, MD: Johns Hopkins University Press.

Williams, Kimberlé Crenshaw (1994) Mapping the margins: Intersectionality, identity politics, and violence against women of color. In: Fineman, Martha Albertson and Mykitiuk, Rixanne (eds.) *The public nature of private violence.* New York: Routledge, 93–118.

Wolcott, Harry F. (1973/2003) *The man in the principal's office: An ethnography.* Walnut Creek, CA: AltaMira Press.

Woods, Angela (2011) Post-narrative – and appeal. *Narrative Inquiry*, 21(2): 399–406.

Yin, Robert (1984) *Case study research: Design and methods.* Newbury Park, CA: Sage.

Zimmerman, Don H. and Wieder, D. Lawrence (1977a) The diary: Diary-interview method. *Urban Life*, 5(4): 479–498.

Zimmerman, Don H. and Wieder, D. Lawrence (1977b) You can't help but get stoned: Notes on the social organization of marijuana smoking. *Social Problems*, 25(2): 198–207.

Index

Printed in Great Britain
by Amazon